THE
BULAWAYO COLLECTION
Series
Volume 3

THE
BULAWAYO COLLECTION

Vol. 1 The Old Transport Road
Stanley Portal Hyatt

Vol. 2 The Passing of the Black Kings
Hugh Marshall Hole, C.M.G.

Vol. 3 The Chronicles of a Contractor
George Pauling

THE CHRONICLES OF A CONTRACTOR

by
GEORGE PAULING

Second impression of the 1969 facsimile reprint of the original 1926 edition with a revised Publisher's Introduction and Appendix 9.

The
Bulawayo Collection
Volume 3

AFRICANA BOOK SOCIETY
BULAWAYO
1996

BOOKS OF ZIMBABWE PUBLISHING CO. (PVT) LTD.
in association with
AFRICANA BOOK SOCIETY
P. O. Box 1994, Bulawayo, Zimbabwe

Publishers of Africana Reprints
and New Southern African Literary Works

ISBN 0-86920-276-6

PRINTED IN ZIMBABWE BY TYPOCRAFTERS

PUBLISHER'S INTRODUCTION TO THE SECOND REPRINT EDITION

A pretty jacaranda-lined street in a quiet garden suburb of Bulawayo bears the name of Pauling — a simple yet ever fresh tribute to a distinguished civil engineering contractor whose company built virtually the entire network of southern Africa's 19th century railway system.

The present reprinting of George Pauling's *Chronicles of a Contractor* heralds the Centenary of the arrival at Bulawayo, on 4th November 1897, of Rhodes's ambitious Cape-to-Cairo trunk railway.

George Craig Saunders Pauling was born at St. Ives, England, on 6th September 1854, and he died at Effingham, Surrey, on 10th February 1919. He was the son of Richard Clark Pauling, a railway engineer, as were his grandfather and grand uncle before him. George's links with contracting reached back to an ancestor, another George Pauling, who was a builder in London in the days of Queen Elizabeth I (1558-1603). His great-grandfather was a partner in the firm which built Somerset House and a part of the British Museum.

George Pauling, destined to win international repute for his engineering accomplishments, came to South Africa from Britain when he was 20, and he was followed by his brother, Harry; and cousin, Harold. The firm of Pauling & Co. Ltd. was formed in 1877 and, in 1881, they completed their first railway construction job — the 65-mile Port Alfred Railway.

The Sterkstroom to Aliwal North, Orange River to Kimberley, Springs to Krugersdorp, and the Crocodile Poort Railway numbered among the major contracts completed in the next decade. By 1892, with the financial backing of the house of D'Erlangers, the Paulings had already extended their activities simultaneously to railway work in Britain, the building of the Johannesburg to Pretoria Railway, the Haifa to Damascus Railway, and to their toughest job of all — the construction of the first stage of the line between Beira and Umtali (Mutare). Hampered by swamps, malaria, tsetse fly and marauding lions, the loss of human and animal life was very heavy. It was to take the Company 5½ years to lay a little more than 200 miles of 2-ft. gauge railway across the malarial swamps and up rugged, forest terrain to 3 500 ft. high Umtali (Mutare).

In 1893, George Pauling was invited by Rhodes to build the Vryburg-Mafeking (Mafikeng) line, the first section of the ambitious Cape-to-Cairo Railway of which, over the next 17 years, his Company was to construct

1 531 miles through Bechuanaland (Botswana) and the Rhodesias (Zimbabwe and Zambia) to Elisabethville (Lubumbashi) in the Congo (Zaire). As already recorded, Bulawayo was the first Rhodesian centre reached by the railway—on the 4th November 1897. Umtali was given its rail outlet to the coast at Beira on 4th February 1898, and Salisbury (Harare) on 22nd May 1899. Salisbury and Bulawayo were linked at Insiza on 6th October 1902. When the main line reached Elisabethville in 1910 an extensive mileage of branch lines had already been completed within Rhodesia — all built by Pauling's Company!

Meantime, the Company had widened its field of engineering operations and was undertaking public works and harbour, dam and bridge construction in such distant places as Greece, the Argentine, Angola, China and India. A review of 49 years of operations by the Company published in 1930— George Pauling had died in 1919 —listed completed contracts worth more than £32 million.

Writing, in 1922, on the History and Finance of the Rhodesian Railway System, in the book *The Story of the Cape to Cairo Railway and River Route,* Baron Emile D'Erlanger said, "The success of the construction and finance was greatly due to the genius of the railway contractor, Mr George Pauling, who never once exceeded his estimate, though cost per mile was kept lower than for any other railway system in the whole of Africa."

In the same book, Mr Hugh Marshall Hole wrote of Pauling: "...he was a man of shrewd business qualities, and indomitable enterprise, and he possessed a flair for gathering around him a staff composed of men of action. When the history of the development of South Central Africa is recorded the name of Pauling will take a place among its Pioneers second only to that of Rhodes."

George Pauling was a most colourful character, noted for his drive, capacity for hard work and physical strength. It was perhaps not unnatural that his qualities should have commended him to Rhodes who, in 1895, appointed him Commissioner of Public Works in the Chartered Company's administration in Salisbury (Harare). He was later given the added responsibility for the Department of Mines, and was also appointed Postmaster-General. As a friend and confidant of Rhodes he was not without influence in shaping the early days of Rhodesia (Zimbabwe) although his greatest contribution was in turning Rhodes's inspired dreams into reality. For his part in building the railway system posterity owes him much. Meantime Mr Arthur Lawley and Mr Harold Pauling supervised the railway construction work, and to the latter goes the kudos for completing 460 miles of track through Bechuanaland to Bulawayo in under 460 working days.

The arrival of the railway at Bulawayo, and the official opening of the line by His Excellency Sir Alfred Milner, High Commissioner at the Cape, drew the largest crowd ever assembled in the town, swelled by four special trains with important guests from South Africa and England for the ten days of festivities. Sadly, George Pauling was not present having gone to England to be with his brother, Harry, during his fatal illness and death which occurred in November. Apart from Harold who responded to a toast to the Railway contractors, the following members of the Pauling family were also present: Mrs Harold Pauling, the two Miss Paulings, and Dr. W.T. Pauling. Rhodes was prevented from attending having contracted "a severe attack of fever" in the wilds north of Umtali while personally supervising the construction of the trans-continental telegraph.

In 1977, Pauling, now a public limited company based in London, celebrated the centenary of the Company's formation and its receipt of a Queens Award for Export Achievement. The Company continues to be involved in major overseas projects with works currently in the Middle East, India and Pakistan.

The book having been reproduced in facsimile, it retains the original place-name spellings, mileages, etc. but these have been brought up to date in Appendix 9 — a most valuable addition to the work.

Louis W. Bolze

Bulawayo
June 1996

MATERIAL NEW TO THIS EDITION

Page

Publisher's Introduction 5

Map: Work of Pauling and Co. Limited in
Southern Africa .... facing page 10

Illustrations: List of Plates .... 9 and 10

Acknowledgements 10

Appendixes 241

Appendix 1 - Minutes of Meeting of Directors of the Bechuanaland Railway Co. Ltd. on 28th July, 1893 242

Appendix 2 - Minutes of Board Meeting of the Bechuanaland Railway Co. Ltd. on 7th August, 1896 245

Appendix 3 - Minutes of a Special Board Meeting of the Mashonaland Railway Co. Ltd. on 21st July, 1897. 246

Appendix 4 - Purchase of Land from Pauling & Co. Ltd. by the Mashonaland Railway Co. Ltd. 248

Appendix 5 - George Pauling's Interview with Joseph Chamberlain 249

Appendix 6 - Letter from David Buchan to Mrs. Booth 253

Appendix 7 - Lawley's Personal Account of his Brush with Rhodes 254

Appendix 8 - Obituary: George Pauling 257

Appendix 9 - Schedule of Railways and Other Public Works Constructed by Pauling & Co. Ltd/Pauling PLC 259

ILLUSTRATIONS

Plates			Page
1	*Top*	BLAAUWKRANTZ RAILWAY BRIDGE	Facing page 32
	Bottom	PAULING WITH HIS FIRST WIFE	
2		"NUGGET" CARTOON: ON HORSEBACK	Facing page 64
3		"NUGGET" CARTOON: "TA-TA BOYS"	Facing page 65
4		"NUGGET" CARTOON: ST. GEORGE	Facing page 80
5		EDITORIAL FROM "THE NUGGET"	Facing page 81
6		"RAND TRAM" ARRIVES AT BOKSBURG	Facing page 104
7		PORTRAITS: RHODES, METCALFE, D'ERLANGER, G. PAULING, LAWLEY AND H. PAULING	Facing page 128
8		"BALLAD OF THE B.M.R." - GOULDSBURY	Between pages 128-9
9	*Top*	A BEIRA RAILWAY GROUP IN 1894	Between pages 128-9
	Bottom	PUNGWE RIVER BRIDGE	
10	*Top*	BEIRA RAILWAY ADVERTISEMENT	Between pages 128-9
	Bottom	ARRIVAL OF FIRST TRAIN AT BEIRA	
11	*Top*	CONVERTING TO 3 FT. 6 IN. GAUGE	Between pages 144-5
	Bottom	BROAD GAUGE REACHES BEIRA	
12	*Top*	"THE PAULINGTON" LOCOMOTIVE	Between pages 144-5
	Bottom	PLAQUE ON UMTALI STATION	
13	*Top*	TRAIN IN THE AMATONGAS FOREST	Between pages 144-5
	Bottom	BEIRA WHARF UNDER CONSTRUCTION	
14		MAP: CAPE TO CAIRO RAILWAY	Between pages 144-5
15		MAP: NEW RAILWAY AND OLD COACH ROUTES	Between pages 144-5
16	*Top*	TRAIN CROSSING TATI RIVER-BED	Between pages 144-5
	Bottom	TYPICAL PLATELAYING SCENE	
17	*Top*	SHASHI RIVER BRIDGE	Between pages 144-5
	Bottom	WAYSIDE STATION: BECHUANALAND	
18		PROGRAMME: OPENING LINE TO BULAWAYO	Between pages 144-5
19	*Top*	HAROLD PAULING'S CONSTRUCTION TRAIN	Between pages 160-1
	Bottom	OPENING THE MAFEKING-BULAWAYO LINE	
20	*Top*	THE LAST COACH TO LEAVE SALISBURY	Between pages 160-1
	Bottom	FIRST TRAIN ARRIVES AT SALISBURY	
21	*Top*	GOURITZ RIVER BRIDGE	Between pages 160-1
	Bottom	HEAVY EARTHWORKS, HOUW HOEK PASS	
22		MAZOE DAM UNDER CONSTRUCTION	Facing page 161
23	*Top*	THE ASSOPOS VIADUCT IN GREECE	Facing page 168
	Bottom	CONCEICAO BRIDGE, SAN PAULO RAILWAY	
24	*Top*	VICTORIA FALLS STATION IN 1900s	Facing page 192
	Bottom	TRESTLE BRIDGE NEAR MATETSI RIVER	
25	*Top*	MR & MRS PAULING AT FALLS HOTEL	Between pages 192-3
	Bottom	VICTORIA FALLS HOTEL IN EARLY 1900s	
26	*Top*	BUILDING THE VICTORIA FALLS BRIDGE	Between pages 192-3
	Bottom	OPENING OF THE VICTORIA FALLS BRIDGE	
27	*Top*	TRUCK DRAWN BY OXEN: N. RHODESIA	Facing page 193
	Bottom	TYPICAL CONSTRUCTION: ENGINEERS' CAMP	
28	*Top*	DONNYBROOK ON THE STUARTSTOWN RAILWAY	Facing page 200
	Bottom	OPENING OF THE OLIFANTS RIVER BRIDGE	

Plates			Page
29	*Top*	FLOATING LOCOMOTIVE ACROSS THE KAFUE	Facing page 208
	Bottom	KAFUE RIVER BRIDGE: FLOATING NINTH SPAN INTO POSITION	
30-31		COMPLETED VICTORIA FALLS BRIDGE "RHODES' DREAM" - GOULDSBURY	Between pages 208-9
32	*Top*	COMPLETED KAFUE RIVER BRIDGE	Between pages208-9
	Bottom	PAULING'S TRAIN CROSSES KAFUE BRIDGE	
33	*Top*	MAP: BENGUELA RAILWAY	between pages 208-9
	Bottom	TEMPORARY BRIDGE: BENGUELA LINE	
34	*Top*	CUANDO DAM UNDER CONSTRUCTION	Facing page 209
	Bottom	BUILDING CONCRETE WELLS, LOBITO BAY	
35	*Top*	PAULING'S RESIDENCE AT EFFINGHAM	Facing page 224
	Bottom	MR. & MRS. PAULING WITH DOLORES	
36-37		PAULING'S LETTER TO DOLORES	Between pages 224-5
38	*Top*	WALWHAN DAM, TATA HYDRO-ELECTRIC SCHEME IN INDIA	Facing page 225
	Bottom	VALVE CHAMBERS, WALWHAN DAM	
39	*Top*	SURVEY CAMP AT YUANCHOW IN CHINA	Facing page 240
	Bottom	MUGADI PIER IN KILINDINI HARBOUR	
40	*Top*	DREDGING FOUNDATIONS, KILINDINI	Facing page 241
	Bottom	ZIWE ZIWE BRIDGE, CENTRAL AFRICAN RAILWAY	

ACKNOWLEDGEMENTS

The publishers gratefully acknowledge the co-operation received from George Pauling's daughter, Mrs. Jane Glass, and his grandson, Mr. George Tabor, who made family photographs and private papers available for publication.

Thanks are also extended to the publishers of the original edition, Constable & Co. Ltd. of London, for permission to reprint it in facsimile; to Pauling & Co. Ltd. of London, for permission to reproduce from *The Works of Pauling & Co. Ltd.* the coloured map, the Schedule of Works (Appendix 9), and a number of illustrations; photographs and original Minute Books for copying purposes; to the National Archives of Rhodesia for permission to reproduce certain early railway photographs, and the cartoons from *the Nugget;* to the Rhodesiana Society for the loan of two blocks from its magazine, *Rhodesiana*; to the Pioneer Publishing Co. Ltd., publishers of the *Cape to Cairo Railway & River Route* for photographic reproductions; and to Philpott & Collins Ltd. of Bulawayo, publishers of *Rhodesian Rhymes* from which Cullen Gouldsbury's two poems were taken.

—FIRST REPRINT, 1969

Since the publication of the first reprint of this title, Pauling & Company Ltd became a public limited company based in London. We gratefully acknowledge the kindly co-operation of Mr. Peter A.B. Prosser, Managing Director, Pauling Plc, in agreeing to a second reprint and for updating the schedule of works constructed by the Company between 1931 and 1996 (see Appendix 9 p.259)

—SECOND REPRINT, 1996

George Pauling

THE CHRONICLES OF A CONTRACTOR

BEING THE AUTOBIOGRAPHY OF THE LATE GEORGE PAULING

EDITED BY

DAVID BUCHAN

WITH AN INTRODUCTION BY

J. O. P. BLAND

CONSTABLE & CO. LTD.
LONDON 1926

PRINTED IN GREAT BRITAIN.
CHISWICK PRESS: CHARLES WHITTINGHAM AND GRIGGS (PRINTERS), LTD.
TOOKS COURT, CHANCERY LANE, LONDON.

FOREWORD

IT is very doubtful whether any man would care to place on record all that he could recollect of a life which had extended over sixty years.

In the career, even of the average individual, there must be incidents which he would be well content to leave buried in the dusty archives of oblivion, although, if they were recorded, they might greatly enhance the interest of his life's story. For my own part, during my threescore and three years, the majority of which have been strenuous and not lacking in excitement, I have been a party to many episodes, which to most of my friends might make palatable reading, but which, possibly from qualms of conscience or fear of reprisals, it is not my intention to set down here. It has taken me many of the later years of my life to establish a reputation as a steady and respectable member of the community: I do not wish to jeopardize that reputation in the writing of this book.

By way of further preface I might add that I have undertaken to tell my story at the instigation of my friends. The idea of dabbling in literature, even in the mild form of an autobiography, had never occurred to me, and consequently I had made no preparation by keeping exhaustive diaries or otherwise. I am therefore dependent almost exclusively upon memory, and it is more than probable that an error in dates or in minor matters of detail will occasionally creep into the text. But for the general accuracy of all the main statements that will hereafter be set forth I readily vouch.

Even now, as I am about to set out on my latest labour, I do not yet appreciate what its ultimate form may prove. It goes, however, without saying that it must contain references to many people with whom I have been connected or come into contact in different parts of the world.

May it be understood from the outset that whatever the nature of these references there shall lurk behind them no suspicion of malice, and that indeed I count it a privilege and a blessing to be able to look back on all these years of varying fortunes and vicissitudes with nothing but kindly memories. For the rest—

But how the subject theme may gang
Let time and chance determine,
Perhaps it may turn out a sang,
Perhaps—turn out a sermon.

GEORGE PAULING.

CONTENTS

CHAP.		PAGE
	Foreword	v
	Introduction	xi
I.	Some Relations	1
II.	Early Struggles	4
III.	A Contractor in the Making	10
IV.	Firbank Associations	15
V.	African Aspirations	21
VI.	The Land of Sunshine	24
VII.	My First Contract	27
VIII.	Side Lines	30
IX.	The Kowie Railway	36
X.	More Side Lines	39
XI.	The Ghosts of Grahamstown and "The Comet"	42
XII.	A Diamond Hunt	46
XIII.	A Feat of Strength	49
XIV.	Sterkstroom to Aliwal North	50
XV.	Orange River to Kimberley	54
XVI.	An Army Contract	62
XVII.	Arduous Days	64
XVIII.	The Lure of the Goldfields	66
XIX.	Barberton	72
XX.	"Holding the Baby" and other Diversions	77
XXI.	Johannesburg	80
XXII.	Placing Properties	84
XXIII.	Other Fields	88

CHAP.		PAGE
XXIV.	Asia Minor	90
XXV.	Biblical Associations	94
XXVI.	The Angora Railway	98
XXVII.	Samos	103
XXVIII.	Back to the Old Love	107
XXIX.	The "S" Syndicate	109
XXX.	Crocodile Poort	112
XXXI.	A Syrian Excursion	120
XXXII.	Syrian Schemes	126
XXXIII.	Vryburg to Mafeking	129
XXXIV.	The Beira Railway	131
XXXV.	Big Game Stories	135
XXXVI.	Lighter Moments	139
XXXVII.	Days of Hustle	142
XXXVIII.	Civil Service	144
XXXIX.	Rhodes, the Raid, Rinderpest, and Rebellion	148
XL.	Mining Laws and Relaxations	153
XLI.	A Transplanted Township	156
XLII.	Mafeking to Bulawayo	158
XLIII.	A Great Bereavement	163
XLIV.	The New Cape Central Railway	166
XLV.	Home Work	168
XLVI.	Greece	171
XLVII.	A Grand Tour	174
XLVIII.	Borneo	181
XLIX.	A Coal Venture	186
L.	Africa in London	188
LI.	More Ventures with Mr. Cleary	194
LII.	The Argentine	198
LIII.	The Transvaal Engineering and Contracting Company, Limited	201

CHAP.		PAGE
LIV.	The Development of Southern Rhodesia	203
LV.	A Grand Trek	206
LVI.	Northern Rhodesia and the Belgian Congo	212
LVII.	The Benguella Railway	214
LVIII.	Wasted Efforts	217
LIX.	China	222
LX.	India	227
LXI.	East and Central Africa	232
LXII.	Au Revoir	238

INTRODUCTION

"He was a man; take him for all in all
I shall not look upon his like again."

TO know George Pauling was a valuable education in courage, kindness, and cheerful philosophy. I had the good fortune to make his acquaintance in 1907, at a time when he was expending much energy and money in the hope of establishing a footing in railway construction work in China, a hope which was never fulfilled. Against the background of those days of high finance and tortuous intrigue, the memory of his sturdy personality and friendship stand out like trees upon the sky-line of a barren land. In the pages of this, his brief and breezy autobiography, the reader may get a glimpse of the human qualities which endeared George Pauling to all sorts and conditions of men—of his indomitable pluck, his shrewd tenacity of purpose, and never failing generosity; but, drawn by the man himself, the picture is necessarily incomplete. George Pauling was staunchly and squarely British, of the breed of the Captains Courageous whose "traffics and discoveries, made by sea and overland, to the remote and farthest distant quarters of the earth," have established and held the far-flung frontiers of the Empire. With the frame of an athlete, the solid common sense of a practical engineer, and (as he says) an inordinate capacity for hard work, he was able to hold his own, against Jew or Gentile, in the rough-and-tumble of the pioneer days of the Rand and in many other fields of outpost enterprise. In the course of his adventurous career, he had occasion to take, and to give, many a hard knock; in his extensive survey of mankind from China to Peru, he found it to contain a considerable proportion of rogues: yet he emerged from the hurly-burly of his early days with the record of a good sportsman and the heart of a boy. Amongst his many lovable qualities, loyalty to old friends and sympathy for the under-dog were ever conspicuous. For the rest he loved his work and was frankly proud of his achievements in opening up the unexplored parts of the earth; also he loved the good things of this life, honest laughter and children and flowers and the fellowship of good companionable men. He was always a *bon vivant* and never happier, in his later days, than when dispensing lavish hospitality in his beautiful home at Effingham, reviving, in the company of old friends, the struggles and adventures of the past—many of which find no place in this discreet chronicle. In many lands George Pauling's work stands as a monument to his memory. This book, edited and prepared for the Press as a labour of love by his friend David Buchan, provides a fitting inscription to that monument.

J. O. P. Bland.

Aldeburgh,
8th January 1926.

THE CHRONICLES OF A CONTRACTOR

I

Some Relations

WHATEVER may be my view on the turbulent problem of heredity—and it shall be my purpose in these pages to avoid controversial matter as I would the plague or a despotic resident engineer—it would be futile for me to attempt to resist the criticism that my connection with the world of public works construction is due to the circumstance of birth rather than to any personal initiative. For was there not a George Pauling a contractor in the City of London in the time of Queen Elizabeth? As became my lineage he was a goodly man, a builder and repairer of churches, and I hold in my possession copies of fragments of his accounts for work which he carried out some centuries ago.

I regret that the chronicles of his career are incomplete. It would have been interesting, if only for purposes of comparison, to learn to what extent he suffered from the exactions of architects, clerks of works, and those other inquisitors whose chief end, from time immemorial, has been to render burdensome the existence of the poor contractor.

From these far-off Elizabethan days I have been unable to identify any branch of the family tree with the business of public works construction until we come to the time of my great-grandfather, who was a partner in the firm which, amongst other monuments to their memory, built Somerset House and a portion of the British Museum. My grand-uncle, an earlier George Pauling, as a member of the firm entitled Brassey, Pauling, and Henfrey, was one of the partners of Thomas Brassey, whose name will long survive among the stalwarts of the contracting world. My grandfather, Richard Pauling, was the contractor for the old Admiralty Pier at Dover, and afterwards went to India as engineer of the Bombay Baroda Railway, but died a few days after reaching his destination. My father, Richard Pauling, was a civil engineer who followed his profession in various parts of the world, and who, during the Crimean War, was engaged on the building of the railway from the sea to the English camp before Sevastopol. When that work was finished he volunteered as an officer of the Sappers and Miners and fought in the trenches before Sevastopol. At the conclusion of that campaign, he, having no private means, was compelled to resign his commission, and to revert to his duties as a civil engineer. In pursuit of his profession he betook himself to India, and it was his lot to be employed there during the period of the Indian Mutiny. It may be claimed as a tribute to his professional ability that for several years he filled the important position of Resident Railway Engineer at Delhi.

My grandfather's brother, Henry Pauling, was for a number of years chief engineer on the Cape Railway system. He had a large family of sons, most of whom have at one time or other been associated with me in my work. Chief amongst these was Harold, who, for some years prior to his death in 1904, had been the principal agent of my firm in South Africa. He was a man of outstanding ability, and his untimely and sudden death not only proved a very severe personal blow to me, but the removal of one of the greatest assets of Pauling and Company, Limited.

Of his brothers only two remain: Willie—who was originally destined for the medical profession, but who has found a more congenial occupation in the contracting world—and Percy, who matriculated as an engineer in the service of the South African Railways. Both of these are now actively identified with me in carrying on the work of Pauling and Company, Limited.

II

Early Struggles

IN the early 'sixties my father and mother were in India. Their four children, Harry, Jenny, Flora, and I, had been left behind under the care of an aunt who lived at St. Ives, in Huntingdonshire, and it was arranged that Harry and I should attend the Grammar School there. My father had mapped out for me a career in the Woods and Forests Department of the Indian Civil Service. Had his scheme matured this book might never have been written and I might now be basking in the sunshine of an insufficient Government pension and a bad liver. But my lines were to be cast in other places. In 1868 my father was the victim of a sunstroke which compelled him to relinquish his Indian appointment, and he had no alternative but to return with my mother to England. As is the case with many professional men he had been none too provident, and by the time he reached home the moderate bonus which had been granted to him by the Indian Railway Company was all that remained of his resources. I was then fourteen years of age and my brother Harry twelve. From lack of funds we were both forced to leave school, but not before I had passed with some distinction the Cambridge local examination. My head master did not at first seem disposed to let me have the certificate because his fees for the previous term had not been paid. His better nature, however, prevailed, and the characteristic sympathy of the provincial "dominie" towards children in unfortunate circumstances induced him to waive his objection, and I became the proud possessor of the parchment. Nor did his generosity go for ever unrewarded. Thirty-five years afterwards the debt was liquidated with compound interest, and I had him to spend a day with me at my home at Effingham. It was a source of great pleasure to me to see the old man thoroughly enjoy himself as my guest, and when, about ten years ago, I heard of his death I was greatly grieved.

My scholastic education had come to a premature end and my parents had to face the problem of my future career. Amongst my father's acquaintances there were the principals of a firm of engineers which took pupils. They were approached on my behalf and I was duly indentured. During the first four months of 1869 I was initiated into the mysteries of engineering office work and also gained some experience in practical surveying in the country. As, however, my father by that time had spent all his reserve funds, my premium remained unpaid and the firm cancelled my articles. The gateway to an engineering profession had thus, for a time, become effectively barred, and I was forced to seek a means of livelihood in other directions. In my somewhat meagre education I had acquired a smattering of French, and a favourable opportunity presenting itself, I endeavoured to graduate as a French correspondent in a kid glove warehouse in Wood Street, Cheapside, but my knowledge of the language failing to prove equal to the occasion my services were dispensed with in less than a fortnight.

I therefore was forced to seek fresh fields, and devoted my energies to what has been the means of making many fortunes—and probably more failures—the India Rubber market. Another of my father's friends endeavoured to accumulate wealth by buying up old billiard-table cushions and disused railway buffer springs, and converting them into small pieces of rubber suitable for sale in the stationery line of business.

He occupied a couple of rooms in Castle Street, Holborn, where he had established a circular knife to cut up the rubber. The knife was operated by a handle, and it was my part of the "profession" to work the handle. At other times I had to accompany my principal when he called at the shops of various stationers to dispose of his goods. We sold the pieces in bags, each containing from ten to twenty pounds in weight. The best samples were always exhibited on top in the same way that itinerant vendors now dispose of strawberries and cherries, and consequently when one bag had been sold it was our custom to mark off the particular shop to which the sale had been made as one in no circumstances to be revisited. We were also careful on no occasion to disclose the whereabouts of our factory. This occupation lasted about two or three months and I did not find it oppressively remunerative. It would be impossible to justify the commercial morality of my work during that period; but much, perhaps, may be forgiven because of the dire straits into which the family had fallen. As a matter of fact, the situation was rapidly becoming desperate not only for me, but also for my mother, brother, and sisters. My father had been unable to obtain any employment. His resources were practically exhausted, and the outlook for all of us was black beyond expression. Fortunately, my father, whatever his weaknesses in other directions, possessed the talent of making many friends, and in the autumn of 1869 one of his companions obtained employment for me in the drawing office of the contractors for the Metropolitan District Railway, a section of which, from Westminster Bridge to the Mansion House, was then in the course of construction.

My wages were but a pound a week, but this modest remuneration proved a veritable godsend in helping us to tide over extremely bad times. Bad luck, however, continued to dog my footsteps, and within three or four weeks my father's friend obtained a better appointment and emigrated to Canada, and I was informed that my services were no longer required. It subsequently transpired that he had really created the temporary opening for me out of friendship for my father. For a moment this cloud of despondency almost overwhelmed me, but Providence, in which, looking back upon my many tribulations, I have always found a sure and safe anchorage, did not fail me. On the very day when I was dismissed, and while my faith in mankind was almost broken, the foreman of the night watchmen happened to see me and, taking compassion on my sad appearance, inquired what was the matter. Being but a boy, in tears I opened my heart to him and told him the tremendous difference the loss of my wages would make to my mother, and the rest of the family. Like the majority of English railwaymen I have met, he was of a kindly disposition and readily volunteered to help me if he could. Luckily, he was in want of a night watchman for the Lambeth Hill yard and offered me the post at a salary of a guinea a week. The only thing that appeared to worry him was my age, and he suggested that although I looked older than fifteen—in fact, I might almost have been taken for a full-grown man—it would be injudicious for me to turn up at the pay office to get my weekly money, so it was arranged that someone else should draw my wages and hand it to me each Saturday night as I commenced duty. I cannot attempt to condone the deceit to which I was a party, but in amelioration of my offence and as an indication of my adult appearance, I may mention that a policeman on the Lambeth Hill beat, with whom I had become friendly, asked me on one occasion if I were a married man. I have now some suspicion that he may have only been attempting to "pull my leg," but I confess to having been greatly flattered at the time.

At the time of which I write my father had disappeared

for some months, and my mother and the rest of the family were living at Nunhead, Peckham. I had to walk from there to Lambeth Hill yard every night and home again in the morning, a distance which I reckon was about four or five miles each way. I should explain that in connection with the construction of the Metropolitan District Railway the buildings on the route were for the most part demolished and a wooden hoarding had been erected along the course of the railway, intersected by the streets which crossed the route. My particular beat as night watchman was a so-called yard, bounded by the hoarding between Bread Street Hill and Lambeth Hill. Part of this yard had been a churchyard and there were times when I felt a bit creepy at the possible prospect of being interviewed by ghosts at the dead of night. I had the usual little box with a coke fire in a brazier in front, and my one diversion consisted in listening to the clock of St. Paul's striking the hours and the quarters all through those very long nights of the early winter of 1869-70.

After I had been acting as night watchman for two or three months I chanced one night to see a man stealing the brasses off a locomotive. Catching hold of a pick-shaft I slipped up behind him and, hitting him with some force on the head, I felled him. Seeing him insensible—in fact I imagined that I had killed him—I whistled for help. Fortunately he recovered, and for this special service I was promoted to the more dignified occupation of brick tallyman at the Carron Wharf on the Thames. There I had to commence work at six o'clock in the morning and to fulfil the task of counting the bricks as they were unloaded into carts from Thames barges; my daily task did not cease until six o'clock in the evening, and the monotony of my new profession did not appeal to me. After two days' experience, having realized that the bricks were being unloaded on piecework by what is called a "butty gang," *i.e.*, under the supervision of one leading man who received a little more than the rest of his fellows, it occurred to me that the butty gang might be willing to let me help in unloading the bricks on terms somewhat less remunerative than they would have had to pay to a full member of the gang. It was quite easy for me to see that the carts were properly loaded, as after a little practice one could tell at a glance whether there was a full load of bricks or not. I, therefore, asked the boss to take me on in the place of a full member and, as I was a very strong youngster, he consented. By this means I was able to supplement by about half a sovereign my weekly pay which had by that time risen to twenty-four shillings. In the harassing circumstances in which we were then living, this little extra added materially to the family comfort.

III

A Contractor in the Making

WHILE I was straining every nerve to increase the resources of our home life my mother had not been idle. In her way she was a remarkable woman. In those days she was subjected to many trials, but she possessed the spirit of a lioness, and the harder her trials the greater were her efforts to overcome them. In her later years she enjoyed the leisure and comfort which she had so well earned, and it was her portion to exceed the allotted span by a dozen years or so. Her later years were spent in Ealing, and during a Christmas visit to my house at Effingham she passed away and was buried within the shadow of the little church that I had built close to my dwelling-place. It was to her womanly instinct and intuition that I owed my real introduction to the contracting world. Without my knowledge she had resumed an acquaintance with former friends of my father and of her own, Mr. and Mrs. Ralph Firbank. Ralph was the principal agent of his uncle, Mr. Joseph Firbank. Of all the English railway contractors Joseph Firbank was perhaps the greatest. He started life as a miner, but by sheer force of character he was able to secure, at the age of twenty-two, a sub-contract in connection with the construction of the great Woodhead tunnel, on the Auckland and Weardale branch of the Stockton and Darlington Railway. From that time in the year 1841 until his death in 1886 he carried out, single-handed, more railway construction work in this country than any other contractor has ever done. I count myself, therefore, particularly fortunate in becoming associated, through my mother's influence, with such a man.

At the time of which I write—I think it was the year 1870—he had just commenced to build the railway from Wood Green to Enfield. My father, who had reappeared, had got some temporary work, so the family treasury was less depleted than usual, and as Mr. Ralph offered to take me as a pupil without premium I was only too glad to abandon the night watchman and brick tallyman lines, and to get to work in the drawing office on this railway. My mother, so as to give me as short a walk as possible, managed to move over to a house in Stoke Newington. From there I had to get to Wood Green by eight o'clock in the morning, remain in the office till six in the evening, and then return home. These daily journeys, however, I regarded as nothing but healthy exercise.

As an indication of how a very little incident may affect the whole future career of an individual, it may be interesting to mention an episode which occurred shortly after I entered upon my new employment. About two or three weeks after I had started I was having my lunch alone by a little stream that ran hard by the back of the office. My modest repast consisted of a slice of bread and a drink of water. It chanced that Mr. Ralph Firbank came out of the office and, seeing me, inquired what I was having for lunch. I could not hide my poverty from him, any more than he could conceal the kindness which was a dominant feature of his character, and he immediately volunteered to increase my wages to twenty-four shillings a week, on the condition that I should have to do whatever I was called upon and that I should have to learn the contractor's business right from the bottom. He then proposed that I should start on outside duty by measuring up some sub-contractor's work, and also that I should become a time-keeper instead of remaining in the drawing office which was, of course, much more respectable and professional and suited to the status of a pupil. But for the fortuitous circumstance of Mr. Ralph Firbank having seen me at my lunch on that occasion, the whole course of my career might have been different and the occasion to record these memoirs might never have occurred.

I remained on the Wood Green and Enfield Railway for a few months when Mr. Joseph Firbank secured a contract for the building of a railway from Sleaford to Bourne in Lincolnshire, which was constructed during the years 1871-2. I was sent there as time-keeper with the reservation that I was to make myself generally useful. The duties of a time-keeper on this work included taking the time four times a day of about four hundred men. The length of the railway allotted to each time-keeper was about four miles, with the result that my work involved walking sixteen miles daily and attending the office every evening, as many of the men wanted a "sub" on account of their pay. These daily "subs" extended from sixpence upwards. The time-keeper had to make up his pay-sheets every Thursday night and have them in the office on Friday morning so that they could be checked ready for the men to be paid on the Saturday. Thus the time-keeper's billet was no sinecure. One or two episodes of more than passing interest occurred whilst I was on the Sleaford to Bourne railway. On one occasion several of the employees came back from a ballast hole about eight miles from Sleaford and took with them in the otherwise empty trucks navvies and other workers on the way to their lodgings. We had to leave on the main road one empty truck to be loaded with bricks. Next morning, just about daylight, we started to take the men back to their work at the ballast hole. I happened to be on the engine with one or two others and we completely forgot the truck which had been left on the track the preceding evening and which, in the meantime, had been filled up. Its existence, however, was brought home to us when we saw it only about forty yards ahead when we had not sufficient time to pull up. I got down on the engine step and just before the impact dropped off. As we were proceeding at considerable speed I fell forcibly on my face. The force of the collision sent the bricks up into the air and it is probable that half a brick fell on my back. At the moment it seemed to me more like half the engine, but the breath was only knocked out of me temporarily and I got up not much the worse for the occurrence. One man was killed and several others were injured. The usual inquest was held when it was proved that the brakes had refused to act properly.

Another interesting incident occurred while I was on this contract. During a circus performance in Sleaford I had had some words with a young architect which resulted in a challenge to a fight with bare fists. I was then rather more than sixteen years of age and he about twenty-one. On the railway we had, as a walking ganger, an experienced prize-fighter named Jack Hewlett. He trained me for about a fortnight before the day of the contest and the architect and I met early one morning. The ground was covered with snow; a proper ring was formed; and we each stripped to the waist and fought with bare knuckles. After four or five rounds I began to feel very sore and downhearted, and when I got to my corner I said to Hewlett, who was acting as my second: "Jack, I have nearly had enough." He replied: "Don't be a damned fool. You are giving him quite as much as he is giving you."

This put fresh heart into me, and after a few more rounds my opponent retired. He must have had a worse drubbing than I thought, because he did not show up in the town for the next week. I, on the contrary, had to go on and get through my time-keeping for that day, and beyond an ornamental black eye and sundry bruises did not feel a great deal the worse for the encounter.

I remained on that contract until after Christmas, when I received bad news from my mother. Whilst at Sleaford it cost me about fourteen shillings a week to live, and consequently I could not do as much to support her and the other members of the family as I had done when we were all living together. I determined to go away without saying anything to anyone, so after the next pay-day, having left all my papers in order, I returned to London. My father had again disappeared for a time and none of us knew what had become of him. For the following two or three months I endured the hardest of my many varied experiences. Tramping about from day to day in search of work, rebuffed and tossed about in the whirlpool of London's unemployed, I had wellnigh abandoned hope. Ultimately, however, I obtained a fortnight's work as a temporary copying clerk at Somerset House. I then became an assistant to an advertisement canvasser, and I shall never forget the many excuses I had to make at my various places of call to try and worm myself into the presence of the manager whose province it was to deal with orders for advertisement. More often than not I only escaped being thrown out by exercising an intelligent anticipation of what was in store for me and by beating a hurried, and none too dignified, retreat.

IV

Firbank Associations

MY mother had never been able to understand why I had left the Sleaford and Bourne railway, and, unknown to me, she enquired from Mr. Ralph Firbank as to the cause of my departure. He replied that he did not know why I had left, and added that it was only out of friendship for her and for my father that he had not taken some steps against me for having broken my pupilage. He also told her that he could not in any circumstances have me back with him, but that if I cared to go to the Settle and Carlisle railway, in connection with which Mr. Joseph Firbank had obtained a contract, he thought he could get me a post under the agent there, Mr. John Throssle.

My position at that time was so hopeless that I was very glad of this opportunity, and by dint of much scraping I managed to collect sufficient money to pay my railway fare from King's Cross to Penrith, where I arrived about two or three o'clock in the morning. To reach Mr. Throssle's office, which was at Appleby, I had to walk, as far as I remember, about nine or ten miles. I reached Appleby at daybreak. A little public-house by the roadside had just opened, and having, with the few pence I had left, bought some beer and bread and cheese, I ascertained where the contractor's office was situated. It did not open until nine o'clock, and at that hour I presented myself and asked for Mr. Throssle. I saw him and the chief accountant, Mr. Cruwys, and told them I had come for a job which Mr. Ralph Firbank had promised they would give me.

Much to my disappointment they professed to know nothing about it. Once more I was very downhearted and begged them to give me work of any kind as I was penniless. They told me that if I cared to go out to the sawmill, which was close by, and carry planks and other timber to and from the mill, I could have a job at three shillings a day. I immediately went out and put in three-quarters of a day's work. In the evening I got a " sub " of two shillings, went back to my little inn, and obtained a bed in a room where three other men were also accommodated. At the end of the week when I went to get my pay, Mr. Throssle sent for me. He told me that he had heard from Mr. Ralph about me, and of my having left without notice, and he had given me the job of sawyer's labourer to see whether I really meant to work or not, that I had satisfied him on the subject, and that he had decided to place me in charge of the time-keeping from Looking Flat quarry to the Helm tunnel. I was also to measure up the piece-work in two quarries and to superintend the preparation of the special stones required for arches, parapets, and other ashlar work. All this I carried out, and more, for in order to keep fit I voluntarily did much actual quarrying and stone-dressing work.

I lodged at Looking Flat farm, had to take the time of about four hundred men, and walk sixteen miles a day over very rough roads which, in the winter time, was no light task. It was, however, a pleasure to me to be able to send half my pay to my mother, and altogether I was very contented. The men employed on the construction of the railway were very rough. By the navvies it was called the " Long Drag." In these days there were the real old English navvies, and it was an ordinary thing for a man to chuck from ten to fourteen cubic yards of dirt into a wagon as a day's work. It would take two or three navvies of the present time to do what one of these men did. Helm tunnel was a big job, and a small township of wooden huts had to be erected to accommodate the miners and the labourers employed at the tunnel, as well as in the quarries. After pay on Saturdays, drinking and fighting were of common occurrence. I have seen as many as twelve rings formed on a Saturday afternoon and twelve couples of good men fighting—in most cases for a gallon of beer. It was very exciting for me, because I rather fancied myself, particularly after my success over the young architect. On Sundays, at Looking Flat and at the neighbouring farms, there were usually wrestling competitions. At that time the three best exponents of the Westmorland and Cumberland style of wrestling were Jamieson, Wright, and George Steadman. Steadman lived at Oakbeak farm, close to Looking Flat. They were all very big men, and George, although only twenty-two or twenty-three years of age, weighed about fifteen stone. He could jump in the ordinary way five feet seven inches high, and with a pole, over ten feet, and I have been told that once or twice he won the hundred yards sprint at Lilley Bridge in London. I took to wrestling very kindly, and have occasionally in after life found my knowledge of it very useful.

After I had been on the "Long Drag" for five or six months, Mr. Ralph Firbank wrote to me that if I cared to come back to him he would risk another effort to make a man of me, so, with Mr. Throssle's permission, I went to a little railway which was being built from Clown to Staveley in Derbyshire. My duties there, in addition to time-keeping, included measuring up a lot of the work for the final certificate. From there I went to Dewsbury, in Yorkshire. The firm was then building a new line from Ossett to Dewsbury and widening the existing line to Wakefield. On this contract my work was somewhat arduous. I had said good-bye to time-keeping, but I had to be in the office at ten o'clock in the morning, and to continue there until four in the afternoon. At that hour I returned to my lodging, but at ten o'clock at night had to put in an appearance in the tunnel. There it was my business to keep the prime costs of the work, do any necessary setting out, and in particular to set the leading frames for the brickwork, and see that the lines and levels of the tunnel were properly kept. My time, however, was not fully occupied with these things, so it was my habit to spend an hour or two helping the miners in the heading, preparing the timber and making myself generally useful. I was always out for physical exercise, so much so that on the Sleaford and Bourne contract I kept myself in condition by swinging the big hammer as a blacksmith's striker for an hour or two every day. I was consequently developing considerable physical strength, but after four or five months the broken rest that I had to endure on the Dewsbury contract began to affect my physical condition.

Fortunately, the tunnel was nearly finished, and one of my most vivid memories of these far-off days is of the junction length being keyed in. It happened very early one morning. We all went to a public-house called the " Spangled Bull," which was situated on the top of the tunnel, and there I was invited to have whatever I cared to choose for breakfast. This breakfast of mine was a record and is still remembered by one or two of my friends. I had four plates of round of beef, a large loaf, a bottle of pickles, and thirty-two glasses of beer, and having done full justice to this modest meal, I was in my place at the office punctually at ten o'clock. Whether it was the breakfast or the broken rest of the preceding four months I do not know, but Mr. Ralph seemed to notice that my health had suffered. He told me that I need not go back to the tunnel, but that I could put in my full time at the office, *i.e.*, from nine in the morning to six in the evening. This continued for a while, but later on he asked me to prepare designs for a pair of villas that he was about to build on some ground at Cricklewood. My ideas of architecture were rather restricted, and I told him so. I have a clear recollection of his reply, which was to the effect that I had been living in houses long enough to know how to design one, and that he expected me to do it. So there was no alternative but to comply with his request, and all that is necessary to add is that the villas were built and are standing to-day.

In 1872 the firm obtained a contract for a railway from Finsbury Park to Canonbury, and Mr. Ralph sent me to open an office at Ashburton Grove. A little later another contract was obtained for the tunnels out of King's Cross—the Copenhagen tunnel and the Maiden Lane tunnel. These were commenced in 1875 and completed in 1878. The firm had at the same time heavy work in Derbyshire on the Erewash Valley line, and were also constructing a junction line from Sedgebrook to Barkston, near Grantham. All this work was under the charge of Mr. Ralph. The contractor's office was supervised by Mr. Edwin Elliott, who was subsequently associated for many years with Pauling and Company, Limited, and who is still carrying out contracts for himself.[1] I was next to Mr. Elliott and, with the assistance of two or three clerks, we did all the commercial side of the business. He had also to measure up the Erewash Valley contract every month, as well as a portion of the Finsbury Park to Canonbury line, for certificate purposes. It was part of my duty to make up the Sedgebrook-Barkston monthly certificates and to help in setting out the work on the London job. My experience on the Helm and Dewsbury tunnels proved very helpful, and Mr. Ralph insisted on my making myself useful on the covered way tunnels at Highbury and on the Copenhagen tunnel. My pay had, of course, increased, but did not then exceed £2 a week. Mr.

[1] Mr. Elliott has died since these Memoirs were written.—ED.

Elliott and I had frequently to put in as much as a hundred hours' work in seven days. When I ventured to suggest to Mr. Ralph that we were being overworked, he retorted that hundreds of young fellows would pay much money to learn what I was learning, whereas I was being trained and receiving pay at the same time. I have long since realized that he was right, but must confess that it did seem hard at the time. I put in about three years at this London work and I recollect taking advantage, early in 1875, of the presence of old Joe—as we irreverently called Mr. Joseph Firbank behind his back—to ask him for an increase of wages. He said, "Why, tha's only a lad."

I was bold enough to reply that I ate as much as a man and did a man's work. I had not been bold in vain, for he gave me a rise of ten shillings a week.

V

African Aspirations

AFTER I had arrived in London and had been given charge of the office I took the opportunity of finding an opening for my brother Harry. About the middle of the year 1874 my father had obtained an appointment as an engineer on the Cape Government Railways. This enabled him to improve materially the circumstances of the family. Early in 1875, having reached the mature age of twenty, I bethought myself very seriously of my own and my brother's future careers. I could see a prospect of earning £600, or perhaps £800, a year as a contractor's agent until I reached middle age, and then the possibility of being out of a billet with an indifferent chance of obtaining another; in fact, such was my frame of mind, that I could discern nothing but an ultimate end in the workhouse if I remained in England. Our grand-uncle, Mr. Henry Pauling, had been an engineer on the Cape Railways from the commencement of their construction, and at that time he was chief engineer of the Western Province Railways. This, however, had nothing to do with the appointment of my father as an engineer in Africa, as all the staff were engaged in England by Sir Charles Hutton Gregory, who was then consulting engineer to the Cape Government. It was, however, because of the fact that Mr. Henry Pauling and my father were both at the Cape that Harry and I decided my brother should seek his fortune in that country. By June of that year we had jointly, by exercising severe economy, managed to save about £10. We took up an assisted second-class passage for him, costing £7, and he reached the Cape in July. In the following September I attained my majority, and Mr. Ralph Firbank considered that I was free from pupilage. I felt that he did not want me to sever my connection with his firm, but the spirit of romance ran strong in my blood and I could not resist the call of the Cape. So it was that I arranged with Mr. T. E. Fuller, who was then Emigration Agent, for an assisted passage similar to that under which my brother had gone to Africa.

In the middle of November I told Mr. Ralph that I was leaving for the Cape in four days. He was more than astonished, begged me to abandon the idea, and offered me more money to remain in England, but on my arguing the matter with him he acknowledged that I was right and concluded by expressing regret that he had not taken the same course when he was young. As a send-off the staff of Firbank gave me a dinner and a memento in the form of a ring. I went to Southampton and sailed from there in the s.s. "Anglian" on the 19th of November 1875. I had to share a cabin with seven other men, most of them railway inspectors and artisans going out to work on the Cape railways.

We had what seemed to me a dreadful storm in the Bay of Biscay, and I was so seasick that I prayed the ship should sink that I might be at rest. By the time I got to Madeira, however, I had quite recovered and was thoroughly enjoying myself. In those days I could rough it with the roughest and hold my own with any of them. So the discomfort of the voyage did not affect me. The "Anglian" was then the crack ship of the Union Company, and it was expected to make the journey in twenty-eight days. There was no electric light, ice, nor other conveniences, and while passing through the tropics the ship got seemingly red hot. We used to lie about on deck sweltering in the heat, and we envied the first-class passengers who were at least a little more comfortable than we were. When, however, we approached land and saw Table Mountain in the distance, all our discomforts were forgotten. I am sure that most of us, being young men, were castle-building and wondering what the future had in store for us in the new land.

VI

The Land of Sunshine

WE reached Cape Town after a voyage extending to thirty days. I expected my father to meet me at the docks. He did not, however, put in an appearance and I began to wonder what I should do. As a stranger in a strange land with only one half-sovereign in the world, my outlook was not inspiring. From the docks I went up into the town, and after making some enquiries found him with some companions in the Fountain Hotel. He seemed very pleased to see me and excused himself for not having met me on my arrival. He asked me many questions about the voyage and inquired how I was off for cash. I told him that all that remained to me was half a sovereign. Whereupon he suggested that I should get a hole bored in it and wear it on my watch-chain, prophesying that in the years that were to come, when I should become an African magnate, I could always regard it with pleasure as a memento of my financial circumstances when I first arrived in Cape Town. In less than half an hour he had borrowed the same half-sovereign to meet his immediate obligations. He was a very forgetful man. After spending a couple of days in Cape Town we went to the place where he was stationed on the railway. At that time, the end of 1875, only about a hundred miles of railway had been built in the whole of South Africa, some eighty miles of which extended from Cape Town to a point near Tulbagh Kloof. The other twenty miles had been built inland from Port Elizabeth, and I think a mile or two had been laid in Natal. A very progressive railway policy had, however, been decided upon, and railways were projected towards the interior from Cape Town, Port Elizabeth, East London, and Durban, so that there were excellent prospects for railway men. My father was stationed as the engineer in charge of a section at Ceres Road, and my brother was employed with him as a field and drawing-office assistant. Afterwards my grand-uncle, Henry Pauling, took Harry as an articled pupil. My father wanted me, before endeavouring to obtain a billet, to get some general experience of South Africa, so I put in at Ceres Road a month of inactivity, except that I managed the domestic department for the three of us, in which capacity I succeeded in materially reducing the cost of living.

I soon became tired of doing little or nothing and went to Cape Town to see Mr. John X. Merriman, the Chief Commissioner of Public Works, with a view to seeking an appointment as an assistant engineer. There were two tunnels about to be built on the Hex River section, and he at first proposed to get me an appointment on these tunnels. There was, however, another tunnel projected on the Grahamstown line in the Eastern Province, and, possibly because there were already three engineers of the name of Pauling on the Western Province lines, Mr. Merriman gave me a letter of recommendation to Mr. Napier, the resident engineer on the Grahamstown line.

I made the journey by sea from Cape Town to Port Elizabeth and had as a travelling companion a Mr. Fred M'Coll, who was also proceeding to Grahamstown to take up a post as a draughtsman in the office there. There was then only a very small jetty at Port Elizabeth, and passengers landed on the beach. It was necessary for one to get on the back of a nigger to be carried through the surf and thereby avoid getting wet.

We remained a couple of days in Port Elizabeth and then went by rail about twenty miles, thence by post cart to Grahamstown. The post cart was a two-wheeled Cape cart, capable of carrying about half a ton of mails and eight passengers, and was drawn by six or eight horses. We changed horses about every two hours, or approximately at each twelve-mile stage. On our arrival in Grahamstown we put up at the Masonic Hotel. Next morning we reported ourselves at the engineer's office. The survey of the line was not quite complete and we were instructed to camp about two miles from the town. M'Coll was rather a heavy drinker, and I am afraid that my habits were not then sufficiently temperate to set him a good example. Fred had been drinking far more than I knew and one night I woke up in the bell tent, in which we had both been sleeping on stretchers, to find him with a candle trying to set light to the green baize lining which, he assured me, was infested with monkeys, snakes, devils, and other fearful creatures. He was a powerful man, and in those days I did not know of delirium tremens or what it meant. However, I knocked the candle out of his hand and tackled him, but he would have been too strong for me had I not shouted for help, and thus obtained the assistance of a cook and two grooms. Between us we managed to secure Fred to the tent pole in an upright position and lash him round with so much rope that he could not move. I then fed him with teaspoonfuls of chlorodyne until he went to sleep. I soon followed suit and very early the next morning sent for the doctor. When he came he told me it was quite possible Fred would never waken as I had given him the greater portion of a bottle of chlorodyne. However, he did awake, pulled himself together, forgave me, and we continued the best of friends; and I do not think he ever went so far on the road to ruin again. He did not remain long on the Grahamstown job. He had wealthy friends, was an adventurous chap, and I heard some years afterwards of his having been killed by a lion in a different part of Africa.

VII

My First Contract

WHILE the survey of the Grahamstown line was in progress I had been seriously ruminating over my position. I could see that there was no fortune to be made out of the engineering profession in South Africa, whereas at the prices that were then being paid for railway work there was ample scope to make a lot of money. I was practically the only man in the Government engineering service who had had any experience of tunnel construction. Mr. Napier had moved to another position and his place had been taken by a Mr. Rose. The Waai Nek tunnel, near Grahamstown, was about to be built. An English foreman named Billy Frith had been sent out to commence operations. My instructions were to supervise the work in the tunnel and on each side of it, but I thought it would be more remunerative if I were to obtain a contract. I succeeded in doing so and took Frith in with me, giving him a one-third interest. Having no money, I was face to face with the eternal problem of finance, but I got out of the difficulty by arranging with a good firm of merchants in Grahamstown to put up a store at the tunnel to supply my men with provisions, and the other necessities and luxuries of life, and I was shrewd enough to make it a condition that they should give me financial assistance to get the work started and that they should also pay me one-third of the store profits. Their assistance was only really necessary for the first month, because the price I had got for the tunnel was excellent and yielded considerable profit. With such success the contracting fever took a severe hold upon me and I began to think that I might make an effort to obtain more work on the Grahamstown line, but Mr. Rose was of opinion that I had enough to attend to at the tunnel. Failing to share his view, I bethought myself of other means to obtain the desired end. Railway construction foremen had by this time been sent to various parts of the new railways under construction, including the Grahamstown railway, so I created a somewhat heterogeneous syndicate, consisting of an Italian, a Scotchman, and an old English navvy. I prompted these men as to the prices they should ask for the different classes of work and they obtained contracts at these prices. The general management of this international combination was under my control, in recognition of which I was to receive a half share of any profits. I had no difficulty with the Italian and the Scotchman, but the English navvy proved a terror. My interest in the work was unknown to Mr. Rose, and consequently I could take no active part in drawing the money every month to pay the men and to meet our other obligations. When the navvy drew his money, instead of disbursing it in the usual honourable way, he developed an unfortunate habit of remaining in Grahamstown and disposing of it in riotous living. Frequently I had to leave Frith to pay our own men and to run the navvy to earth in his haunts of doubtful repute. On one occasion I found him in a house where he had been robbed of over £400, which he had drawn to pay the men. By dint of very harsh measures towards the landlady I managed to get nearly all the money back. I took him out to his camp, locked him up, and kept him in a room on very short commons for a few days, and for some time afterwards he behaved himself. With all his faults he was an affectionate old chap and was really very fond of me. He was incapable of bearing malice, and during the intermittent periods when he was sober he invariably acknowledged that I was his best friend.

After some time the Italian got homesick, and when he had squared up he left. I then got Mr. Rose to take over his work, which consisted of a short tunnel and some heavy work about nine miles from Grahamstown, at a place called Ross's camp. I write it, not in any spirit of vanity but more of thankfulness for the strength and endurance given to me, that these were really strenuous days. By four o'clock in the morning I was generally out of bed and away on horseback to inspect the work that was in progress beyond Ross's camp. I then visited practically every bit of work that was being carried on and was back to my camp at Waai Nek tunnel before breakfast. After a bath and a morning meal I supervised my own work in the tunnel until the middle of the day. Then a snack and on horse again to ride right through the work and back to my camp. But I was not indifferent to the enjoyment of ordinary pleasures and, considering myself entitled to a little recreation, it was my habit to go into Grahamstown to the Masonic Hotel, enjoy a good dinner, drink freely with congenial spirits, and play billiards till the hotel closed. Riding back to camp I usually arrived there before midnight. Whenever a favourable opportunity occurred I put in an hour or so sleeping in the daytime, but generally speaking I was at work at least thirteen or fourteen hours a day. By the time the tunnel was finished the other work on the line was also completed, and I got a contract to lay the rails, and ballast the line from Highlands, about eighteen miles away, into Grahamstown Station. When this was finished the railway was opened and a through route was established from Grahamstown to Port Elizabeth via Alicedale Junction.

VIII

Side Lines

RAILWAY work in the Colony then slackened off, and for the moment my occupation as a railway man was gone. I had attained the ripe age of twenty-four years, and had made about £15,000. In 1877, as a side line, I entered into my first matrimonial contract.

In Grahamstown I had, in the nature of things, made several business friends. I had never indulged in social friendships, although when I first arrived in the town I thought the social circle might be of advantage to me. The Wesleyan fraternity appeared to present the best social opportunities, and I frequented the church of that community and even took a class in the Sunday school. On the first Sunday we arrived in Grahamstown M'Coll and I paid a visit to the Wesleyan Chapel. His worldly wealth consisted of half a sovereign and a sixpence. We were sitting in a front pew and when the collection plate was handed round Fred, to the eternal discredit of his Caledonian origin, put in the half sovereign instead of the sixpence. I grasped the awful situation, and when the plate came to me I looked the collector in the face, and whispering that my friend had made a mistake, took out the half-sovereign. Had I not done so we should have been on a compulsorily teetotal diet for several days. I shall never forget the surprised and horrified look of the man who took up the collection.

Amongst my business friends there were a saddler and a baker, and when I was in a position to do so, I put some money into each of their businesses. Ostrich farming was then outgrowing its infancy, and there was a boom in that industry. A friend of mine named Bill Upsher, who had been at school with me at St. Ives, chanced to come to Grahamstown. He had been brought up as a farmer in England, and before removing to Grahamstown had held an agricultural appointment near Port Elizabeth. He knew something about ostriches, and by his advice I took a farm of 16,000 acres called Bucklands, situated on the Great Fish River, about sixteen miles from Grahamstown. There I started Upsher with a few ostriches and three hundred head of cattle. I had also commenced business as a builder and contractor in Grahamstown and had obtained contracts to build two wagon factories, an extension of the Diocesan Girls' School, and the Dundas Bridge in the town; and having become a Freemason I was entrusted with the work of building the Masonic Temple. With a considerable portion of my money thus distributed in various directions I decided to have a trip to England, and in the autumn of 1879 I took my wife and our baby, George, to the Old Country.

We travelled home in the s.s. "Arab." It was just after the Majuba affair and the Zulu war, and there was quite a number of officers on board. Mrs. Pauling was a very bad sailor and was confined to her cabin during practically the whole of the voyage. The night before we were due to arrive in Plymouth there was much noise and ragging outside our cabin. About half-past ten someone banged at our door. I opened it and was immediately hustled by two or three people. I was at a loss to know what to make of the situation and struck out generally, at the same time making full use of that forcible vocabulary which is one of the necessary assets of a contractor. To a man immediately in front of me I dispensed the upper cut, which lifted him off the floor, and his head broke the lamp in the alleyway. I then barged into another individual, named Bouchier, and, believing him to be one of the rowdy officers, I hit him in the midriff and put him out of breath for about a quarter of an hour. By this time there was a general pandemonium raging in the alleyway. All the passengers, more or less in deshabille, were emerging from their cabins. The captain arrived in due course, and probably judging from my language that I was the principal culprit, he sent for quartermasters to put me in irons. Luckily for me, however, Mr. Watson, the chief engineer of the Eastern Province Railways, who, with his wife, occupied a cabin near to us, had heard the riot. He told the captain that the fault was altogether on the side of the youthful military officers. The captain accepted his assurance; I escaped durance vile; and an honourable peace was concluded all round. Next morning Bouchier came to me and suggested that in future when I felt in the mood to hit a man I might at least inquire if he had connection with the trouble. It transpired that he had been quite an innocent victim. I, of course, apologized most profusely and was really heartily sorry. Next morning we reached Plymouth and I was grieved to learn that one of the officers whom I had assaulted the night before, and who subsequently attained great distinction in his military career, had on arrival received news of the death of his father. His face had been severely bruised and cut and I could not refrain from expressing my sorrow at what had occurred. As became a gentleman, he insisted that the apology should have come from his brother officers and himself. In fact, the whole disturbance had been the outcome of a mistake. The young bloods had intended to rag a brother officer who occupied the cabin opposite mine, but they had knocked at the wrong door. When I came out they at first thought that their victim had been delivered into their hands, and when the alleyway light went out and I started hitting all round, everyone lost his head and it developed into a free fight. This episode on the " Arab " was remembered for very

BLAAUWKRANTZ BRIDGE ON THE KOWIE RAILWAY.

GEORGE PAULING WITH HIS FIRST WIFE PHOTOGRAPHED IN GRAHAMSTOWN.

many years by the officers of the ship and I frequently heard of it on later voyages.

On arriving in England I took a house near Finsbury Park, where I established a temporary home for my wife and son. I lost no time in ascertaining the whereabouts of Mr. Ralph Firbank, who was then living near Manchester. He had severed his connection with his uncle and had gone into partnership with Mr. Baker, who had been one of Mr. Joseph Firbank's foremen. Mr. Baker had had the fortune to gain the goodwill of the Duke of Portland of that day, who was a recluse and a mystery to most people. The Duke gave Mr. Baker a lot of work, including the making of an underground riding school, and the construction of the tunnels under the park at Welbeck. Out of this work he made much money, and, as he knew that Mr. Ralph was an exceptionally able contractor's agent, I imagine he found the capital to start the firm of Baker and Firbank. Mr. Ralph told me a good deal about this, and suggested that as I had done well in South Africa I might try to obtain contract work in England. I did not tell him that I had invested nearly all my money in South Africa, but the idea of carrying out work in this country appealed to me, and under his advice I tendered for several small jobs. Indeed, I was on the point of taking a contract, when I received news from the lawyer in Grahamstown to whom I had deputed the management of my affairs, that if I did not return at once I should probably lose all my money. I therefore took passages for my wife, child, and self, and returned to South Africa with the least possible delay.

Amongst my other Grahamstown investments I had lent £5,000 to the landlord of the Masonic Hotel, who was a great friend of mine. He had, during my absence, got into difficulties, and with the object of making an effort to save my money I took over the premises. Except as a patron I had had no previous experience of the public-house line of business, but I was young and enthusiastic, and prepared to take my chance in any commercial proposition that came my way. Saddlery and baking had both gone wrong and had taken my money with them. The boom in ostriches was over, and the value of breeding birds, for which I had paid as much as £600 a pair, had depreciated to about a sixth of that figure. In partnership with another man I had chartered a sailing vessel and sent Mr. Upsher to Australia with about three hundred ostriches on board, and we had high hopes of making a fortune out of the venture. Our vessel took a long time to get to its destination, and two others on a similar mission arrived before it, with the result that our birds did not yield enough to pay expenses, and our dreams of opulence were dissipated.

Mr. Upsher then came back to me on the farm. There was in that year a big drought in the Eastern Province and nearly all my cattle died. The tower of the Masonic Lodge in Grahamstown, which I had undertaken to build, fell just after it had been erected. I had protested against its construction because of the unsuitability of the substructure, and I was therefore not liable. This was admitted, but to oblige my masonic brethren I undertook to re-erect the temple properly and relied upon them to pay me the cost. They, however, only paid a quarter of it and I lost the rest. From that time I ceased to take an active interest in freemasonry, although I had been Senior Warden and had reached as far as the Thirtieth Degree.

This accumulation of misfortune reduced me to a state of desperation and, about the middle of the year 1880, I had no alternative but to call a meeting of my creditors. They had, however, sufficient faith in me to think that I would pull through, and I was permitted to carry on. Railway work had, as I have already stated, practically ceased throughout South Africa, but about the end of that year, there was some talk of its resumption. Tenders were invited to build a railway from Cookhouse to Cradock. I combined with three other working contractors and we put in what was really a very good tender. The work, however, was not given to us on the plea that we were too small, and the contract was obtained by Faviell, who had previously completed the railway to Graaf Reinet. My friends and I, rightly or wrongly, considered that we had not received fair play, and I afterwards tried, as I believe successfully, to put a spoke in the wheel of the big contractors.

IX

The Kowie Railway

RAILWAY access from Grahamstown to the sea was then through Port Elizabeth, a distance of about a hundred miles. The natural outlet was, however, Port Alfred, at the mouth of the Kowie River, only about forty miles away. The Government had, in previous years, spent something like £200,000 in making the river accessible to ships of small draught, and big vessels were unloaded in the roadstead into lighters which were brought into the river by steam tugs. One of the Members of Parliament for Grahamstown was Mr. Cron-Wright, with whom I was on terms of intimate friendship, and I suggested to him that, if the Government could be induced to grant a subsidy of approximately £2,000 per mile for building the railway from Kowie River to Grahamstown, I might be able to raise the rest of the money in England. I had in mind to get Mr. Ralph Firbank to join me in this venture, and had previously written to him on the subject. Mr. Cron-Wright, and other members of Parliament for Grahamstown and Albany, thought well of the proposal, and during that session the Cape Parliament passed a Bill giving a subsidy of £1,500 a mile for its construction. Leaving the management of the hotel and my other affairs in the hands of my wife, I lost no time in sailing for England. As she was not able to look after all my local interests, I obtained six months' leave for my brother Harry, who was then an engineer in the Western Province, and he went to Grahamstown to help Mrs. Pauling.

I took with me to England full particulars of the

trade of Grahamstown and of Port Alfred and the district through which the railway would pass. I had figures to show that in the preceding ten years the trade of the Port had increased by several hundreds per cent. I also took with me a photograph, showing thirteen sailing vessels lying in the river at the wharves which had been constructed by the Government. These sailing vessels were, of course, of comparatively small tonnage, most of them being boats which had brought sugar from Mauritius, and were being loaded with maize and other produce from the Grahamstown district. I had the photo enlarged to about six feet in length, and it made a beautiful picture, showing the noble river with much shipping, indicating a centre of commercial progress, and I have no doubt that the photo assisted us greatly in our efforts to raise the necessary capital for the railway. I also brought home with me several photos of the magnificent scenery along the Kowie River which nowadays attracts many visitors to that part of the country. I knew that whatever I might be able to arrange at home would have to be completed with the utmost dispatch. Having the utmost confidence in the ability and wisdom of Mr. Ralph Firbank I at once referred to him. He took to my scheme with enthusiasm, and in less than two months we had formed a company with which on my estimates he had made a contract, in the name of Firbank and Pauling, to build the railway, and I returned almost post-haste to the Cape. There I saw Mr. Cron-Wright, and we had no trouble in fixing up an arrangement with the Cape Government.

The survey of the railway presented many difficulties. A very bad piece of country had to be crossed and it took some time before it was decided to cross the worst spot on the route called Blaaukrantz, about thirteen miles from Grahamstown, by a high level bridge. This bridge was subsequently built on the cantilever principle, with a central span over three hundred feet above the bottom of the gorge. In point of design it has been described as the most graceful in the Colony. It was designed by Mr. Max Am Ende, of Westminster, and to my mind it was at the time the strongest and lightest bridge of its kind in the world, and so long as it is properly maintained it will continue to fulfil its purpose. For a time the work progressed satisfactorily, but ere long I experienced much delay and trouble in obtaining money from home. When about two-thirds of the work were finished an arrangement proposed by Mr. Ralph Firbank for finding further capital fell through, and I had great difficulty in raising sufficient cash to carry on. I had reckoned on the probability of getting the Government to advance money against the subsidy of £1,500 per mile. But the department concerned resolutely refused to part with a fraction till the railway was completed, and I had no alternative but to acquaint my partner, Mr. Ralph Firbank, of my miscalculation in this connection. He wrote me that this fact had upset his arrangements, but that he was making others which, he had no doubt, would be carried through, and by which sufficient funds would be forthcoming. About a fortnight after this letter was written he died suddenly from heart failure. He left as executor his brother Christopher, who tried to complete the arrangement which Ralph had initiated. Unfortunately it fell through and I was put to all kinds of devices to manage to carry on. This would have been impossible had I not in the meantime obtained other contracts, of which I propose to write in succeeding chapters. We saw it through to the end, but it proved a sore drain on our resources. We had financed it to completion and had taken part payment in paper, which was never of any value to us. The Kowie Railway Company got the Government subsidy, part of which ultimately came back to us. The railway was opened in 1884 and was purchased from the Company by the Union Government in 1913.

X

More Side Lines

WHILE the Kowie Railway was under construction, and while I was gradually becoming involved in other large projects, several events of greater or less interest to me were occurring in Grahamstown. Rink skating had become a craze in South Africa, and a man arrived in our town with several hundred pairs of skates. He hired, as a skating rink, the Albany Hall, which had a fairly large floor space. He took a room at my hotel and, thinking that there might be some profit in the business, I asked him to allow me to participate in his speculation. He flatly refused, and probably partly from that reason and partly from his having offended me in another direction, I decided to build an opposition rink. I leased a vacant piece of ground in the High Street, close to the hotel, and in a fortnight I had erected on it a wood and iron building with about double the floor space of the Albany Hall, and a concrete floor with a smooth cement surface. This at once dislocated his show, and I had the satisfaction of buying all his skates at about a shilling a pair, subject to discount to the extent of his hotel bill. Naturally, in a small place like Grahamstown, the skating furore did not last long, but I had judiciously acquired the patronage of the élite of the town, who paid me handsomely for the privilege of having the rink at their exclusive disposal for three days a week. For the remaining days the rink was at the disposal of the plebeian element; and altogether, from a financial point of view, I had no cause to regret the temporary skating enthusiasm of the people of Grahamstown.

Just about the time that the skating fever began to wane, Mr. Frank Fillis, the well-known South African circus proprietor, arrived in the town with one or two horses, a few dogs, and two or three men. He had fallen on evil days and had lost nearly all that he had ever possessed. He put up at my hotel and it occurred to me that he might to some extent retrieve his fallen fortunes by giving circus performances in the rink. We accordingly set to work to convert the rink into a circus, and our wisdom was justified. For a month or two Fillis had a good time and he left Grahamstown with much more money than he had brought into it; in fact, I think his visit put him on his feet again.

Although it afforded me a considerable amount of amusement and through it I had made many friends, the licensing business was not one which had any great attraction for me, and I had been trying for some time to get rid of the Masonic Hotel in Grahamstown. Ultimately I succeeded in getting a Port Elizabeth firm to supply a good man to take it over. He did not, however, pay me anything, and not only did I fail to retrieve the £5,000 which I had put into it, but I also lost a considerable additional sum. When I returned from England to commence the construction of the Kowie Railway I was practically free from all other business troubles except the carrying of the mails and the running of the passenger cart between Grahamstown and Port Alfred. This I had obtained on a yearly contract in partnership with a man who kept an hotel about fourteen miles from Grahamstown.

I had not only lost my first fortune of £15,000, but through ill-luck and foolishly helping other people by backing bills and similar indulgences, I had incurred very considerable obligations. By the time I got rid of the Masonic Hotel and had commenced the Kowie Railway I had cleared off practically all my debts, with the exception of one for furniture which I had had to buy to set up a private residence. My creditor for this furniture had once or twice asked me for payment, but as he professed to be a friend of mine I had not taken serious notice of his requests and it was with astonishment that I learned he had obtained judgment against me for the debt. I was made very painfully aware of it, however, one evening when, after returning from the Kowie Railway about six o'clock, I found my wife and children in great distress on the hillside near our house and, between her sobs, Mrs. Pauling told me that a man had come and taken possession of the house. She had been so frightened that she went outside with the children to wait for me. I was furious, entered the house, kicked the bailiff out, and threatened to " half-kill " him if he ever tried to come in again. This was a most drastic and illegal action on my part, and as soon as the man had gone away I went into the town and hunted up my lawyer. He took a very serious view of what I had done to the bailiff, but said he would try to make things all right. Fortunately I had the money to pay off the furniture debt, otherwise I might not have escaped my deserts so easily.

XI

The Ghosts of Grahamstown and "The Comet"

AMONGST the heterogeneous visitors to the Masonic Hotel there arrived one day a man of the name of Houghton. A journalist by profession, he possessed an outstanding, if none too scrupulous, personality. He had had a very varied experience in commercial life, and after having been in the hotel for some weeks and having acquired considerable local knowledge, he asked me to let him have the skating rink in which to deliver a series of lectures. These, he told me, were to be entitled "The Ghosts of Grahamstown." It should be explained that Grahamstown is called "The City of Saints," and contains many chapels, churches, public-houses, and other inducements to virtue and vice. My first conclusion was that such a series of lectures as Mr. Houghton contemplated would prove particularly interesting. On being shown the introductory lecture, however, I had occasion to change my mind. It commenced by stating that for some time Houghton had hesitated between dedicating the lecture to Judas Iscariot or the Impenitent Thief, but that he had found a solution of his difficulty by addressing it to a local gentleman whose name he did not hesitate to introduce, and who was a very important member of the community. I knew trouble would ensue if the lecture was delivered, and I therefore refused Houghton the use of the rink. He became somewhat abusive and insulting; and as he had neglected to pay his hotel bill and had offended an acquaintance of mine to whom he also owed money, friendly relations ceased and we got judgment against him in the Magistrates' Court, and paid a shilling a day to have him locked up as a civil prisoner. He was incarcerated, I think, on a Wednesday. On the Friday morning the local dean, in company with the Congregationalist minister, came to interview me. They told me that Houghton had asked them to come to the prison, and in a very contrite and beseeching manner had requested them to implore the prayers of their respective congregations on the following Sunday for a poor prisoner. What was probably more material to Houghton, they appealed to my humanity that I should allow him out of prison. Neither his other creditor nor I was devoid of a sense of humour and the situation tickled us immensely. So on the Saturday morning I went to fetch Houghton out and restored him to the dignity of a guest at the hotel. This occurred about the time when our tender for the line from Cookhouse to Cradock had been rejected. I told Houghton of the incident and also of our suspicion that we had been unfairly treated by the Government, acting under the advice of its engineering department. He suggested that if I would lend him a little money he would start a small newspaper and take the matter up. This proved the humble origin of "The Comet" which, I believe, became the most libellous newspaper ever published in the Cape. The paper was entitled "The Comet" because of the uncertainty of the intervals at which it would make its appearance. No printer would take the risk of having any connection with it, and Houghton set up the type and printed off about 1,500 copies of each issue on a hand printing machine in a little building which he rented and the whereabouts of which was known only to a select few. He was a very good compositor, and being always keen on learning all I could I helped him to set up the type.

Houghton's personal grievances against different people were much more extensive than I had been aware of, and in addition to fighting our battle he carried on a campaign on his own account. He had engaged as the nominal editor of the paper a man to whom he paid £20 a month. We called this man the "Prison Editor" because, for some months, he was constantly serving short terms of imprisonment for libellous articles which had appeared in "The Comet." The railway articles, however, served their purpose. They resulted in Houghton being prosecuted for criminal libel against one of the Government engineers. He defended himself, and for a week gave the engineer a most outrageous time in the witness-box before the resident magistrate. He was committed for trial, which in due course took place at the Eastern Districts Court. He again acted as his own counsel, and by challenging various members who had been called on the jury, succeeded in getting included on that body a young man who, being under twenty-one years of age, was not qualified to serve in that capacity. This was a precaution in case the verdict should go against Houghton, when a fresh trial would have been demanded on the ground of the incompetence of the jury. However, this was scarcely to be feared as the sympathy of the public and of the majority of the jurymen was with us, because of the unfair treatment our tender for the Cradock line had received. When all the evidence had been given, Houghton addressed the jury on his own behalf. In his speech the prosecuting barrister called Houghton many unpleasant names, and amongst other things had stated that as they could not take damages out of his pocket they were determined to take punishment out of his hide. Houghton was very much enraged, and in his defence called attention to the fact that under Roman Dutch law the offence of criminal libel could be punished with death. He said it was very hard for a man of pure English blood to be insulted by an individual having black blood in his veins—he referred to the prosecuting counsel—and he went on to state that under that law, by which he was being tried, both the judge on the bench and the prosecuting barrister could be whipped through the streets of Grahamstown at the end of a cart. Grahamstown races were then taking place, and the lotteries associated with them were advertised as being under the patronage of the judge and the solicitor-general. By Roman Dutch Law lotteries were forbidden, and anyone taking active part in them was liable to be treated as a rogue and a vagabond, and to be whipped at the tail of a cart through the public streets. Houghton's speech caused immense excitement and amusement in the court. The jury retired, but did not take long to return with a verdict of " Not guilty." Houghton was carried from the court to the Masonic Hotel, where I reaped a rich harvest dispensing drinks and other refreshments to half the population.

XII

A Diamond Hunt

AN amusing and interesting episode occurred on one of my voyages to the Cape. I was travelling again by the s.s. "Arab," the chief engineer of which at the time was an Irishman named Cassidy. In those days, while travelling to or from the Cape, nearly all the passengers became more or less intimately acquainted, and the community developed into a gigantic family party. Amongst the passengers on this particular ship there was a Mr. Lowenthal, an old Kimberley man of very striking appearance. There were also two young Scotchmen, making a maiden voyage and going out to seek their fortunes. They appeared, as far as I remember, about twenty years of age, very nice young fellows but intensely inquisitive, and they never lost a chance of seeking information about their future country, South Africa. They pestered Mr. Lowenthal with questions to such an extent that he asked Cassidy and me to join in getting up a "rag" for them. The day after the boat left Madeira, Mr. Lowenthal, in the smoking-room and within hearing of the Scotchmen, asked the chief engineer if we might go down to have a look over the engine room. Mr. Cassidy, as had been arranged, readily acquiesced, and the inquisitive Scotchmen were permitted to join us. After looking well over the engines we went down into the stokehole. On arriving there, Mr. Lowenthal looked interestedly at the coal coming from one of the bunkers, and said: "Cassidy, where did that coal come from?"

Cassidy replied: "Oh, we took it on board at Algoa Bay last voyage."

Lowenthal then innocently observed: "I believe it is coal from my farm near Kimberley," and, stooping down, took up a handful of its dust. With extreme care he turned it over in the palm of his hand and amongst the dust appeared to discover three or four rough diamonds which, of course, he had dexterously secreted there. Pretending to be very surprised, he said: "Why, Cassidy, it is just as I have always thought, this coal is diamondiferous. Now, this must be kept a great secret and you must not burn any more coal from that bunker. We will have it discharged at Cape Town and well searched. There might be thousands of pounds in it, and if there are you shall all have a share in the profits."

The engineer replied: "All right, Mr. Lowenthal, I will see what I can do."

The Scotchmen were palpably very much impressed. We all went up to the smoking-room, and after we had had several rounds of refreshment, Mr. Cassidy went to his cabin followed closely by the Scotchmen, whose national avidity had been fully aroused. In the course of a general conversation the engineer told them that he was in a quandary; that he did not know how to break the news to Mr. Lowenthal, but that he could not possibly keep the coal as it would be necessary to use it all to get to Cape Town. The only solution he could suggest was to restrict the burning of the coal from the particular bunker to one furnace for so many hours each day, and to have the ashes carefully examined, but he was afraid he could not trust the firemen if any diamonds should be discovered.

By this time Mr. Cassidy had completely captured the Scotchmen. They begged to be allowed to be present at the examination of the ashes and undertook to accept full responsibility if any diamonds were found. The engineer, who would have made a name for himself as an actor, protested that this would violate the strict regulations of the ship, but after what appeared a great deal of persuasion he consented to accept £50 to allow the Scotchmen to disguise themselves as firemen. It was arranged that one should be below in the stokehole and the other at the top of the ash lift to examine the contents of the ash bucket each time it was brought up and to make sure no diamonds were lost before the ashes were thrown overboard. The Scotchmen were quite content with this arrangement, and for two of the hottest days of the voyage, in the region of Cape Verde, one was down below for about four hours a day, and the other on top diligently searching the ashes. Meantime we had let a few of the other passengers into the secret and we spent the Scotchmen's £50 in the smoking room standing drinks to all and sundry. After two days Mr. Lowenthal thought they had endured sufficient penance for their curiosity. One or two of us accordingly went down to interview the Caledonian on the ash lift who, with a black face, a sweater, and a swab round his neck like an ordinary fireman, was engrossed in his search. His friend was brought up, and Mr. Lowenthal moralized to both of them on the evils of too much inquisitiveness and explained to them that at a cost of £50, which they could well afford, they had learned a lesson which would probably be of infinite value to them in after life. Notwithstanding their nationality they took the joke in splendid part, and we were all the best of friends for the rest of the voyage.

XIII

A Feat of Strength

SINCE, if not before, the days of Solomon, it has been an accepted axiom that all mankind is vain. At the time of which I write I was particularly proud of my physical strength, and many were the opportunities I had of demonstrating the extent of my muscular power. While "mine host" of the Masonic Hotel in Grahamstown, I possessed a Basuto pony which weighed about four hundred and fifty pounds and which was capable of carrying me as many as sixty miles a day, and in fact did so. The animal had been so trained to allow me to get my head and shoulders between its front legs and to lift it on my back. In this position I frequently carried it from the stable into the billiard room and round the billiard table in the hotel. My clients at the hotel, like most colonials, were irresponsible gamblers, and from the uninitiated I won many rounds of drinks by carrying out this feat. One day, however, I had a literal demonstration of the Biblical adage that "pride goeth before a fall." Being vain enough to think that I could do so, I attempted to carry the pony upstairs, but my strength was insufficient for the task and I fell with the pony on top of me, and had a very narrow escape from having my brains kicked out. This proved to be the last performance, for from that day the animal refused to be a party to its repetition.

XIV

Sterkstroom to Aliwal North

IN the early 'eighties the Cape Government invited tenders for the construction of a railway from Sterkstroom to Aliwal North through a district which afterwards became historic in the days of the Boer War. There were about ninety miles of very heavy work, and I submitted a tender in the name of Firbank and Pauling, Mr. Christopher Firbank having agreed that he would find the two sureties asked for by the Government when tenders were sent in. Three or four firms competed, amongst them my old opponents, Messrs. Faviell. I, however, succeeded, my tender being about £500,000, with the Government supplying the permanent way materials. A peculiarity of this contract was that the Government, to save time, had already let to small sub-contractors some of the heavy work at a place called Bushman's Hoek, and a clause in the contract provided that this work would be measured and that credit would be given at scheduled prices to the successful contractor, who would be debited with the prices paid to the sub-contractors. I had spotted this clause as the probable means of obtaining the working capital necessary to carry out the contract, for both Mr. Firbank and I, with all our efforts, could only raise about £3,000 for that purpose. This tided me over the few weeks necessary to have the sub-contractors' work measured up and to hand in the account to the Government engineers for the difference between the credit due and the debit against it. The difference meant that I got £17,000 practically before

I did any work. The chief engineer objected very strongly to this money being paid to me, but he could not help himself, as it was a condition of the contract, and, as I pointed out to him, it really made no difference because my tender was for a lump sum based on a schedule of prices, and if I got something more for one class of work I certainly got a bit less for another class, as my lump sum tender was the lowest the Government had received and was well within the estimate the engineers had made of the cost of the line. So I did not consider I had done anything wrong in making use of a clause so favourable to me. This contract I knew to be one out of which £100,000 to £150,000 might be made, and after I got the £17,000 on the first certificate I was able to keep on financing the Kowie job, which otherwise would have been a source of continual worry to me.

A curious event, and, so far as I was concerned, one of considerable importance, occurred in connection with the landing of the material necessary for the construction of this railway. About 60,000 tons had to be brought from England. The shipment was entrusted partly to the Union and partly to the Castle line, which had not then been amalgamated. Before I tendered I had ascertained that the landing charges of the boating companies at East London for discharging cargo from the steamers lying in the roadstead into the lighters and bringing it ashore was about four shillings and sixpence per ton. In my tender I had allowed about five shillings and sixpence, but I had omitted to make any arrangement beforehand with the boating companies. When I got the contract I asked them how much less than four and six they were prepared to charge. To my surprise they replied that their price would be ten and six a ton. This was a disturbing feature which I had to take immediate steps to overcome. At the time I had on the Kowie River a tug and several lighters belonging to a little company which I had formed there for landing cargo, and having obtained the concurrence of my friends interested in it, I arranged to send the tug and lighters round to East London. Each time a steamer arrived there with cargo I instructed my agents, Messrs. Robert and John Stroyan, that they were to send out the tug and lighters with a letter addressed to the captain of the steamer demanding any cargo it might contain for the railway. The two East London Boating Companies had arrangements, one with the Castle and the other with the Union Company, by which they discharged all cargo, so that the captain of each steamer as it arrived refused to allow my tug and lighters to take any of our materials. I insisted on getting the refusals in writing, and so the game went on. The East London Boating Companies brought the cargoes ashore, and as the material in which I was interested was Government property they could not, although they tried hard to do so, prevent me from obtaining possession of it without paying their landing charges. This went on until about 20,000 tons had been landed, when they sued me for the landing charges at ten shillings and sixpence a ton. The case came before Judge Shippard. My counsel was Mr. Dick, afterwards Sir Richard Soloman, the Agent-General in London of the Cape Government. I lost the case, the judge deciding that it was the custom of the Port for the East London Boating Companies to discharge the cargo, and consequently the steamship companies were justified in refusing to put the material into my lighters. My counsel was absolutely certain that the decision was wrong, and by his advice I appealed to the High Court, depositing security in case judgment should be given against me. It took some considerable time before the appeal was heard, and by then all the cargo for the contract had been landed and forwarded to the work. The High Court gave a decision in my favour, consequently the East London Boat Companies had landed 60,000 tons of cargo, for which they got nothing. My Kowie Boat Company was quite satisfied when I gave them half a crown a ton for their trouble in sending out the tug and lighters when the steamers came in.

XV

Orange River to Kimberley

WHILE running the Masonic Hotel in Grahamstown I had made the acquaintance of Mr. George Garcia Wolf, who afterwards became a very great friend of mine. He went to Kimberley, opened a big furniture business there, and became senior member for that town in the Cape Parliament. About the same time Mr. Rhodes became Member of Parliament for Barkly West. As I had been successful in obtaining an Act of Parliament and a subsidy for the construction of the Kowie Railway, Mr. Wolf and I thought it might be possible to get the Cape Government to give a concession for the extension to Kimberley of the Cape Railway. The idea appealed to Mr. Rhodes, but after sounding Members of Parliament and of the Government, we were persuaded that there would be no chance of getting an Act through Parliament, so abandoned the idea.

Some time, however, before I finished the Aliwal North contract, on which I had reason to believe I had given satisfaction to the authorities, some of my Cape Town friends told me that the Government wished the Kimberley extension to be built as rapidly as possible, and that, although they could not give my firm the contract without calling for tenders, they would favourably consider my tender if it were at all possible. The one essential condition was rapidity in construction. The expedition to the Rooi Grond in Bechuanaland was about to be sent under Sir Charles Warren, and it was realized that every mile that could be laid northwards would obviate many transport difficulties. There were four competitors for the Kimberley railway, including my oldest friend, "Jimmy" Butler. My tender was successful and I immediately set to work to organize a competent staff and to commence operations.

At the outset I had to build a temporary bridge over the Orange River. The erection of the permanent structure had been commenced and was being built departmentally by the Government. One of the noblest bridges in South Africa, it cost about £60,000 and was opened for traffic in 1885. Consisting of nine spans, its total length is 1,230 feet, and it is one of the few bridges in that part of the country that remained intact at the end of the Boer War. I made a deviation and crossed the river about a mile above the site of the permanent bridge. At the place which I selected there were many rocks and rapids, and I was able to throw across a bridge built of heavy baulk timber. After we had made a fair start with the Kimberley contract Sir Charles Warren's expedition arrived at our Orange River camp, and had to be forwarded from there up to what was called the Rooi Grond, in Bechuanaland. A number of Dutchmen, encouraged, it was said, by President Kruger, had taken possession of a large tract of country and had formed what they called a republic. This was objected to by the British authorities, and the mission of the Warren expedition was to put an end to the republic. The Dutchmen constituting the republic, were all farmers who had trekked over to the Rooi Grond with their wagons and oxen, and had marked out farms for themselves. When they heard that an expedition had arrived at the Orange River and intended to proceed to the Rooi Grond, the bulk of these farmers brought their wagons and oxen down to the Orange River and hired themselves to the military transport authorities at £1 10*s*. to £2 a day for the use of their wagons to transport the military troops and stores up to the Rooi

Grond. Naturally, when the Warren expedition arrived at its destination a somewhat Gilbertian situation was created, inasmuch as it was found that there was no one to fight with because they were paying the majority of their enemies good money for transportation work. The expedition, therefore, after settling that there should be no Dutch republic, returned to Kimberley. By that time the railhead was only ten or twelve miles from that town, and I was able to take Sir Charles Warren and his forces back and to deliver them to the open line of railways at Orange River. I believe that some of the military forces were given farms along the Transvaal border in the Rooi Grond, and that within a very short period they sold their farms for very little money to the same Boer farmers who had intended to form a republic. These farmers thereby became possessed of their land under a British title, which was better for them than a small republican title, and the price they paid for the farms and for stocking them was realized from what they had earned by transporting the Warren expedition. One has to be up early to get the better of a Boer farmer.

The Kimberley contract was a peculiar one. No final definite survey had been made. The survey on which I tendered I had understood to be provisional, and I was aware of several places where much work could be cut out without adding to the working costs of the line, and I naturally considered that I should be allowed to make these deviations. I had not reckoned, however, on the consistent hostility of the Government engineers who, as has been the case with practically every Government engineer with whom I have come in contact, invariably desired the departmental, in preference to the contract, system of carrying out public works. The latter system minimized their influence and robbed them of much patronage in the shape of dispensing billets which, had the work been under their control, would have been at their disposal. And thus it happened that I was not allowed to make any deviations. Two of the most material items in determining the ultimate result of this contract were the station buildings and station yard at Kimberley. There had been no time to prepare designs for the buildings and the yard, and a clause was inserted in the specification that the station accommodation was to be similar to that at Graaf Reinet, but somewhat larger. I was aware of the cost of the station accommodation at Graaf Reinet and in my tender had allowed for more than double what had been provided there. When the Kimberley Station plans were presented to me I found that the required accommodation exceeded that at Graaf Reinet by more than seven times, and that the rail level of the whole of the station yard was to be from two to four feet below the surface of the ground. The ground surface was practically dead flat, covered with a few inches of sand, and under that sand there was the hardest kind of rock, much of it being agate. I at once protested against the sinking of the rail level, and pointed out that by an alteration of grade, which would in no way increase the working cost of the traffic, the station yard could be laid on the surface of the ground, thereby avoiding the removal of any of the hard rock. The engineers, however, refused to agree to my suggestion and I was forced to lose from £15,000 to £20,000 in the unnecessary excavation of the adamantine rock. I also protested against the quality of the masonry which had been stipulated for the station. The engineers insisted that every stone should be dressed and that no joint should exceed a quarter of an inch. The stone was very hard basalt and its dressing cost several thousand pounds. I argued that no similar work had been done on any station constructed of stone on the Cape Government railways, nor on the stations at Orange River, Modder River, or other small stations on the Kimberley Railway itself, but all my protestations were in vain. In point of fact, the goods sheds at Kimberley contained more than ten times the space of the Graaf Reinet sheds, and I think I am safe in stating that to this day more than one half of it has never been used in that capacity, but as a bonded warehouse for the Customs Department. If I had had then the experience that has subsequently come my way I would not have allowed the railway to be opened for traffic until these questions had been settled in my favour, but I foolishly listened to the advice and assurance given me by several Cape Town friends—including Members of Parliament and of the Government—that I should receive fair play, and I consequently allowed the railway to be handed over for traffic in November 1885. The station accommodation at Kimberley was not at that time finished, but goods and passengers were taken as far as De Toit's Pan, two or three miles south of Kimberley Station. My financial position was rapidly becoming desperate. I had an overdraft of £30,000 at the Cape Town branch of the Cape of Good Hope Bank. This was secured to some extent by a ten per cent. retention fund which the Government held back from my monthly certificates. My partner, Mr. Christopher Firbank, was in Cape Town, and it was his advice, combined with that of all my Cape Town friends, that prevented me from holding up the opening of the railway until a settlement had been agreed. The Government engineers were extremely exacting, and it gradually became increasingly difficult for me to find money to pay even my men's wages. Apart from the Bank overdraft I did not owe much to creditors, probably about £15,000. In view of the circumstances I was forced to call a meeting of my sub-contractors at Kimberley. They were all very loyal and sympathetic, and, being satisfied that I could complete within the sum still coming to me, they entered into contracts for all that remained to be done to finish the Kimberley work. I submitted this arrangement to the engineer and asked that I should be financed to carry it through with my men. He, however, absolutely refused to give the least assistance. I was also being pressed by one or two outside creditors to whom about £2,000 was owing. I had no means of satisfying them unless to the detriment of my other creditors. This I refused to do, and one of them got judgment against me in the courts. I shall never forget the day on which old Moses Cornwall, the High Sheriff at Kimberley, and a very good friend of mine, came to me and said, "Pauling, you will have to keep indoors from sunrise to sunset or I shall have to arrest you as I have a judgment against you." This settled the question. I immediately wired to one of my friendly creditors to make the firm of Firbank and Pauling bankrupt, and Christopher Firbank saw our lawyers in Cape Town and we sent in our papers. My uncle, Mr. Henry Pauling, was then chief engineer of the Cape Government railways, and, according to our contract, he was the sole arbitrator. I had previously seen him about the Kimberley Station question. He told me that the Attorney-General of the day, whose advice he had taken, maintained that I was obliged to provide at Kimberley whatever accommodation the Traffic Department of the Cape Government railways might deem to be necessary, and that it was they who had stipulated the size of the station buildings and yard, but it was the resident engineer who had stipulated for the class of work to be carried out.

When the firm became bankrupt there was a fortnight's pay due to the white masons, carpenters, and other employees at Kimberley to a total number of about 300. I called a meeting of the whole of them in Kimberley goods shed and explained the circumstances to them, telling them that I knew the Government would pay the wages if they would wait a week or two. Some of them became very restive and insulting, and some even talked of " going for " me. I had, however, some friends among the men. These I asked to stand by me, and as far as the others who, in their own words, had expressed a desire to " take it out of me " were concerned, being something of a pugilist, I invited them one by one to a bout. But the challenge was not accepted. My friends rallied round me; and the meeting terminated without any trouble. A week afterwards the men were paid their wages by the Government.

I was very anxious to prove that I could get the work at Kimberley finished in the way I had proposed to the resident engineer, and was confident that if I were allowed to do so there would be enough to pay all our creditors and the bank overdraft. I appealed very hard to be allowed to work out my own salvation, but the engineer would not let the men become parties to the sub-contracts they had offered to take, and determined to finish the job by day work. I realized that this would absorb all the remaining money, so by pressure in Cape Town I compelled the engineer to allow me to protect the interests of my creditors by seeing that the balance of the work was economically completed. It follows that I was continually calling his attention to the waste of money resulting from the day work method. Many of the men who had been faithful and trusted servants of mine were keen to help me to pull through. From them I learned much about the waste that was going on. The engineer came to hear of this, and one morning, while going round the work, I was informed by one of my old foremen that instructions had been issued that no one was to speak to me. I naturally enquired who had given such instructions, and was informed that an inspector was responsible for the edict. He had been a fellow passenger with me in the "Anglian," and we had had a slight altercation on the voyage.

Practically at the moment I received this information, I saw the inspector coming out of his house. Mad with rage, I went up to him, and after a few brief but incisive words I knocked him down. He refused to get up. I gave him one or two gentle kicks, just to help him up, when his wife appeared on the scene. I was so enraged that I picked him up off the ground and, although he weighed over twelve stone, I threw him against his wife and both of them fell into the doorway of the cottage. It all seems very funny now, after the lapse of years, but I saw no amusement in it at the time. The cottage was just opposite the office from which the engineers had been watching the scene. Having administered Draconian justice to the inspector I returned to the engineers' office and found its occupants, each armed with a massive ruler, prepared to resist to the uttermost my anticipated onslaught. I had, however, no intention of making a physical attack, but only wanted to tell them what I thought of them, which I did, succinctly if profanely, and then left them. It took nine months to get the rails through from Orange River to Kimberley. Previous to my commencing to build railways in the Cape by contract, the rate of construction had been very slow, and this at the time was considered a big record in Cape railway work. As a performance, however, it was far eclipsed by what we subsequently accomplished on the Rhodesian railway system.

XVI

An Army Contract

When the Warren expedition, referred to in the previous chapter, was about to be sent from the Orange River I joined two friends of mine in making contracts for the supply of forage for animals, as well as potatoes, and onions, and the like necessities for the troops. My partners were Messrs. James Butler and "Jimmy" Ferguson. Mr. Butler had been our engineer on the Kowie Railway. The Grahamstown district offered exceptional advantages in which to buy agricultural produce, so Mr. Butler did the purchasing part of the arrangement. "Jimmy" Ferguson was a well-known Kimberley man and he had made the contract with the military authorities. My particular function was to get the goods as far up the railway towards Kimberley as possible, and to obtain transport to send it on beyond the Vaal River at Barkly West, where the army base was situated. Mr. Ferguson took charge of the goods at Kimberley and was responsible for their ultimate delivery. One of our consignments consisted of about eighty tons of potatoes. They were beautiful potatoes when they left railhead, but the wagons were unduly delayed on the road to Barkly, and by the time they reached their destination some of them had become odoriferous. The army commissariat officer refused to accept delivery. His action was quite unjustifiable, because when offered to him only a relatively small quantity of the potatoes were bad, and Mr. Ferguson at once stated that he would only expect payment for the good tubers. Red tape intervened and the matter was referred by the officer to higher authorities. Meantime, the potatoes deteriorated and the odour increased to such an extent that by the time the Army authorities had decided definitely not to receive them the stench was so great that it was impossible to approach them. The commissariat called upon Mr. Ferguson to remove them, but it was humanly impossible to do so. The ultimate result was that the authorities lost all round, for not only did we successfully sue them, but the potatoes beat them also, and the camp had to be shifted about ten miles to escape from the evil smell. We came out of our Army contract on the right side, but in those days such ventures were no great catch and we did not make much out of the deal.

XVII

Arduous Days

UNTIL he came out to help me while the Kimberley railway was under construction, I had never seen my partner, Mr. Christopher Firbank. Socially he was a charming fellow, but he did not take a very active interest in the work, and consequently the major responsibility of all our interests devolved upon me.

I had made my home in Queenstown, where my wife and children were living. I managed to join them about once in six weeks, generally arriving on a Saturday afternoon and leaving on the following Monday morning. It was part of my routine to ride and drive through the line from Sterkstroom to Aliwal North and to supervise nearly every detail of the work. I had two sub-agents on the job, but I personally checked practically all the measurements of the work carried out by the sub-contractors. I had a secretary, Ben Curtis, who afterwards became a big racing man, and when the contract was more than half finished, I got my cousin, Harold Pauling, to join me, chiefly with the object of educating him to become a contractor's agent. I paid the men once a month and handled the money myself right through the job. After going through the Aliwal North contract, it was my habit to drive across to Kimberley, visit the Vaal River Bridge at Barkly West, which I was building for the concessionaires, Messrs. Hill and Paddon, then go back to Kimberley, carefully go through the details of that contract, thence seventy-five miles to the Orange River, where I took the train to Worcester. Occasionally, of necessity, I enjoyed a

FACSIMILE OF A CARTOON OF GEORGE PAULING PUBLISHED IN "THE NUGGET", AN EARLY HANDWRITTEN SALISBURY NEWSPAPER.

The Nugget Dec 25, 1896

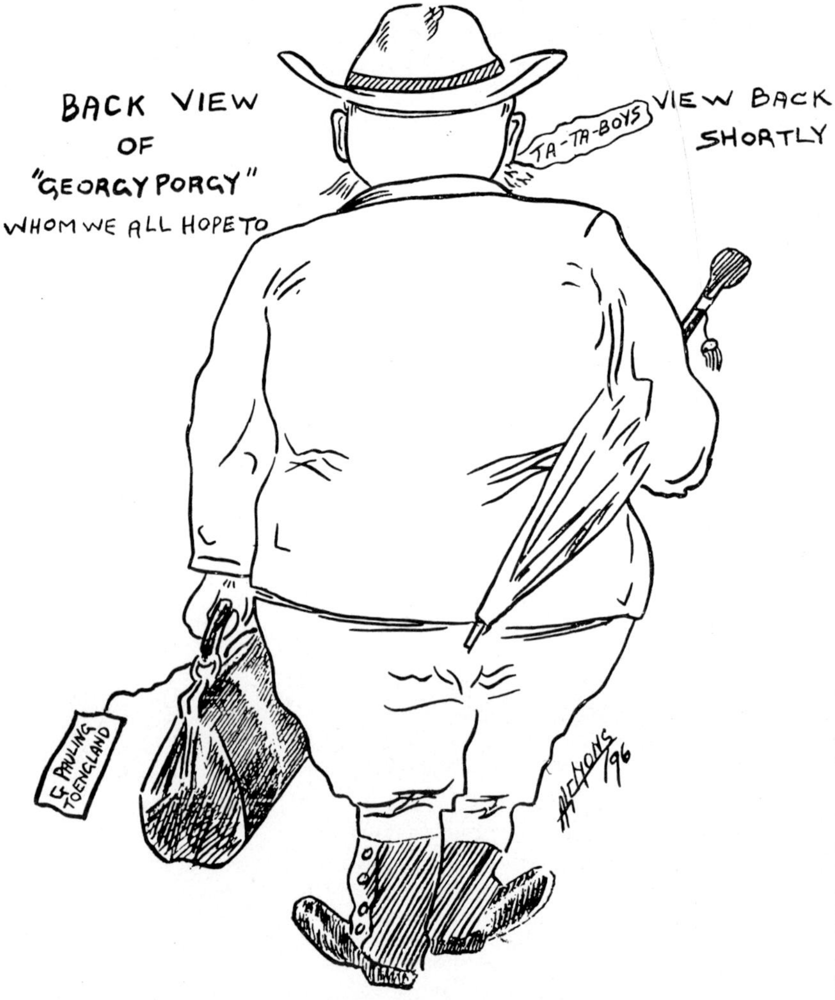

FACSIMILE REPRODUCTION FROM "THE NUGGET".

little variety by paying a visit to Cape Town to interview my bankers. I would then proceed by train to Grahamstown, visit the Kowie Railway, thence by post-cart to Kingwilliamstown, train to East London, where all the material for the Aliwal North contract was landed, and then by train on to Queenstown for a day's rest. I was almost incessantly on the move, and on a conservative estimate covered an average of from two to three thousand miles a month by rail, cart, and horseback. Every day I was up with the sun, and seldom went to rest before eleven o'clock at night. My sleep was generally taken in a cart or on the railway, and I do not believe that I enjoyed the comfort of a bed on more than seven days in every month.

During the time the Kowie, Aliwal North, and Kimberley contracts were being carried out I kept control of everything in my own hands. I had under me several very good assistants, and my secretary, Curtis, was invaluable. I had agents for the purchase of materials, etc., in several places—Johan Jansen at Cape Town, John Keith at Port Elizabeth, Stroyan Bros. at East London, and George Farrar, who was subsequently knighted, in Queenstown. Farrar and Curtis were both powerful athletes, good at running and jumping, and on my initiative they competed, with considerable profit to all of us, in events at Grahamstown, Kingwilliamstown, Burghersdorp, and other places. My principal contractors' agent on the Kimberley line was an engineer named Wilcox, who had been in the Cape Government service, and who had also had much experience in Australia, chiefly in gold mining and railway building. He was one of the old Ballarat crowd. By the time the Kimberley job was in full swing the Aliwal contract was finished, and I had made for myself and my partner about £150,000 out of the contract.

XVIII

The Lure of the Goldfields

AFTER my episode with the inspector at Kimberley, recorded in a previous chapter—strict chronological sequence in relating my tale is impossible—I went down into Kimberley and was having a cup of tea in a tea-room when Dr. Rutherfoord Harris came in. He had been practising in Kimberley, and I had given him the position of railway doctor between Modder River and that town. We were on very friendly terms and he knew most of my worries and troubles. In my mood of the moment I told him there was but one thing I desired, and that was to shake the dust of Kimberley from my feet for a time. He condoled with me and, probably in sympathy with my sorrows, told me that he had made up his mind to give up his practice in Kimberley and to proceed to Barberton in the Transvaal to try his luck at gold mining. I immediately made up my mind to accompany him.

We went round to the coach office and found we could get seats for Barberton in the coach which was due to leave the next morning. All I had in the world was about £70. I had tried to borrow £100 from an old engineering friend of mine, whose association with me had not been unprofitable, but he would not "part." I have, however, got more than my own back by reminding him on every possible occasion in later years of his refusal.

The Barberton goldfields were then the Mecca of the mining community. The Sheba reef had been discovered and fortunes had been made for those who were lucky enough to be in the original syndicate. Two brothers named Thomas, old railway men, had found what was afterwards known as Thomas's Reef, and had received about £60,000 to buy them out. The Victoria Gold Mining Company had commenced work under the control of Mr. Alfred Leonard Lawley, who has long been one of my greatest friends. It was thought that a new Eldorado had been discovered, and people of all trades and no trade were rushing up to Barberton from every part of the colony. At that time all public travelling was done by coach. The coaches were an improved type of the old Cobb's Australian coach. They were hung on leathers instead of springs, and could carry about fifteen passengers and about a ton and a half of mails and baggage. They were drawn by from ten to fourteen horses or mules, and the stages were about twelve miles or two hours apart. They ran right through by night as well as day. There was about half an hour's stoppage at each place, where the animals were changed, and perhaps a little more at the stages where meals were procurable, but there was no rest through the night, and one had to get sleep as best one could. It took three days and three nights to get from Kimberley to Pretoria, a distance of about 300 miles by the coach road. An amusing incident occurred at the breakfast stage on the second morning of our journey. In these days the staple diet consisted of mutton chops, which were served at almost every meal. Occasionally, however, a fowl or a few eggs were forthcoming. On this particular occasion, when we got down from the coach to breakfast, one of the passengers, a Jew, was first in at the table. In front of him there was a plate with six boiled eggs on it, all in their shells. When the rest of the passengers came in it was noticed that the Jew had broken the tops of two of the eggs and had put them on one side. Then he took up another, smelt it, and put it with the other two, and with the fourth he followed the same procedure. In the suggestive circumstances, all the other passengers barred eggs and went on to chops. Presently, however, the Jew was seen to collar the four eggs which he had tapped, but before he could get the other two someone else realized what he had been up to, and anticipated him. It transpired that all the eggs were perfectly good, but his artful method of tapping them and then smelling them was very successful, inasmuch as it kept the other people away from that particular food.

On our way to Pretoria—I think it was at Christiana—we met the down coach, and among the passengers there was a man named Alexander, a Kimberley butcher, with whom Dr. Harris and I were acquainted. He showed us a piece of quartz which we afterwards knew as the Banket rock, in which is found the gold that has made the Witwatersrand mines so famous. The butcher told us that quite a large quantity of this material had been found; that it contained heavy gold; and that he was on his way to Kimberley to tell his friends and form syndicates to take up claims in the Rand. This was, of course, very interesting to the doctor and myself, but it did not alter our purpose to proceed to Barberton.

Next day—I think it was near Wonderfontein—we met a young Dutchman, Mr. Pieter Mostert, a friend of mine who had been in charge of the provision stores on the Kimberley line. He informed me that his uncle, Mr. Bantjes, had pegged out several claims on the Banket formation. This was the origin of what afterwards became the well-known Bantjes Gold Mining Company. Pieter begged of us to linger awhile to look into this new proposition, but he did not know how hard up I was at the time. He had great, if misplaced, faith in me, and I honestly believe he thought that if I could be got to join him in pegging out ground on the Rand all our fortunes would be made. I arranged with him that he should make use of his relationship to Mr. Bantjes, keep his eyes open, peg out some claims, and get hold of valuable ground. Meanwhile, Dr. Harris and I would go to Barberton, where the doctor had what he considered good prospects; and that one of us would return to the Rand as soon as possible to join forces with Mostert with a view to making our fortunes.

We remained in Pretoria only a few hours, and the coach went on through Middleburg to the top end of the Eland's Valley. There we had to alight for the connection to Barberton. The coach itself went on to Lydenburg and Pilgrims' Rest, the latter being then the centre of the old-established Transvaal Goldfields. From Eland's Valley to Barberton there was only a post cart with four mules, a Kafir driver, and room for four people and a few bags of mails. Immediately on the arrival of the coach I had secured a seat and so had three other passengers, so that there was no room for Dr. Harris and two other travellers on their way to Barberton. The doctor, however, thought he would be more comfortable on horseback and managed to obtain a horse. The two remaining passengers had to accept the alternative of waiting for the next coach or walking a distance of about 70 or 80 miles. It was late in the afternoon when we left the top of the Elandsburg. We had not travelled far before the shades of night fell upon us. Presently, however, the moon rose. To a man of less material instincts than my own the conditions of our journey would have provided some elements of romance. Some 7,000 miles from home, practically at the end of my means, far from the habitation of a civilized community, jogging uncomfortably over an impossible road, with the entrancing prospect of an Eldorado at the end of it—such surroundings suggest a fitting theme for poets to perpetuate. To the unfortunate travellers there was, however, but little occasion for sentiment. The road was atrocious, the jolting dreadful, and the mules, true to the traditions of their kind, too sluggish for words. Amongst the passengers was Mr. "Sammy" Marks, of the firm of Lewis and Marks, which has contributed so much to the development of the South African mining industry. "Sammy" held the reins while the Kafir driver got down and ran alongside to lambaste the mules. In view of the awful condition of the road I had tied myself to the cart with a rope to prevent the possibility of being jerked off. The passenger sitting next me, a Mr. Foxwell, declined to take this precaution, and in a very short time the cart nearly capsized and he was thrown off. As he fell, somehow or other he grabbed the spokes of the cart wheel, and when the cart righted itself, as it did almost instantaneously, the wheel passed over his jaw and smashed it.

Dr. Harris was riding a mile or so behind. We waited for him to come up. We all blamed Mr. Marks for the mishap, which we attributed to his incompetent driving. He was greatly disconcerted about the accident and thought he might have to pay heavy damages to Mr. Foxwell. When the doctor overtook us he found that the jaw had been very badly fractured. We had to proceed a few miles to reach the only farm in the Eland's Valley, which was owned by a Dutchman named De Jaeger. When we reached the farmhouse, Dr. Harris had another look at the jaw. Mr. Foxwell was in terrible pain, and it was evident that he could never reach Barberton. The doctor and I held a kind of court martial on "Sammy" and succeeded in getting him to promise us a big interest in a mine named "Wheel of Fortune" on condition that Harris would take charge of Mr. Foxwell and get him down to Pretoria. The doctor got a Scotch cart and a pair of oxen from De Jaeger and offered to go back with Mr. Foxwell to Middleburg, or even to Pretoria, to place him under proper medical treatment so that his jaw could be repaired. Through the care and attention of Dr. Harris this was accomplished. It took him eight days to get to Pretoria, and all the while he fed Mr. Foxwell with brandy and egg through a reed tube, which was the only means of providing him with sustenance. During the period Dr. Harris was away Mr. Marks was most anxious to get on to Barberton, as he had expectations of making much money out of the "Wheel of Fortune."

On the morning after the accident the rest of us proceeded on our journey, and the same evening arrived at the Devil's Kantoor, at that time a mining camp where men were working alluvial ground.

It seemed extraordinary to find good alluvial wash on the top of mountains such as the Devil's Kantoor, but it is a well-known fact that better alluvial gold has been found in the hilly districts in the Transvaal than in the river valleys. The Devil's Kantoor stands up almost sheer from the De Kaap valley, where Barberton is situated. There was no road in those days beyond the Devil's Kantoor, and one had to do the distance from there to Barberton, about thirty miles, on foot.

XIX

Barberton

FROM the Kantoor I walked to Barberton, which I reached late one afternoon. As I approached the town I met a man whom I had known at Kimberley as one of the old brigade and who was very fond of other people's horseflesh. A new road was in the course of construction, and my friend was standing with his foot resting on a shovel. According to the colonial custom I invited him to come to the nearest bar and have a drink. He pointed somewhat consequentially to the other men at work on the road, and said, " I cannot leave these chaps. I have got a Government contract and they would do no work if I went away." I afterwards discovered that my friend was one of a gang of prisoners employed in making the road. A couple of guards, armed with rifles and standing some distance off to ensure that none of the prisoners would run away, had escaped my notice.

I arrived in Barberton with a capital of about £20, and soon found a lot of people whom I had known in the Cape Colony. Amongst them was Ramsay M'Nab, who had been proprietor of the Molteno Hotel on the Aliwal North Railway. I also met a man named M'Gregor, who had been one of my masonry sub-contractors on that contract.

I had only been in Barberton a few days when the first races were to be held, and M'Nab suggested that he, M'Gregor, and I should take a contract from the committee to put up a grand stand and supply refreshments for the races. We had practically no money but managed to hire the timber for the stand, which I designed, and M'Nab and M'Gregor contrived to build. We also bought on credit, for sale or return, a considerable amount of liquor. There was two days' racing, and the result was that we divided between us a profit of about £200. My share was the first money I made on the Barberton goldfields.

There were only two hotels in the town, the Crown and the Phoenix, and the whole place was crammed with people, everyone expecting to find another "Sheba," "Thomas's," "Wheel of Fortune," or some such mine. Meals were being served at the hotels three deep, and one had literally to fight one's way into the dining-room, to make sure of getting something to eat.

For a few pounds I bought small interests in ground that had been pegged out. I was waiting to hear from Dr. Harris, and at last I got a letter saying that he was joining Pieter Mostert, and, in accordance with an arrangement I had previously made with him, he had cabled in my name to my brother to come out to the Rand. This Harry did, arriving there about the middle of 1886, and I went down from Barberton to meet him and arrange our programme. Both Harry and the doctor had a few thousand pounds, but were careful not to take any very serious risks. In company with five or six others, all workers, they had formed a syndicate and had pegged out the Banket Mine claims and the Evelyn Mine. Both these were floated in Kimberley, and the syndicate received a considerable number of vendors' shares. Meantime, I had met my old engineer, Mr. Wilcox, in Pretoria. I was very keen on getting him to come up to Barberton with me, so as to make use of his Australian experience. We purchased an old cart and a pair of horses in Pretoria and started to drive the two hundred odd miles to Barberton where, after a somewhat slow and adventurous journey, we arrived without any serious damage to our cart, horses, or selves. We were amongst the first to get a wheeled vehicle through from Devil's Kantoor to Barberton, and we sold the cart and horses for three times what we had given for them in Pretoria.

We then established ourselves as mining engineers and prospectors, and I put a little money into several working syndicates as, having so many old friends and acquaintances, I had a better opportunity of doing this than almost anyone else in Barberton. One little group in which I was interested was composed of several betting men and an old prospector named Tom Osborne. Four of these men were engaged in prospecting in the hills beyond Jamestown. Osborne had a Hottentot boy who came to him one day with a piece of gold-bearing white quartz, about as big as a man's fist and containing literally nearly fifty per cent. of gold. The boy refused to tell anyone except his boss where he had found the quartz, but Osborne, who was a very fair chap, insisted on his partners sharing with him the secret. It ended in the boy taking them all to the hillside where, amongst the grass and rank vegetation, they found a huge piece of white quartz weighing about half a ton and covered with gold. They broke it up and brought the pieces into Barberton, and the bank credited them with 1,600 ounces of gold out of this one piece of quartz. I think there were six or seven in the syndicate, and instead of dividing up the proceeds from the bank we formed the Hottentot Gold Mining Company, set to work, and pegged out a lot of ground in the vicinity of the spot where the boulder had been found. Other people also subscribed capital. Every effort was made to find the supposed reef, adits were put into the hillside, shafts were sunk, and various other operations carried out, but to cut a long story short I believe that ultimately a sum of between £40,000 and £50,000 was spent trying to discover the reef from which the white quartz had come. Our efforts, however, proved unavailing, and the origin of the boulder remains a mystery to this day, because, although there are many reefs in those hills, there is none of white quartz. Some of us came to the conclusion that the Hottentot boulder must have been deposited there, possibly by glacial action in the very dim past.

Wilcox and I did a lot of prospecting on the hills beyond the Queen's River. Our usual procedure was to spend two or three days among the hills and whenever we came across what appeared promising rock, we broke off a piece, tried to locate, as well as we could, the spot where it had been found, and then, when we had got perhaps twenty or thirty of these specimens, we went down and camped by the river to crush and wash them. Once or twice we found very big prospects in the pan, and then we spent days trying to find the reef from which they came, but failed to locate it. We also worked for alluvial near the Devil's Kantoor, and were lucky enough to find a little pocket containing nuggets, some of them as big as small potatoes. From one of these pockets we took out four hundred ounces of gold. For some little time we continued to work there, but finding nothing more that was payable, we gave it up. I mention these incidents to illustrate the difficulties of a gold prospector.

In those Barberton days my old friend "Bill" Upsher turned up and he and I entered into a prospecting partnership. We worked together sinking a shaft on a reef near Queen Mac Mac's Kraal, about forty miles from Barberton. On more than one occasion I walked the whole distance from there to Barberton, starting early in the morning and arriving late at night. I took the short cut by Fever Creek and over the top of the Sheba. This meant a rise and fall of nearly two thousand feet in the course of a forty-mile walk, with a temperature, during part of the day, of over one hundred in the shade. The track was as rough as it is possible to imagine. This was not at all an unusual tramp for a prospector, as we were all in good condition in those days. I was, however, a bit handicapped, as I weighed over sixteen stone.

One day when I arrived back at the camp, I found Upsher had had a very narrow escape from a violent death. Some years previously he had, as the result of fever, lost all his hair, and he wore a wig. He was occupied in sinking a shaft, about twenty feet deep, on the reef. We had some six boys working for us, one of whom had been with Upsher for several years. Several holes had been drilled in the rock at the bottom of the shaft, and Upsher went down to charge them with dynamite and to light the fuses. A rough windlass had been provided with a rope and bucket to carry tools and other materials up and down the shaft. After lighting the fuses Upsher, as usual, put one foot in the bucket and shouted to the boys to haul up the windlass. It was a terribly hot day, and while being pulled up he took off his wig to get some relief from the heat. There were four natives on the windlass, one of them luckily being his own boy. When the others saw Upsher's bald white head appear out of the shaft—his face was always brick red from weather and sun—they were so frightened that they let go the windlass and started to run away. His boy was unequal to the task of holding the windlass by himself, and Upsher started going down the shaft again. His boy, however, knew that the fuses were lighted, and in their own tongue yelled to the other boys to come back. Seeing him undaunted they recovered from their fright and returned to pull up the windlass. Upsher just managed to get away from the top of the shaft as the explosions began to take place. If he had not then been clear of the shaft he must have been blown to atoms.

XX

"Holding the Baby" and other Diversions

ABOUT this time I had secured a big interest in a block of ground containing claims which were expected to become of great value. I sent particulars of these to Kimberley, and asked my brother to come up and confer with me about our future prospects. He came and remained about a week, after which he returned to the Rand. This project was floated in Kimberley. I received about 30,000 shares, but had promised the promoters of the flotation that I would not sell until they agreed that vendors' shares might be disposed of. I did not then know my Kimberley friends well enough, for I afterwards found that I could have sold my shares at thirty shillings each, as had been done by several of my co-vendors. The mine turned out a failure and I was left in the dignified position of what was then known as "holding the baby." Harry and I had to buy our experience from the gentlemen, Jew and Gentile, who have made the gold and diamond mining industries of South Africa. Mr. Wilcox had left Barberton for the Rand, and I began to think seriously of joining my brother there, but I was interested in too many Barberton ventures to get away at a moment's notice. I had joined Messrs. George Eaton, Gordon Cameron, and an old man named, as far as I remember, Boult, a working compositor, as owners of the "Barberton Herald," the first newspaper to be published in that town. The "Herald" was produced under constant difficulties. Of some type letters we had but a limited supply, while we had a surfeit of others; consequently, the letter " r " had not only to fulfil its alphabetical mission, but had to do duty for the letters " e," " p," and " q." It followed that our words were frequently spelt with little regard to phonetics and less to orthography. We were also short of paper, and several issues were produced on thin white blotting paper, foolscap, and punjum, a thin white cotton cloth. After a time Mr. Gordon Cameron, who was the editor and leader writer, received a number of shares in the Imperial Mine. We did not at first know of this, or we should probably have claimed a proportion of them. One day, however, Mr. Cameron disclosed the information to us and added that he was about to leave for England. We protested, but in vain. I believe he sold his shares for something like £6,000. After Mr. Cameron had left for England Mr. Eaton proposed that he should go down to the colony to endeavour to form a company to take over the " Barberton Herald," and send up a proper press with type and other necessary plant for an up-to-date printing office. He went, and I was left to fulfil the function of editor, leader writer, and all the multifarious duties of newspaper production, with the exception of printer, which remained in the hands of Boult. I endured it for a few weeks and then, having heard nothing from my partners, with Boult's consent I sold the paper to an American doctor named Woolf. The " Herald " is still in existence, and I have often regretted neglecting to keep copies of the issues printed on the blotting paper, foolscap, and punjum.

Amongst other claims I had pegged out a very large but low-grade proposition near the Kaap River, which I christened " The Big Golden Quarry." Afterwards, when I went to the Rand, I took with me the documents relating to this and to one or two other blocks of claims. The Christmas of 1886 I spent with " Bill " Upsher on our claims. To remind us of home and holly we made a massive pudding. In our inexperience we boiled it in a bandana handkerchief which belonged to Upsher, and which rivalled Joseph's coat in the number and variety of its colours. All the dye came out of the handkerchief. As a thing of beauty our pudding left the rainbow a very inferior second. Unfortunately, the colouring had penetrated well into the pudding and we had to cut away the outer sections till there was only a bit left about the size of an orange. This we enjoyed very much, and it is not improbable that the colouring proved a blessing in an artistic disguise, for if we had been able to consume the full-sized pudding we might have been overcome by pain and sickness.

I was very sorry to leave Barberton. The physically hard life suited me, and it was a real rest to be free from all the anxieties I had had on my shoulders for practically the preceding ten years, when I had been struggling hard to make a big position and a lot of money. If in Barberton I did nothing more I at least earned a good living and was free from worry.

XXI

Johannesburg

I LEFT Barberton towards the end of December 1886, and on New Year's night we had to cross the Eland's River, which was then in flood. There were only four passengers in the coach. The driver was a Dutchman, and the leader, *i.e.*, the man who held the reins of the ten or twelve mules in the team, was a nigger. In view of the condition of the river we had to use very strenuous means to induce the Dutchman to make an effort to cross it. As the water came right over the wheels and half-way up the windows we all got on top of the coach. The river was not very wide and luckily the first four mules got a foothold on the other side before there was a chance of the coach being absolutely swept down the river. After tremendous yelling and very heavy work with the whip we managed to get through all right, and the remainder of our journey to Pretoria was uneventful. My brother met me there, and I went on with him to his camp at Van Wyk's Vlei. There he lived with Dr. Harris, Mr. Mostert, and one or two others who were all, as it were, partners in mining business. They had pegged out and floated the Banket and the Evelyn Mines, and Harry had received a considerable number of vendors' shares in both these companies.

In those days Johannesburg was a very small place. A few single-storied brick houses, some offices with iron roofs, and a number of wood and iron huts and tents, constituted the town. The township had been surveyed and laid out by the Transvaal Government,

FACSIMILE REPRODUCTION FROM "THE NUGGET".

EDWARDS AND C^o. LARGE STOCK OF SPLENDID NEW GOODS — JUST ARRIVED

For its Labby this, an Labby that, an' "Hit 'im when 'es down!"
But its Welcome Mr Labouchere, "when I come back to town
An' its "Labby this, an Labby, an' Labbys lost 'is name":
An' Labby aint no bloomin fool you bet 'e knows is game

G. C. S.

A large amount of transport has reached Salisbury during the last few days and the Merchants are jubilant once more, but their jubilation would appear to be short-lived for I hear many loud and bitter complaints and invectives levelled at the heads of Mr George Pauling and those in authority on the line between Beira and Macequece for their gross and arrant callousness and carelessness, in knowing full well that merchants are robbed right and left all along that line, and yet winking at such robberies. Many cases that were of correct weight on leaving Beira have reached Salisbury empty — notwithstanding full freight has been paid — and many cases and bales of general merchandise, when opened here, are found to contain about a half of their original contents. Mr Pauling when approached by one merchant or another airily tells them to "go to Lisbon and sue him", which is about equivalent to telling them to go to — elsewhere. The consequence is, to come out on the winning side, the Merchants have to increase their charges for the goods, and the Public have to pay through the nose for the ordinary necessities of life. This is a howling shame, and one that will not be remedied until Mr Pauling's control over the railway is dispensed with. Much as it is to Mr Cecil Rhodes' benefit to "keep in" with George Pauling he makes himself nothing but an accessory to this wholesale robbery, by his indifference to the complaints of the Salisbury merchants and . . .

FACSIMILE REPRODUCTION FROM "THE NUGGET".

and in September 1886 the first sale of stands or building lots had taken place. Harry bought forty of these stands at £10 apiece. One side of this block faced Market Square and the other Commissioner Street, and I should think that now these stands, at a conservative estimate, are worth at least £1,000,000. Harry bought them with the intention of erecting a few brick and iron-roofed shanties to be let as living rooms and offices, and he had relied on one of my old masons coming up from Kimberley to do the work. This man, however, failed him, and a couple of weeks afterwards Harry accepted an offer of £50 profit on his deal. If he had hung on he would have made a very handsome fortune out of this one venture.

A few days after I arrived at Van Wyk's Vlei, Mr. Rhodes, Dr. Hans Sauer, and some other Kimberley people arrived in Johannesburg, and I had a long conversation with Mr. Rhodes about the prospects of the Rand. It should be understood that up to this time only a few rich propositions had been struck. The Jumpers Mine, the Simmer and Jack, and one or two others with very rich stuff on the surface had been found. What is now called the main reef was the only reef then known, and I told Mr. Rhodes that I was sure it would not yield more than eight or ten pennyweights to the ton. The existence of coal had not at that time been definitely established, although it was believed to exist in the Middleburgh district, about a hundred miles away. The gold in the reef was very fine and floury and difficult to catch. The south and other leaders which were ultimately found to be very rich, and which established the success of the Rand, had not by that time been discovered, so that at the beginning of 1887 the prospects of the Rand were by no means encouraging. It was years afterwards before I learned that Mr. Rhodes agreed with my view. We happened to be fellow passengers on a ship from Delagoa Bay to Beira.

Walking up and down the deck together one night he said to me in his characteristic, abstracted way: "You were right, Pauling." This enigmatical observation was beyond my comprehension, and I asked him what he meant. He replied: "It was right what you said about the Rand at Van Wyk's Vlei."

No one had then dreamed of the possibility of the leaders being found, of the existence of coal which could be produced plentifully and cheaply, and of the potentialities of the cyanide process. Had these elements not materialized the Rand main reef would never have been worked and the leaders themselves could never have produced Johannesburg.

Dr. Harris, Harry, and I held a consultation as to our future interests. At that time the claims on the Rand had only been pegged out one—and, in a few cases, two—deep. We pegged out about a thousand claims on the dip extending from beyond the "May" claims right through to beyond Roodepoort. We also acquired the right to purchase from the farmers fourteen farms extending from Langlaaghte out towards the west. I had all the papers giving the right to the "Big Golden Quarry" claims at Barberton, and also to some claims adjoining the Sheba Mine, which we called the "Great She." I had also, through my Grahamstown friends, acquired an opportunity of dealing with a concession of about 5,000 square miles between the Shashi and Macloutsie Rivers, which had been given by Lobengula to old friends of mine named Chapman, Francis, and Clark, who had been hunters and traders in Matabeleland for many years. As a result of our conference we came to the conclusion that Dr. Harris should go up to Barberton and carry on further prospecting work in connection with the "Big Golden Quarry" and the "Great She" properties, and that Harry and I should proceed to the Cape with a view to promoting a syndicate with a capital of £12,000 to provide the £1 per month licence necessary to keep alive for twelve months the right to the thousand claims we had pegged out. Our idea was that after this was done we should proceed to England with the object of floating all, or as many as we could, of the various properties we had in our hands. This programme was carried out. Harry and I did our utmost in Cape Town to raise the necessary licence money to protect our claims, but nobody had sufficient faith in the Rand to support us. This happened about the end of January 1887. If we had been able to hold these claims for twelve months we should have laid the foundations of a fortune amounting to many millions of pounds, for it was during that year that the Rand was really proved. Failing to do anything in Cape Town we cabled to our agent on the Rand to give up the claims because we had already spent between us about £2,000, and we had not enough money to warrant us carrying on. Neither would Dr. Harris nor my brother have agreed to do so, even if I had wanted, and in those days they had the money and I had practically none.

XXII

Placing Properties

IN June 1885 my wife died and my two boys were then aged five and seven respectively. At the beginning of 1886 Harry took them to England and placed them in charge of my mother, who was living in Huntingdonshire, her native county. My father had left South Africa at the time when the temporary stoppage of railway construction had occurred, and from that time he had been enduring a hand-to-mouth existence. It was very difficult then, as now, for a civil engineer of over fifty years of age to get a billet of any sort, so Harry and I looked upon the old man as retired for the rest of his life, and I am glad to be able to state that we were in a position to make his remaining years comfortable.

When I joined Harry in England we set to work at once to deal with our African gold properties. We got into touch with sundry company promoters and, through our Kimberley acquaintances, had introductions to people connected with the Stock Exchange who could, and did, give us good advice. We found afterwards, as in Cape Town, that whilst Barberton was known and liked there was no chance of doing anything with Rand properties. To our surprise the most likely thing to be taken up was the 5,000 square miles proposition.

First of all, however, we managed to float the "Great She" and the "Big Golden Quarry," and an old friend of mine, Mr. Ethelbert George Woodford, who had been the engineer to the Kimberley Mining

Board, was sent out to take charge of the "Big Golden Quarry" for the new company. I do not know who was sent out to the "Great She." These flotations were accomplished in a few weeks from the time we arrived in London. Dr. Harris was advised of them, and he left the Barberton district to meet Mr. Woodford and the "Great She" man on their way up, so that he might give them all the information within his knowledge about these properties. Unfortunately, neither of them turned out successful. The doctor, Harry, and I received no money from these flotations. All we got were vendors' shares which we neglected to sell at the psychological moment. The net result was that not only did we spend much valuable time without remuneration, but the preliminary money we had put up "went west."

Harry and I had also started negotiations for floating simultaneously in London, Glasgow, and Paris the 5,000 square miles concession. By arrangement, the Glasgow and London groups were in my hands, while Harry was entrusted with the more delicate task of wooing Paris. It had been decided that whichever group was the first to make an acceptable offer should have the concession. The Paris group included Baron d'Erlanger, with whose firm I have enjoyed a long and honourable association. The London and Glasgow groups consisted of Exchange people. One day Harry wired me that he had fixed up the business and the same night he came over to London to see me. I immediately notified the Glasgow and London groups that arrangements had been made elsewhere. They were very angry and threatened me with dire and diverse penalties. I invited them to do their utmost, but heard nothing further in the matter. Harry did not carry out the Paris negotiations without considerable difficulty. He had to attend several meetings of the French group. At the last interview matters remained indefinite, but old

Baron d'Erlanger walked away from the meeting with him and told him that if he liked to leave the group alone, he would settle with them and see that they got what participation they desired, and that he would at once accept our terms, subject to the stipulation that Harry should go out to report on the concession and take charge of it. Harry, as the vendor, objected to this proposal, maintaining that it was a most unusual proceeding. However, the Baron was insistent, and Harry ultimately agreed.

The concession of 5,000 square miles was not the only Matabele project in which we were at that time interested. Messrs. Francis and Chapman had also obtained a promise from Lobengula that if they brought up to him the next time they came to Bulawayo a certain sum of money and a few guns he would give them the mining rights over the whole of Matabeleland, except the Tati Concessions, which had been granted years previously. Harry mentioned this matter to Baron d'Erlanger. All the relative documents were signed in Paris and Harry was instructed to proceed to South Africa to report on the concession and to take with him to Lobengula the cash and the guns he had asked for. Harry left for the Cape—I think in March or April 1887—went to Grahamstown and arranged an expedition composed of Mr. Joseph Wood, M.L.A. for Grahamstown, "Bill" Francis, "Bill" Upsher, and himself. Bill Upsher had turned up again and was taken with the expedition as a general utility man, and particularly to look after the wagon and oxen and to shoot for the pot. They went to Kimberley, bought wagons, oxen, provisions, and other requisites, and were soon ready to start. Harry would not allow liquor to be included in the commissariat, as he was a teetotaller and knew the dangers of drink on such an occasion. Unfortunately, when the expedition was ready to set out from Kimberley, word was brought that it would not be allowed to go through to the Shashi-Macloutsie Concession on the ground that there was a dispute between Lobengula and Khama, a Bechuanaland chief, as to whom the territory belonged. This upset all the arrangements. Harry and his friends sold the wagons and oxen at once and went to Pretoria by coach. There they fitted up another expedition and determined to go through the Transvaal and across the Limpopo River; proceed by Tuli to Bulawayo; there see Lobengula; give him his cash and guns; secure the Matabeleland mining rights; and then see what could be done about the Shashi-Macloutsie Concession. They started on their journey, and after trekking for about two months arrived within sixty miles of Bulawayo. There they were met by a Matabele impi, or regiment of warriors, who, on encountering Harry and his friends, threatened them with drastic treatment and gave them to understand they were only waiting instructions from Lobengula to kill the lot. Harry had with him an assay plant, including a quantity of methylated spirits. He made friends with the leaders of the impi, and as he had nothing else to offer them he gave them tots of methylated spirits, which they described as the most potent brandy they had ever tasted. After about a week's delay messengers arrived from Bulawayo with instructions to the impi to escort Harry's expedition to the southern boundary of the Tati Concessions, and to hand them over to the Bechuanaland police. They were then taken before the authorities and, after being bound over under a penalty of £3,000 each not to go back into the country again, were sent under escort to Kimberley. Thus ended Harry's expedition, and he returned to England towards the end of 1887.

XXIII

Other Fields

After I had floated the " Big Golden Quarry " and the " Great She," and Harry had proceeded to South Africa, I had to look around for work for myself. An English group had been formed in London to endeavour to obtain a concession for a railway from Alexandretta *via* Aleppo to the Tigris River, on to Bagdad, thence across Persia through Beloochistan, and on to Kurrachee in India. I was asked to go to Constantinople and arrange with the group's agent there, a Mr. Alexander, to make a reconnaissance survey from Alexandretta to Kurrachee. This was a very big undertaking for one man, and I did not then anticipate the difficulties that were likely to be encountered. I accepted the invitation and proceeded by Orient Express through Vienna, Budapest, to Giurgevo on the Danube, across that river to Rustchuk and through Roumania by rail from Rustchuk to Varna, thence *via* the Black Sea and Bosphorus to Constantinople. On arrival there I was kept waiting a few weeks to get the necessary special passport for my journey, and I had the novel experience of being insured against brigandage, for Mr. Alexander had to arrange with a brigand agency to pay a sum of money to ensure that I should not be obstructed by the brigands who operated in the vicinity of Alexandretta. On several occasions I had to go to Kiamil Pasha, then Grand Vizier of Turkey, to explain the object of my journey. He was a very fine type of man and spoke English perfectly. I had instructions not to tell him anything about going through Persia, but only of my mission as far as Bagdad. I ascertained that some years previously surveys of a considerable portion of the route beyond Aleppo had been made by German engineers for the Turkish Government, and after much trouble and some well directed bribery, I managed to get from the Turkish Public Works Office access to these surveys, from which I took all the information I required. Kiamil Pasha was exceedingly kind and urged me to see him immediately on my return to Constantinople and to give him any information I could as to the country and the manner in which the Government officials were discharging their duties within the area I traversed. At last I got away from Constantinople in a Russian steamer belonging to what was known as the Volunteer Fleet, which traded from Odessa down the Asia Minor and Syrian coast to Alexandria in Egypt. These steamers returned by Salonica and the Piraeus to Constantinople. Our ship was crowded with deck passengers, but there was only one other cabin passenger, a Turkish colonel. We left Constantinople in the evening and I had as good a dinner on board as I had ever enjoyed. The captain was a Dalmatian by birth. He spoke about ten languages, was the commodore of the Russian Fleet, and when he saw how I enjoyed my dinner and my narghile, or Turkish hubble-bubble, which I had afterwards smoked, we became great friends.

I had been asked to examine and report upon the Mersina and Adana Railway and thought I should therefore have to land at Mersina and take another steamer to get to Alexandretta. The captain, however, offered that if I could make my examination within twenty-four hours he would wait for me so that I could get another day of his company and one or two more good meals.

XXIV

Asia Minor

I GOT a special train from Mersina and ran through to Adana, making notes of the railway *en route*. I stopped at Tarsus for a few hours as I was interested to see the birthplace of St. Paul. We arrived at Alexandretta very early one morning and I went ashore. It was a miserable place—no hotel and no one who could speak a word of English. I had letters to the British Vice-Consul there, a Greek named Catoni, who could speak French but not my native tongue. My knowledge of the French language, although it had improved since my London office days, was by no means first-class, but I managed to make myself understood and asked him if he could find me an interpreter who could speak some English. He had no hesitation in replying that he could. That day I bought three horses, one for my interpreter, one for baggage, and one for myself. My special Turkish passport ensured for me the attendance of a zaptieh, or Turkish soldier. I left Alexandretta the following morning. I rode on a Turkish saddle, very much resembling one of the pads one sees on a circus horse. I wore a fez, carried an umbrella, had a pedometer attached to my horse's leg to record the distances travelled, a couple of aneroid barometers for judging altitudes, a prismatic compass, notebooks, and the miscellaneous paraphernalia of a flying survey. Nor did I neglect to bring my narghile with me. In all my journeys, whatever the vicissitudes or vagaries of my mission, there has always been one companion who has never left me—" My Lady Nicotine." With advancing years I have overcome most of the vices of youth, but I have always (except for a period after my Kimberley misfortunes when I absolutely gave up smoking and the use of alcoholic liquor) been, and remain, an inveterate smoker, realizing the wisdom of the dictum of a reverend friend of mine, that it is better to smoke in this world than in the next.

After travelling a few hours we came to some trees and water, where I made a halt with the view of obtaining some breakfast and a good rest. After waiting some time and finding no preparations for breakfast, I approached my interpreter and realized that about the only English he knew was " Yes, sir," which he spoke with an accent no Englishman could beat. Apart from this his English vocabulary was restricted to seafaring lingo, the predominant characteristic of which was profanity, which he had picked up on the steamers in Alexandretta, where he had been employed as a stevedore. It would have been futile to turn back, so I had to make the best of the circumstances. Luckily, I had with me a Turkish dictionary and phrase book, which gave the Turkish and English words and the phonetic pronunciation of the former. I occupied my leisure time in making the interpreter talk to me slowly in Turkish, giving the names of articles, numerals, and short phrases which I judged might be useful. These I corroborated from my Turkish book and committed to memory, and after a few days I had managed to memorize about 200 words.

It took me several days to find the best crossing for the railway over the Armanus range, and I came to the conclusion that it could not be negotiated without providing for a tunnel about seven or eight kilometres in length near a village called Beilan. I also had to make various detours to get the best line to Aleppo, and it took me nearly three weeks before I reached that town. The English Consul there at that time was a

Mr. Henderson, to whom I had letters of introduction. He was very kind to me and I enjoyed his hospitality for several days.

I had arranged to keep Mr. Alexander informed by telegram of my progress. Even in those days nearly all the Turkish towns and villages and the military stations throughout Asia Minor were connected by telegraph. Special permission had, however, to be obtained to use it, except for Government purposes. This permission had been obtained for me in Constantinople.

I left Aleppo with the intention of proceeding to Diarbekir Aintab to choose a suitable route for the course of the railway to Bagdad. Near Diarbekir there was a very big copper proposition, named Arghana, which I had been instructed to visit if at all possible. No European knew much about it, except perhaps that it was worked about every fourth year, and all the copper, not only for the Turkish coinage but also for the culinary utensils for the Palace and for high Government officials, was extracted from it. It was Church property, under the control of the Sheik Ul Islam. The ore was of a very high grade, yielding as much as from sixty-five to seventy per cent. of copper. This mine was afterwards organized into full working order, and I am under the impression that it must have been of great value to the Germans during the late war.

I had no sooner left Aleppo than I received a wire from Constantinople instructing me to return and, on my way, to examine a route *via* Antioch to a port called Suediah, the ancient Roman port of Seleucia. I stayed a day or two at Aleppo, and Mr. Henderson offered to accompany me as far as Antioch. There was no necessity for me to make any further survey between Aleppo and Antioch, and we proceeded along the old Roman road which goes as straight as the crow flies. Although at least 2,000 years old, this road was in a remarkable state of preservation, with stone guard-houses about every twelve miles, and although not perhaps suitable for vehicular traffic, it was quite good for camel and horse transport. Mr. Henderson lent me a very fine grey stallion which one day fell dead beneath me. Its decease was probably attributable partly to the great heat and it may have been to some extent to my excessive weight. Anyhow, I was immediately surrounded by the natives accompanying us, and Mr. Henderson's groom, who was passionately fond of the horse, became greatly excited and seemed to be threatening me. Mr. Henderson advised me to be very careful to stick close to him until we reached Antioch, where he proposed to leave me and to return to his station. The groom and his native friends were of the opinion that I possessed the " evil eye," and had been responsible for the horse's death, and there was no doubt that if they had been presented with a favourable opportunity they would have ended my days.

XXV

Biblical Associations

A FEW miles from Antioch we were met by a procession of the notabilities of the place. They had heard of my projected visit, and as the railway was a subject over which they had long been agitated, they were more than pleased to see me and, I suppose, they regarded the construction of the railway as a practical certainty. On the night of our arrival Mr. Henderson and I were the principal guests at a banquet, and I confess to having enjoyed myself very much, even if I did not understand a single word that was spoken. Apart from my friend, no one knew a word of the English tongue, and he told me that in the whole sixteen years he had been at Aleppo no other Englishman had visited the place. The next day he turned back to Aleppo. I remained a day or two in Antioch, selecting a site for a station and picking out the route through the town. I expected to find only a very small town, but I found that Antioch contained about 60,000 inhabitants. The old walls were still standing, and I entered the town by Paul's Gate, so named after Saint Paul. The Orontes River runs partly through, and partly past, the town, and I saw what I suppose are the biggest wooden water wheels in the world, which were being used for irrigation purposes. These wheels were between fifty and sixty feet in diameter and raised the water to that height so that it might be conveyed into the canals which had been made to provide the necessary irrigation for the surrounding country.

On leaving Antioch I passed through the groves of

Daphne and spent a couple of days exploring them. I occasionally came across statuary which had been there almost from time immemorial. Not far from Antioch there was a tribe of Yezidees, or devil-worshippers. I followed the valley of the Orontes River down to Suediah. I found the remains of the old harbour or docks of Seleucia about a mile from the sea and many feet above it. They were, of course, very small docks as compared with those of modern times, and I do not suppose were ever big enough to deal with vessels of much more than two hundred or three hundred tons. I also discovered the aqueduct which in Roman times supplied the town with water. Part of it was underground and I penetrated nearly half a mile into the old tunnel which had originally been part of the aqueduct.

I then returned to Antioch and crossed again to Beilan. It had been suggested that it might be possible to find a better crossing of the mountains between Alexandretta and Aleppo, so on reaching Alexandretta I discussed the suggestion with Catoni. He introduced me to a retired brigand who for many years had pursued his occupation amongst these mountains. He and I spent about a fortnight in the country of his escapades, trying to find a better crossing than that of Beilan. We went to the edge of the Plain of Issus and through the pass down which Darius came to fight Alexander the Great. It was most interesting, but I failed to find a better crossing. I left Alexandretta by sea and returned to Constantinople. There I went to see the Grand Vizier and gave him my candid opinion of the Turkish officials. I told him of some of the abuses which I thought ought to be discontinued. It may have been a coincidence, but I heard not long afterwards that both the Pasha of Aleppo and the Kaima Kan of Alexandretta had been removed.

I happened to have with me a piece of the rich Hottentot gold quartz of which I have already written.

This I gave to the Grand Vizier. He was greatly interested in all I told him about the gold and diamond fields of South Africa, and about the future of that country. I seemed to impress him very favourably, for he did me the honour of introducing me to the Sultan, with whom I had a brief interview. I confess to a great admiration for the old Sultan, Abdul Hamid. He did his best for his country and I know that through his instrumentality there were built, principally out of his privy purse, over 10,000 miles of roads in Asia Minor.

It transpired that I had been recalled because considerable difficulty had arisen in connection with the efforts to obtain the concession beyond Aleppo. The matter had passed the Council of State and was only awaiting the Sultan's firman. In business of this kind I have found that while it takes a very big official to get a concession, a very small one can block it. Such proved the case in this instance. My friend, Mr. Alexander, gradually became tired of doling out £10 here and £20 there to these minor officials which had become necessary to secure audiences with various ministers and other people in authority.

It is a time-worn axiom that every man has his price, more especially a barber. Not even a Sultan can afford to ignore the exactions of a Figaro, and it so happened that Mr. Alexander neglected to oil sufficiently the palm of a brother to the honoured individual whose chief function in life was nominally to trim the Sultan's locks, but in reality to keep him alive to every sort of gossip that was being related in Constantinople. One morning he told the Sultan of a report that the English were endeavouring to obtain possession of the northern part of Syria, and that they had already, as a first step, acquired a railway concession to Aleppo. He produced a map on which Cyprus was painted red, the admitted English colour, a small piece of blue representing the sea between Cyprus and Alexandretta, and a big red mark leading into Aleppo and down through Syria. I fancy this induced the Sultan to think furiously. Anyhow, the firman was refused, my mission came to an abrupt end, and I left for England.

XXVI

The Angora Railway

I ARRIVED home about the end of September 1887. I immediately set about to find something to do, and in partnership with Mr. G. H. Leane, a surveyor, took on the preparation of a survey and plans for a railway at Blackheath. Having been a widower for some time I married again early in November of that year and went to St. Ives to spend a few weeks with my mother and my two sons. My brother Harry was then on his way to England, and joined me at St. Ives in December. He and I had made a little money, but as it was limited to a few thousand pounds, we had to look round to plan out our future careers. Harry again proceeded to South Africa to join Dr. Harris with the object of making a fortune in the goldfields.

When I was in Constantinople I had met a Mr. Zeefelder who, with his partner, Mr. Alt, had some time previously obtained a concession and had built a railway from Haidar Pasha, opposite Constantinople, to Ismidt. He had told me much about the interior of Asia Minor, and about the fertility of the country, and had persuaded me that the construction of railways in that part of the world would be a very profitable undertaking. I repeated this to my London friends, and we had several interviews and examinations of the map of Asia Minor. I had traced a route from Ismidt *via* Angora, Kaiserea, down to Diarbekir, and thence to Bagdad; and it was determined that we should make an effort to obtain the concession from Ismidt to Angora, about three hundred miles, as a first step towards a railway to Bagdad, going through the middle of Asia Minor. My friends had also information that antimony was to be found in large quantities in the island of Samos, in the Grecian Archipelago, and I was commissioned, first to make a flying survey to Angora, then to put matters in the hands of Mr. Alexander, our Constantinople agent, and, if time permitted, to go to Samos and obtain a concession for the antimony mines.

I left for Constantinople again by the same route as before, and there met Mr. Alexander. After some delay, occasioned by the necessity of obtaining a Turkish passport, I went to Ismidt and equipped an expedition similar to that which I had proposed for my Aleppo adventure, but on this occasion I had as interpreter a young German who spoke English and Turkish almost with the same facility as he did his native tongue. The survey to Angora was not so difficult as that to Aleppo had been, because there was no big range of mountains to negotiate. We proceeded to a point near Kuplu, which was the centre of the silkworm industry. The whole country for many miles around was covered with mulberry trees, and silkworms were bred on a gigantic scale. Kuplu contained many factories, in some of which at least a thousand girls were employed, mostly Greeks and other foreigners. They were occupied in winding off the raw silk from the cocoons. The produce was all exported to Lyons. I forget how many tons of raw silk were exported yearly, but it was a very large quantity.

From Kuplu we traversed rough country to Eski-Cheir. I found it a difficult problem to get through this piece of the work, and I recollect having to follow a stream through a gorge with limestone cliffs three or four hundred feet in height on each side. This was, so far as I could then see, the only route by which to get the railway through without having to make a tortuous and steeply graded line over the hills through which the gorge passed. It is in the district around Eski-Cheir that meerschaum is obtained. It is found in pockets in the ground at depths varying from five or six to about twenty feet, and is exported in large quantities, principally to Vienna. I saw some pieces about as big as my head which, having regard to the size of my hats, is apparently above the normal, and I brought away with me two particularly fine samples. At Eski-Cheir I went to a Turkish bath which, according to report, has been in existence for two thousand years and was largely patronized in the time of the Romans. The distance between Eski-Cheir and Angora is about one hundred miles and the whole country is well cultivated. Corn of various kinds is grown, not only in that area but, I believe, for two hundred miles beyond Angora as far as Sivas.

I had a letter of introduction to a Mr. Newton who occupied the position of English Vice-Consul at Angora and who represented there the firm of Messrs. Whittall of Constantinople. Angora is a city of considerable size. Mr. Newton lived about three miles out of the town, and in the evening of my arrival the Pasha, or Governor, sent out his band to give me a serenade. To my untutored ear the music seemed most weird, and in deference to my British nationality included a combination of " Annie Laurie " and " God Save the King."

In the interior of Asia Minor the cost of living was extremely cheap, so much so that Mr. Newton was able to run the whole of his establishment, consisting of himself, wife, four servants, two or three horses, and a lovely garden, several acres in extent, for about £40 a year. In all my travels in Asia Minor it was my habit to take with me a big bag of money of the lowest coinage which we called metalliques. They represented tenths or twentieths of a piastre, which was then worth about twopence. It cost me only about the equivalent of

£13 in English money for the whole of my trip to Angora and back, covering a period of nearly three months. From Angora to Ismidt I returned by practically the same route as I had taken on my outward journey, and I halted occasionally to re-inspect a few places where the railway work was likely to be heavy. On reaching Constantinople I again saw Kiamil Pasha, the Grand Vizier, who evinced a great interest in what I told him about my journey and my views about the condition of the country. By that time the Germans had heard of our idea of a through railway from Ismidt to Bagdad and we learned that they were making proposals to the Turkish Government. I therefore returned to London to report progress to our syndicate. The consulting engineer to the syndicate whose office, then as now, was within a few doors of my own in Westminster, was Mr. Charles Meik.

It had by the time I returned to England become necessary to invoke the co-operation of a contractor, willing to undertake the construction of the Angora line at my estimate. I was not then in a position to take the contract as I had not the necessary capital, nor had I been established as an English contractor. Mr. Meik and I both knew the controlling spirit of Messrs. S. Pearsons and Sons, Ltd., who was then Mr. Weetman Dickinson Pearson and is now Lord Cowdray. At my suggestion the group opened negotiations with his firm. Considerable delay occurred, during which I was engaged in other work, but ultimately I met Mr. Pearson and discussed the position with him. Our representative had been informed that the only way in which a concession could be obtained quickly and without trouble would be for our English group to come to an arrangement with the Germans so as to obviate the element of competition, and that the Sultan would in that event give the concession to the Germans without delay. It having been agreed that the English group should divide equally with the Germans, Mr. Pearson proceeded to the scene of our operations. He had, on my estimate, undertaken to build the railway for about £10,000 a mile. My arrangement with him was that I should carry out the work, as his chief agent, at a high salary plus a substantial percentage of the profits.

As the concession was German, the work had to be carried out under German engineers, and we were accompanied on our trip to Eski-Cheir by the German chief engineer, whose name was Kapp and who had been engineer for the Corinth Canal. I pointed out to him all the salient details, and we arrived back in Constantinople sometime early in December.

Further delays took place and, to my great disgust, our English group in the end sold their birthright to the Germans for an inconsiderable sum. I believe Messrs. Pearson were offered the contract by the Germans if they would reduce their price by about £2,000 a mile. I begged them to do this, because even then there would have been a considerable profit in the contract. They, however, erroneously thought that the Germans would come up to their price, and held out accordingly. As it transpired, they failed to understand the disposition of the Teuton, who decided to build the railway himself, and all I received for my labour and interest in the business was a very small sum.

XXVII

Samos

WHILE the Angora proposition was being hung up through procrastination in Constantinople I was asked to fill in my time by going to Samos to examine the antimony mines there. I had previously studied mineralogy and had taken out a certificate as an assayer, particularly for gold. My experience of mining on railway tunnels and in the Transvaal rendered me quite capable as a mining engineer. I went overland to Marseilles, thence per steamer to Vathy, which is at once the capital and the port of Samos. I had a letter to a Mr. Marc, a Greek, who occupied the position of English Vice-Consul, and who had an excellent knowledge of the English tongue. I presented my credentials to him and he told me it was quite possible that I might get the concession for the mines, if I were prepared to pay for it. Samos, which is situated in the Aegean Sea, is an island extending to nearly two hundred square miles. Although its governor, the Prince of Samos, is a Greek and the majority of the islanders entertain Greek sympathies, it is under the suzerainty of Turkey and is compelled to pay tribute to the Porte. The Governor is advised by a Native Council, consisting of five members, and Mr. Marc explained to me that three out of the five constituted a majority and that, therefore, it would only be necessary to ensure that three of the councillors were in favour of the concession. On the morning following my arrival I, by arrangement, met Mr. Marc and three councillors. After a lengthy argument I agreed that it would be worth my while to pay £400 for the mine concession. The councillors were gracious enough to say that they considered it would be to the benefit of the islands if the antimony could be worked, and therefore their consciences would be quite clear if they gave me the concession and accepted a small present for their kindness and goodwill. This meeting, which took place at ten o'clock, was, of course, unofficial. I found that a meeting of the full Council had been summoned to meet an hour later and, after our understanding had been arrived at, I adjourned with Mr. Marc into an adjoining room. After a brief interval we were invited to attend the meeting of the Council. I was then called upon to state the whole of my case through Mr. Marc, and, with the support of our three senatorial friends, it was unanimously resolved that the concession should be given to my group. I had had some experience of how concessions are negotiated and flattered myself on having succeeded so far so quickly.

That evening I had been invited by the Governor, Prince Alexander Kara Theodori, to dinner at the palace. I found the Prince, who spoke English perfectly, very friendly. Although I did not know it at the time, he had been the Turkish representative at the Berlin Congress and was, I was told, practically in exile because he had not been able to obtain the terms which Turkey expected to get at that Congress. We talked much about Africa, as well as about Asia Minor and other parts of the Turkish Empire, and in view of his friendly and confidential attitude, I decided to tell him all about the meeting with the Council. He was less surprised than amused, and congratulated me on having adopted the correct course. In a few days the necessary documents were completed and approved by Mr. Marc, and I went in a small steamer to the other port of the island, called Carlovassi, the antimony deposits being about five miles from that town. In Carlovassi there was no hotel, but

PRESIDENT KRUGER WATCHES THE ARRIVAL OF THE "RAND TRAM" AT BOKSBURG IN 1888.

I secured a room in a café for myself and Mr. Marc's son, who accompanied me and acted as my interpreter. I had got together tools and explosives and proceeded to the hills where the antimony was supposed to exist. A small quantity of the metal had been found in certain spots and I went to work and followed up the indications. It did not take me long to discover a number of stringers of antimony and several large pockets, some of which contained several tons of the stuff. I found, however, that the amount of deadwork that had to be accomplished in order to find these lenses or pockets would be very costly, and as I failed to strike the principal reef I came to the conclusion that it would be inadvisable for me to recommend more money being sunk in the venture.

At the café where young Marc and I put up quite an amusing incident occurred. It was my habit when I got up in the morning to sponge myself down in a small wooden bath. One morning the water and the wooden tub were not ready, so I asked my interpreter what was the reason. He replied that the owner of the café had been late in getting up that morning. I naturally enquired what that had to do with it, and was informed by young Marc that the tub had to serve more purposes than one. In the early morning it was used for making bread in, after which it was passed on to me for my bath. On the morning in question the proprietor had been a late riser and the bread had not been made early. Hence the delay. I immediately ordered a tin bath from one of the tinsmiths in Carlovassi. A friend of mine who visited the island some years later told me that my bath was then in existence, although kept more as a matter of curiosity than for utility.

The cost of living on the island was ridiculously small. A dozen eggs could be purchased for a piastre, which was equal to twopence, and a fowl or more wine than one could drink in two or three days, at the same price. When I came to pay my bill at the café, however, I found that the proprietor had charged me a medjidi a day, equal to three shillings and fourpence of our currency, for myself, Mr. Marc, and a servant. My bill happened to be handed to me while I was having a farewell breakfast with the Judge President and the captain of the Gendarmerie. Having by accident discovered the extent of my charges, they were very angry, sent for the proprietor, called him a robber and a thief, asked him how he expected that visitors would come to the island if they had to submit to such extortion, and insisted that he should return to me a half or two-thirds of the money. To me the scene was extremely amusing, and I told them that, while I could appreciate their point of view, I should prefer that the manager should keep what I had paid him as he had been more than kind to me.

I had no alternative but to condemn the mine, which I did on my return to London, and thus ended unprofitably another chapter in my history.

XXVIII

Back to the Old Love

ONCE again I was face to face with the problem of my future career. Realizing that if I remained in England the prospects were very meagre, I determined to revisit South Africa. I mentioned my intention to Baron d'Erlanger, who was flattering enough to suggest that I should go out as a mining expert to represent his firm, and with his usual generosity he offered me a good salary and very liberal commission on any business being accepted through my introduction. This was arranged, and I left England in the autumn of 1889, going straight through to Johannesburg which, by that time, had developed into a large town. My mission soon became known and I found quite a number of people who wished to interest my principals in various Rand mining schemes. All these propositions I looked into, and having arrived at the conclusion that the terms asked for were invariably far too high, I communicated my decision to Baron d'Erlanger and, while awaiting instructions, went to Pretoria and spent some time with Mr. E. G. Woodford, who was then State Mining Engineer for the Transvaal. He was at that time busily occupied in compiling a Mining Law for the Transvaal. He had made himself possessed of copies of the Mining Laws of other countries, including those of the United States, and together we went through and selected what we considered the most suitable clauses to obviate big lawsuits such as had occurred in the United States and elsewhere. His report met with great approval, and very much of it was embodied in the

Transvaal Mining Law which, I believe, was then, as it is to-day, the fairest mining law in the world. I had, of course, told Mr. Woodford my position, and that I was only waiting to hear from Messrs. Erlangers before deciding what to do next.

In view of my expressed opinions to them that the prices being asked for all mining propositions were far too high, I had requested that if they did not object, I might be permitted to resign my appointment.

Just about that time the Transvaal Government had called for tenders for what, although really a railway, was known as the "Rand Tram" from Johannesburg to Boksburg. I was not in a position to submit a tender myself, but others had done so, including Mr. James Butler. One of the competitors, a Mr. George Gray, had submitted a tender about £10,000 lower than Butler's and had secured the contract, but after doing some little work, found that he could not see it through. M. Verwey, the chief engineer of the Netherlands Railway Company, then approached Mr. Butler and asked if he would undertake the contract at his price. The latter agreed to do so, and, happening to meet me in one of the streets of Johannesburg, told me what he had done in securing the contract and asked if I would care to have a participation. After looking through the documents I agreed, but my difficulty at the time was money. However, my brother, who was then in Kimberley, was willing to help us to the full extent of his resources, and as Mr. Butler was also in a position to put up capital, it was arranged that we should establish the firm of James Butler and Company, and the work was carried out in that name.

We started work early in 1890, and after finishing the line to Boksburg, we obtained from the same source two further contracts, one from Johannesburg to Krugersdorp, and the other from Boksburg to Springs.

XXIX

The "S" Syndicate

ALTHOUGH actively engaged on railway work, I did not neglect to keep in close touch with my friend Mr. Woodford, who continued to occupy the position of State Mining Engineer. In these early days it was the opinion of very many mine owners and mining engineers in the Rand that the banket deposit carrying gold would not continue to any considerable depth, and, consequently, very few mining companies had pegged out their claims more than one, two, or, in a few cases, three claims deep on the dip of the reef. Mr. Woodford had access to the plans and workings of the previous mining companies, and had come to the conclusion that the reef would continue more or less indefinitely in depth. He and I had frequent conversations on the subject, and as he succeeded in persuading me and two other friends of his, Mr. David Benjamin and Mr. J. S. Curtis, to accept his view, a small syndicate was formed with a capital of one hundred and twenty shares of one pound each.

We pegged out a number of claims, extending from close to the "May Consolidated" property, past the "Simmer and Jack," "Jumpers," and other mines, right up to, and just beyond, Johannesburg. The claims, as pegged, formed the shape of the letter "S," which inspired us to call our group the "S" syndicate. I did not take any very great interest in the project, but in consideration of my holding, undertook to beacon the claims with masonry beacons. Mr. Benjamin was the financial genius on whom we relied to turn our syndicate into a big company. Mr. Curtis was a mining engineer, whose particular function was to make any necessary reports.

Efforts were made to dispose of the property in England, but they miscarried, chiefly, in my opinion, because of mismanagement.

The history of the "S" syndicate is well known. It was one of the principal items in the formation of the Rand Mines Company. I have heard that Messrs. Benjamin and Curtis each received at least for one £1 share £8,000, and I know that I sold the only one share standing in my name for £1,500. If the business had been well handled there is not the slightest doubt that each of the four holders in the original syndicate would have become a millionaire from this single deal. This was the third occasion on which I had missed amassing a fortune through entrusting the care of my interests to others instead of looking after them myself. I am confident that in the case of my brother's original purchase of the forty Johannesburg stands at £10 each; in that of the fourteen farms which passed into other hands after our option on them had expired; and in that of the "S" syndicate I had a head level enough to have made big fortunes out of each of these transactions, but following the old adage of "cobbler, stick to your last," I contented myself with pursuing my own line of business. Nor do I now regret failing to become a millionaire through any of these channels, but am glad that I have been spared to enjoy comfortable circumstances chiefly through hard work and attention to my own business.

In connection with the "S" venture it is interesting to recall that a year or more afterwards, when the Rand Mines Company was floated, Mr. Beit, who, I think, was unaware of my connection with the "S" syndicate, offered me 3,000 shares in the original flotation at bed-rock price. On my refusal to take them he told me I was very foolish, and predicted that they would go to £25 each. As a matter of fact they went up to over £40, and Dr. Rutherfoord Harris, who was with me at the time Mr. Beit made me the offer, and who received a similar offer, took up his 3,000 shares and sold them at practically top price.

XXX

Crocodile Poort

WHILE we were engaged in the construction of the Rand trams, the Netherlands Company was building the line from the Portuguese frontier to Pretoria, and had entrusted the work to a firm of Hollander contractors named Van Hattum. This firm was making indifferent progress, and the construction involved a very heavy piece of work in the Crocodile Poort. It so happened that about that time Mr. Woodford had proposed that he and I should see President Kruger. He stated that the latter entertained very friendly feelings towards him and suggested that as the President was greatly in favour of railway development, the chance of further contracts might come my way, and it was only natural that Mr. Woodford's suggestion should appeal to me.

Our interview with President Kruger took place at what, in England, would be considered the unusual hour of 5.30 a.m. We found the man, whose name will ever be associated with the history of South Africa, sitting on a chair in the verandah of his house, sipping coffee. He genially invited us—in the Dutch tongue—to join him in his morning cup. It is a well-known fact that, although he was familiar with it, he consistently refrained from conversing in the English language. Mr. Woodford, who spoke Dutch much better than I, acted as an interpreter between the President and myself. Having ascertained my name, he stated that it was not unfamiliar to him, for a Pauling had once befriended him and had given him coffee and a place to sleep in at a time when he was sadly in need of it.

It has been my general experience that acts of kindness, however small, seldom go unrewarded. So it was in this instance. My brother Harry had told me of the episode of which the President spoke, and which had occurred while my brother was a Government railway engineer at Krankuil, about five hundred and fifty miles from Cape Town, when it was the railhead on the line towards Kimberley. The President and two other Dutchmen, named Dutoit and, I think, Smit—known as the Triumvirate—had previously gone to England to protest against the British annexation of the Transvaal. It was, of course, known who they were, and on their return the English and other people at the end of the rails were very rude to them, so much so that the hotel keeper refused to give them accommodation. The night before they were due to leave Krankuil by passenger coach for Pretoria, my brother chanced to see them wandering about just as darkness was approaching, and he took the liberty of speaking to them. They told him that they had been refused accommodation at the hotel, and in his usual good-hearted way he offered them a shakedown in his office and promised that they should be called and given a cup of coffee before the coach started in the morning. They thankfully accepted his invitation.

Through Mr. Woodford I told the President that the Pauling to whom he referred was my brother, and that I had heard from him of the occasion of which he spoke. The old man, who, whatever his faults in other directions, possessed within his breast the milk of human kindness, immediately volunteered to render me any help within his power in recognition of my brother's service to him. I told him that I was a railway contractor and that I was on the look out for work. Without hesitation he replied that I should have all the contracts at his disposal, and he thereupon sent for Mr. Verwey, who was at that time the chief engineer of the Netherlands Company. Whilst we were awaiting the arrival of Mr. Verwey, Mr. Woodford told the President of my trips to Turkey and to Asia Minor, and the old gentleman showed great interest in the story of my wanderings. When Mr. Verwey arrived, he introduced me as "George Pauling" and instructed him to give me all the railway contracts that he could.

When I left the President, Mr. Verwey came with me and showed an immediate desire to comply with the instructions of his chief by expressing his willingness, if we could come to terms, to let me have a contract; and the failure of Messrs. Van Hattum to fulfil their obligations opened up a very favourable opportunity for him to do so. He told me of the circumstances and implied that he would like my firm to do the work, but stated that he would have to call for tenders. He furnished me with much useful information and we tendered in the name of James Butler and Company. There were several competitors, but our price was the lowest and was accepted. Crocodile Poort enjoyed a most unenviable reputation. It was regarded, not without some justification, as one of the most unhealthy parts of the country. Fever was rampant in the district which, of course, would materially increase the cost of the work, already known to be very heavy. My partner, Mr. Butler, made it a condition that he would only remain on the work for a limited period, which he did, but agreed to allow his £3,000 capital to remain in the business until it suited me to return it to him. We remained on the Rand to square up the accounts for the Tram contract, which was then approaching completion.

I went to Barberton, from which the Crocodile Poort contract was distant about thirty miles. One man who stuck to me was my old friend John Scott, to whom I should have referred at a much earlier stage in these records. I met him first in the early part of 1878, when I was carrying out work in the Wei Nek tunnel, not far from Grahamstown. He was then working under Mr. E. R. Carolin, who was district engineer in the construction of the line from Alicedale to Grahamstown. He had had considerable previous experience with the Cape Government Railways, and in 1879 we again met in Grahamstown when he was with a Mr. Jordan, for whom I built a wagon factory. He subsequently rejoined the Cape Government Railways, and after we commenced work in Johannesburg, I engaged him as our head office man, and he came with me to the Crocodile Poort job to occupy a similar position. From that day to this he and I have been actively associated. He has been the secretary of Pauling and Company Limited since the inception of that company, and I have received from him invaluable assistance in regard to all the projects in which I have been interested. I also engaged an engineer named Richard Pizzighelli, who is to-day in the employment of my firm, and my cousin, another Harry Pauling, who had been employed with me for a time in connection with the construction of the Rand trams. Harry, although he had been brought up as a farmer, turned out a first-class contractor's man and proved very useful to me. When Mr. Pizzighelli and I went to inspect the route we found that the heavy nature of the work had been by no means underestimated. Our first visit consisted of a fearful walk, or rather a combined scramble and climb, and it took us eight hours to cover eight miles, or approximately half the distance, through the Poort from the Barberton end.

After carefully examining the country we returned to Barberton and I made the necessary preliminary arrangements for carrying out the contract.

We established our main camp, called the Middle Camp, about two-thirds of the way through the Poort. I had been under an obligation to a Port Elizabeth firm, Messrs. Hansen and Schrader, and in order to liquidate my indebtedness I made an arrangement with them under which the supply of provisions and stores for the men was placed in their hands. It was a condition of the arrangement that I should receive ten per cent. of their profits. For the purposes of their business they erected a couple of stores in suitable places. While this was being done I received a notification from Mr. (now Sir) Percy FitzPatrick that he had obtained the right from a Mr. Pott who, he said, held a concession from the Netherlands Company, to supply provisions and other goods for the men engaged on this particular part of the railway. I told Mr. FitzPatrick that my contract with the Netherlands Company contained no reference to any such concession, and that consequently I could not recognize his claim. He, however, persisted in his contention and sent out materials and men to erect a store at what was called the Waterfall, about half-way through the Poort. This was a most unapproachable place, in fact the only way to reach it was by a surface path which I had had cut out at a cost of £1,000, in order to get my supplies, plant, and material delivered along the work. I maintained a studied silence until Mr. FitzPatrick had erected and stocked his store. Then I gave him notice that I was about to open a big quarry close to his establishment and that there was every probability that it would be blown to pieces. It may have been because of this incident that the "Barberton Herald" at that time published a number of very slanderous articles in which I was described as the Great Crocodile, who swallowed up smaller men in my line of business, and in which I was generally portrayed as a very unpleasant person with whom to have any dealings. I ignored these articles, but chancing on one occasion to meet the editor, I caught hold of his arm, and by dint of a little gentle pressure on his wrist, induced him to come to the club with me and to buy me a drink. The "Barberton Herald" of that morning had contained a particularly venomous attack on me. The astonishment, however, with which the people in the club saw the editor treating me, and both of us apparently on the most friendly terms, completely robbed it of its sting.

It did not take us long to realize the immense difficulties that we should have to contend with in carrying out the work. These consisted notably of fever amongst the men, which we had been led to expect; of tsetse fly, which prevented ox wagon transport; and of lions which found frequent, and apparently satisfying, meals among our donkeys. In consequence of the tsetse fly I had to depend to a great extent on donkey transport, and through illness and the fly I lost over 500 of these beasts. They are not immune from fly, but they withstand its ravages better than any other animal.

It was excruciatingly hot in the Crocodile Poort and all my work had to be done on foot, but notwithstanding these conditions I was never able to reduce my weight below sixteen stone. I did not suffer much from fever, but Scott and all my other assistants, with the exception of Pizzighelli, had a very bad time. One night some of us were playing poker at the Middle Camp while Scott was lying in the room next to us with a temperature of about 107 degrees. Old Dr. Williams put down his poker hand, went into the next room, and returned shortly to tell us that poor old Scott was out of his hands and in the hands of Providence. Fortunately, Providence was kind and John Scott, who did not take long to recover from his malarial attack, has since enjoyed, and continues to enjoy, robust health. Dr. Williams was my medical officer. He was, in his way, a great character, and in his professional capacity had had much experience of malarial fever. At one time he had served with the Servian Army in the Turko-Servian war. He was shot in the foot and thereby made permanently slightly lame. Mr. Pizzighelli, curiously enough, had served on the Turkish side as a Bimbashi or Major, and had also been wounded in the foot, slightly affecting his walking gait.

Not the least difficulty in a fever country is to keep up the spirits of the men, and to prevent them from dying through sheer funk of the fever. With this object Dr. Williams instituted a very helpful game in our hospital at Middle Camp. The hospital was made of native timber, thatched with grass, and consisted of one room, large enough for twenty-four patients. It was generally more than half full. The doctor had a number of thermometers, and in the afternoons he created a pool, into which was placed a shilling collected from each patient. If a patient was too ill to subscribe, a shilling was put in on his behalf. Then the temperatures were taken, and the man registering the highest "scooped" the pool. Frequently several of the patients with temperatures of from 105 to 107 or 108 were off their heads when their temperatures were taken, but with a falling temperature the first indication of incipient consciousness was an inquiry as to the result of the previous pool.

Although the work was carried on under extremely trying conditions, we occasionally contrived to find recreation and amusement. It was at the Poort, either at Christmas or New Year 1890-1, that we held a sports meeting. As the temperature at three o'clock in the afternoon was about 115 in the shade, the circumstances were not favourable for record breaking. Feeling it my duty to take an active part in the programme, I entered for the half-mile race. Carrying, as I did, over sixteen stone, I did not fancy my chances, but the indulgent handicappers had given me a big start and I got home first. I was the more pleased with my success because there was among my men a flyer named Nash, who held a record for the half-mile distance.

Towards the middle of 1891 I had practically finished the Crocodile Poort contract and had left Messrs. Scott and Pizzighelli to complete and hand over the line to the company. Some time before the work was finished I had repaid Mr. Butler the £3,000 capital he had left in the business. I was asked to tender for other work, but by that time many competitors had entered the contracting field and were prepared to accept prices which did not appeal to me. I therefore decided to keep what I had made, which was a very considerable sum, and to leave the Transvaal. I went down to the Cape, and from there to Kimberley to meet my brother, and he and I decided to return together to England. Meanwhile, at the request of Mr. Rhodes, I had looked into the question of a proposed railway from Kimberley to Vryburg, which, however, was built departmentally by the Cape Government, a section of it being completed under the supervision of my cousin, Mr. Harold Pauling.

XXXI

A Syrian Excursion

ABOUT September 1891 Harry and I arrived home. One of our first visits was to my old friend Mr. Edwin Elliott, with whom I had been in Firbank's office before I went to the Cape. He was anxious to start contracting on his own behalf, and after considering the matter, Harry and I agreed to put up capital to start English work in conjunction with him. Our first contract, which was taken in the name of Pauling and Elliott, was obtained from the Great Western Railway, and consisted of the erection of bridges and some other minor railway work.

Towards the middle of 1892 I was offered a contract to build a railway from Haifa to Damascus in Syria, and I went out to look over the route before coming to a definite decision. At the end of July I returned to England and accepted the contract. Whilst I was at Haifa there was a severe outbreak of cholera and people were dying almost like flies. It was nearly impossible to get away from Haifa, as the Turks had placed soldiers at all the drifts leading from the town. Before I left England I had again encountered Houghton. He spoke Arabic and Turkish with considerable facility, and was one of the few Christians who had managed to make the pilgrimage to Mecca—of course, at the risk of his life. When I told him of my proposed visit to Syria he begged to be allowed to accompany me, and I took him as my secretary and interpreter. He determined to make an effort to get away from the cholera. He was a very resourceful person and, proceeding on foot over the mountains, accomplished his purpose and reached Beyrout.

I had engaged at Haifa a Roumanian youth named Sam Sherratti. He had been in England and knew the English language well. He was also, I think, familiar with all the eastern languages and certainly spoke Arabic and Turkish perfectly. He told me that he knew of a drift on the road towards Jaffa where he thought we could bribe the Turkish soldiers to let us get across. Very early one morning we left on horseback, and I gave Sam fifty Turkish pounds in gold. As we approached the drift he rode forward and asked the sentry to request the Turkish officer to speak to him. When the officer came Sam showed him the gold. I did not know what had happened, but I heard Sam shouting to me to gallop away. His horse was turned round and he came in full haste after me, followed by a shot from a Turkish rifle, which did not hit either of us. When we had reached a safe distance we pulled up and Sam told me that he had never before known a Turkish officer to refuse gold. When he told the officer the object of our mission the immediate reply was that the sentry would be ordered to fire on us. Hence the hurried retreat.

The cholera was still rife in Haifa when a French tramp steamer came into the port, and by dint of persuasion, combined with a liberal cash payment, I induced the German consul, Dr. Schmidt, to arrange with the French captain to take Sam and me to Marseilles. The steamer had been originally a sailing vessel, but engines had been dumped into her stern part, and she could make about six or seven knots under steam. After leaving Haifa we had bad weather all the way down the Mediterranean. The captain was almost continuously drunk. The mate, who was the only other officer, proved a very decent fellow. The rest of the crew consisted of an engineer and his assistant, about four firemen, and a couple of deck hands. There were some nuns on board and one or two other passengers. As we were sailing towards the islands of Corsica and Sardinia, the chief officer came up to me, and from the perturbed expression on his usually unemotional countenance I inferred that there was something seriously the matter. It transpired that the captain had given orders to go through the Straits of Bonifacio. In view of the gale that was then raging this course would, in the opinion of the chief officer, have proved calamitous and could only have one result—the loss of the ship. He was at his wits' end to know what to do, and, as a forlorn hope, suggested that I should overpower the captain, who was in his usual drunken and boisterous condition, force him into his cabin, and lock him in. With the skipper thus imprisoned, it was the intention of the chief officer to assume command and to turn the ship across so that we might proceed *via* the Gulf of Lyons instead of through the Straits. The suggestion did not at first commend itself to me, because I could not quite foresee what trouble might be in store at the end of the voyage. I was literally between the devil, in the person of the captain, and the deep sea, which meant a watery grave in the Straits of Bonifacio. So I was the more easily persuaded when the chief officer explained that if he refused to obey orders or took it upon himself to lock up the captain it would be mutiny, whereas, if I did it, the mutinous element would be eliminated and he and all the other members of the crew would swear that I had only done what was necessary for the protection of the ship. Accordingly, when the captain sat down to have more drink and some lunch, I went more or less stealthily behind him, caught him in my arms, dragged him out of his seat, threw him into his cabin, and locked the door. For some time the row in the cabin reminded me of a miniature menagerie, but after a while the captain quietened down and went to sleep. The chief officer altered the course according to his programme and next morning I, with some misgivings, opened the captain's door. Contrary to expectations and much to my surprise, he was most affectionate, thanked me for saving him from a stupid action and from probably losing his ship, and thus a very unpleasant episode had a happy end. We arrived at Marseilles without further excitement, and as our voyage had taken thirteen days from Haifa we were free of quarantine, and I was permitted to proceed straight through to London.

On returning to England I found many difficulties to militate against the commencement of the work from Haifa. For one thing the finance had not been completely arranged and consequently it was possible to enter into a definite contract only for the first five or ten miles. However, the directors, who were Manchester people, the concessionaire being a Mancurian named Pilling, determined to make a great flourish at the ceremony of cutting the first sod, and it was arranged that I should leave England again for Syria in company with three of the directors and two or three newspaper men. On arrival at Haifa I was instructed to provide a big entertainment for about 500 notables and 10,000 natives. I put this business in the hands of Messrs. Thomas Cook and Son and they sent from Egypt a steamer with several hundred waiters, all kinds of provisions, refreshments, and the various necessities and luxuries for such a feast as I had been commissioned to provide. For the consumption of the natives quite a big quantity of sheep had been secured. Large marquees were erected to accommodate the notables; about a ton of fireworks had been imported; and altogether a most elaborate outfit had been supplied for the delectation of everyone during the few days over which the ceremony extended. Everything went off admirably. Pashas and other high officials from Jerusalem, Acre, Constantinople, Beyrout, and other places were present, and a big impression was made on the Turkish mind of the wealth and capacity of the people to whom the railway concession had been given. After the ceremony of cutting the first sod was finished, the directors and their friends were taken charge of by Messrs. Cook and made a trip to Jerusalem, thence to Damascus, and back to Beyrout, and then on to England. I accompanied them as far as Nazareth, where I left them to return to the scene of operations.

This railway passed over most interesting ground. Haifa is situated at the foot of Mount Carmel, where there are two caves, each of which is claimed to have been the cave of Elijah. The one cave is situated under the high altar of the Carmelite monastery, the other about three or four hundred yards farther down the mountain. Both of these caves were then and, I believe, are still visited by as many as several hundred thousand people yearly—Christians, Mohammedans, and Jews—because Elijah was venerated as a great prophet by the followers of each of these religions. I spent a very enjoyable, albeit quiet, week in the Carmelite monastery. The Superior was a man who spoke English, and who had at one time been at the Carmelite church in Kensington. He was apparently very pleased to see me and did all he could to make me comfortable.

After spending some time in completing the preliminary organization I started the construction work. It was impossible to look very far ahead because the finance for the whole line had still to be arranged, and as a matter of fact the concession was ultimately lost through the company's inability to carry out its financial obligations.

Practically every mile of the route over which it was intended to build the line was fraught with interesting Biblical associations. We had a bridge over the Brook Kishon, from which one could see the traditional site of the altar of Baal on the Carmelite ridge. Thence we passed across the plain of Armageddon into the valley of Jordan. One of the stations was called Nazareth Road, Nazareth itself being in the hills about five miles distant; another, Endor, traditionally named after the Witch of Endor; a third Nain, believed to be the scene of the raising of the widow's son. The railway then crossed the River Jordan, close by an old Roman bridge which had been built over 2,000 years ago, and which still carried the traffic across the highlands of the Houran to Damascus. Skirting the Sea of Gallilee or Lake of Gennesaret, it passed up the ravine where, it is locally believed, the Gadarene swine ran down into the sea. I looked forward with a great deal of pleasurable anticipation to carrying a railway through these world-known places on to Damascus, but it was not to be.

A few months after starting work at Haifa financial difficulties began to arise, and I did not receive payment for the work I was doing, so I reduced expenditure to a minimum and returned to England.

XXXII

SYRIAN SCHEMES

WHILE the work at Haifa was in progress Mr. Houghton came to me with what we both thought was a money-making proposition. The World's Fair was due to be opened at Chicago in the following May, and his idea, with which I was in accord, was that if we could manage to transport to Chicago—America being a country pretty full of cranks, religious and otherwise—a couple of million bottles of Jordan Water, we should be able to sell them at a dollar each for the purpose of baptizing children, and what might not be used for baptismal purposes could probably be utilized for diluting whisky. The idea of "a whisky and a Jordan water" seemed quite a happy one, and we thought it would probably take well. Amongst the acquaintances of Mr. Houghton was Sequah, the celebrated Yankee tooth-puller, who then happened to be in Egypt. We had a conference and, Sequah thinking well of the idea, he and Mr. Houghton worked out the details of the scheme. They succeeded in obtaining the approval of the American Government, and also got the American authorities to send over to the American Consul in Haifa 5,000 official sealing machines. My friends provisionally engaged about 10,000 men, women, and children for water-bottling purposes, and commenced to erect at Haifa wood and iron sheds in which it was proposed to do the bottling. They also arranged for the supply of 500 wooden casks, suitable for being carried on camels, because the water would have to be brought to Haifa from the Jordan, about forty miles away. Meanwhile we had approached the Turkish Government in Constantinople for their permission to export the waters, and if that had been granted in time we should have sent to Chicago two million bottles of Jordan water, officially sealed and guaranteed genuine by the American Government. We should probably have made about £80,000 out of the deal. Time went on, however, and owing to the usual Oriental dilatoriness we could not obtain permission from Constantinople, and when it became too late to send the water for the Chicago Fair we abandoned the scheme, and from a financial point of view the waters of Jordan conferred no blessing either on Sequah or on myself.

While in Syria I became very friendly with the colonel in charge of the Turkish troops at Acre, which is on the opposite side of the bay and about twelve miles from Haifa. I frequently visited him at Acre, and he returned the compliment to me at Haifa. On one of my visits he told me that there were huge quantities of old cannon lying in the vaults under the citadel at Acre and took me to see them. It struck me that most of these cannon, or at any rate a large proportion, were of bronze, and I had several of them chipped to see; and this corroborated my view. I asked the colonel if the Turkish Government would sell these cannon as they were useless and only worth the price of old iron. He urged me to ask the authorities at Constantinople, and promised strongly to recommend the sale himself and to get the recommendation endorsed by the Pasha at Acre. As far as I could judge, there were about 3,000 tons of metal in the vaults, and I authorized an offer of £3 a ton to be made. Meantime I had communicated with one of the biggest English firms in the iron and steel trade, who had agreed to participate equally with me in the venture. I believe we should have got the matter through in Constantinople had it not been for the obstinacy of the Turkish War Office Department. The people in authority seemed to think that these obsolete guns might still be of use in some future war. Anyhow, the deal failed, and once again I lost the opportunity of making a fortune.

CECIL JOHN RHODES.

SIR CHARLES METCALFE, BART.

BARON EMILE D'ERLANGER.

GEORGE PAULING.

A. L. LAWLEY.

HAROLD PAULING.

A BALLAD OF THE B.M.R.

Down in the land where heathens are,
Down in the swamps where white men stew,
Amid the woods that stretch afar,
Amid the creepers dank with dew
The Line ran out — perchance, askew,
And drunkenly designed — but, ah!
In days gone by was work to do
Upon the lonely B.M.R.!

The Gates of Death were held ajar —
The pegs that marked the mileage too
Have stood for tombstones — near and far
Ghosts of a grimy, shrivelled crew,
The sun looked down from out the blue—
Out of the night looked down the star,
And marked where men had drifted through
The death-trap of the B.M.R.

Each bolt, each nut, each metal bar,
Could tell a story — grim but true —
And where the gangers' houses are
Maybe are ghosts of dead men too —
Ghosts of the men who worked and knew—
The fever-swamp, the sickening jar
That came when life was rusted through
Upon the lonely B.M.R.

L'Envoi.

Lo! — we may scoff — we often do —
And jest at engine, truck, and car —
But — must we then forget the few
Who made for us the B.M.R.

—Cullen Gouldsbury

(In 1900 the Beira-Umtali-Salisbury sections of the Beira Railway Company and the Mashonaland Company combined under one management at Umtali and became known as the "B.M.R.")

A BEIRA RAILWAY GROUP IN 1894. CENTRE ROW, LEFT TO RIGHT: MR. A. L. LAWLEY, MR. THOM, SIR CHARLES METCALFE, BART., AND MR. GEORGE PAULING.

BRIDGE OVER THE PUNGWE RIVER

BEIRA RAILWAY.

PASSENGER SERVICE.

Until further notice a passenger train will leave the 75 mile Station every Wednesday at 6.30 am connecting with the Mail Steamer at Fontesvilla

A passenger train will also leave Fontesvilla for the 75 mile Station on the arrival of each Mail

FONTESVILLA

GEORGE PAULING
CONTRACTOR

ADVERTISEMENT FROM "THE UMTALI ADVERTISER" OF 1895.

THE FIRST TRAIN AT BEIRA ON THE OCCASION OF THE OPENING OF THE BEIRA-MASHONALAND RAILWAY.

XXXIII

Vryburg to Mafeking

WHILE I was about to leave Africa in 1891, and indeed after I had made arrangements to go home by the east coast route, I was summoned by telegram from Barberton to Cape Town, where Mr. Rhodes wished to see me about the extension of the railway from Vryburg to Mafeking. Vryburg is the capital of Bechuanaland, and had for some little time been the terminus of the line northwards from Cape Town. I accordingly abandoned my plans and, accompanied by Harry, I went to Delagoa Bay, and thence by sea to Cape Town. On arrival there I saw Mr. Rhodes, and at his suggestion Harry and I proceeded to Mafeking, travelling by rail to Vryburg and then over the route of the proposed extension by cart to Mafeking. On our return we made a proposal to Mr. Rhodes, but he insisted that we should proceed at once to London to see his directors. I was in some ways rather pleased as I was anxious to ascertain the financial conditions then existing. Harry went to England and I followed shortly afterwards.

In London I found that it would not be possible to proceed with the Mafeking work as speedily as Mr. Rhodes had expected. Financial troubles delayed its commencement for a time. In April 1893 I went out by the s.s. "Dunottar Castle," and one of my fellow passengers was the late Sir James Sievewright, with whom I discussed the question of the building of this line. On my arrival in Cape Town I saw Dr. Rutherfoord Harris, who was then secretary of the Chartered

Company, and Sir Charles Metcalfe, one of the consulting engineers to that company, and ascertained that it had been definitely decided to commence construction. We had some differences as to the price to be paid, and I understood that we had as competitors the firm of Messrs. Lucas and Aird. I was not satisfied with the price suggested by the consulting engineers for this work and made another tour over the route, after which I decided upon terms and ultimately, through Mr. Rhodes, I entered into a contract (which I remember was signed at midnight after a dinner at which Sir Charles Metcalfe and I were the guests of Mr. Rhodes) with the Bechuanaland Railway Company, Limited. The fulfilment of their obligations was guaranteed by the British South Africa Company, and its construction, extending to 106 miles, was completed in the following year. This section is of especial interest to me inasmuch as it is the commencement of what is known as the Rhodesian railway system, with the construction of which I have since been so closely connected.

I appointed my cousin Harold, who, after my Kimberley debacle, had entered the Government service and had been in charge of a section of the line from Kimberley to Vryburg, as agent in charge of the construction of the line; and my brother Harry who, with Mr. Scott, had been looking after our affairs in England, went out to see the work started.

XXXIV

The Beira Railway

SOMETIME in the year 1892 Mr. Beit sent for me and asked if I would be prepared to build a railway in Portuguese East Africa from a place up the Pungwe River, known as Fontesvilla, about fifty miles by river from Beira, to a point about seventy-five miles distant towards Rhodesia. There was some competition for this job, Mr. Lawley being one of my opponents. However, I in the end obtained the contract and engaged him on fair terms, including a share of the profits, to manage it. I knew it was a bad fever country and that he had no fear of fever, and very little of anything else. I did not want my brother to go there to take charge of the work, and I could not go myself. During the negotiations Harry had come home, and, as soon as the contract was signed, he left with Messrs. Lawley and Butler and some other engineers to make the survey. It was understood that Harry should only remain to see the survey work properly started, and Butler agreed to go only on condition that he could come away again before the following December, when the fever season was supposed to start. Butler left in accordance with the terms of this arrangement and the survey was placed under the charge of Mr. Mansergh, a very capable surveyor, and Lawley was left to take charge of the construction, my brother returning home. Having then left him and Scott to look after our affairs in London and to decide what should be done about the Haifa contract, I went to South Africa, and after fixing up the contract for the Vryburg-Mafeking line, I proceeded in May 1893 *via* Port Elizabeth to Beira. Before arriving there I received news that Lawley was down with fever. I found him at Beira, where he had been sent down from the railway, desperately ill with malaria, so much so that his weight was reduced from a normal fifteen to under ten stone. I got him on board a steamer and sent him for a sea trip to Quilimaine and Zanzibar, and it was arranged that he should keep up and down the coast in steamers until he got well enough to resume his duties on the railway. Meantime I went up to Fontesvilla to take charge of the construction. At one time practically every white employee on the job was suffering from fever, and then I fervently wished that I had never heard of the Beira railway. In one fortnight we lost six white men, including my book-keeper.

We had brought round from Delagoa Bay and East London two steam tugs and some lighters to convey the construction material from the ships at Beira up the Pungwe River to Fontesvilla. Our first rainy season there was a very heavy one, nearly all the country was under water, and, as a matter of fact, from the Zambesi to the Pungwe, a distance of about 200 miles, the whole area was converted into a huge river. One of our tugs, the " Agnes," got out of the track of the river and grounded some considerable distance above Fontesvilla and about seven miles away from the bed of the Pungwe. As is usual in these parts, the water went down as rapidly as it had risen, and the " Agnes " was left high and dry in the bush. There she remained for three years before we had another flood high enough to get her away, and even then we were only able to do so with the help of a canal which we had cut for several miles. The sand banks on the River Pungwe were constantly shifting, and it was invariably a matter of great difficulty to ensure reaching Fontesvilla without running aground and thereby losing much time.

Fontesvilla was a very unhealthy place and intensely

hot, so as soon as the railhead reached Siluvu Hills, about forty miles up the line, I made my head-quarters there.

While the first section of seventy-five miles was being built, negotiations took place for an extension of the railway for a further forty miles in the direction of Rhodesia, to a place called Chimoio, and a definite arrangement for this extension was entered into in the spring of 1894. The contract for the construction of the line from Fontesvilla in a more or less direct line to Beira was not entered into until about the middle of the year 1895. In these early days, however, it sometimes happened that a considerable amount of work had been finished before the definitive contracts were executed. In 1895 the section was also commenced from Chimoio to Umtali, on the borderland of Portuguese and British territory, and when it and the Beira sections were completed, a total length of just over 200 miles of railway had been laid.

The original Beira Railway was of two feet gauge, with rails twenty pounds to the yard run. It looked like a toy railway, but was quite capable of dealing, and did deal, with a very large amount of traffic, and we had trucks for special mining machinery with a capacity of twenty tons per truck. My cousin Harry was Mr. Lawley's principal assistant and proved most useful to him. We had many thousands of natives working on this job and feeding them was a big question. Harry was a great shot, and I have known him at Fontesvilla go out before breakfast, get into the middle of a herd of buffalo, and shoot eight of them. We had a Dutchman, named Neumeyer, who was placed in charge of providing the natives on the line with meat. This he did easily. He usually took about twenty boys with him to bring in the game, and he generally shot as much game as the Kafirs could eat. This was a good thing for us, because Kafirs are very fond of meat, and I am sure it was an important factor in securing our labour that the boys could stuff themselves with as much meat as they cared to eat.

While on this work I had several attacks of fever, including a mild dose of blackwater, but the doctor pulled me through. Unhappily, it was not so with my cousin Harry, who took fever badly and died at Beira. His death was a very sad loss to me and to all those who were engaged on the Beira Railway, as he was one of the best and kindest-hearted men that ever lived.

In those days one steamer a month or six weeks was all the communication Beira had with the outer world as compared with about forty a month for some time preceding the beginning of the War. Ice was unheard of and fresh vegetables very scarce indeed. It was the lack of these and similar luxuries that made 1892-3 so fatal for our white men on the railway. In each of these years we lost by death sixty per cent. of these men, including all the teetotallers. According to my experience, teetotallers do not stand a fever country even as well as excessive drinkers.

The narrow gauge railway from Beira was eventually completed to Umtali in 1898. In the meantime I had negotiated with Mr. Rhodes for the extension of the railway, of standard 3 feet 6 inches gauge, from Umtali to Salisbury, and this extension was finished towards the end of 1899. All the permanent way and other materials necessary for this extension were carried over the narrow gauge railway from Beira to Umtali.

Meanwhile, arrangements had been made with the Beira Railway Company to change the gauge of the railway from Beira to Umtali from 2 feet to the standard 3 feet 6 inches gauge. The widening and relaying in connection with this work was placed in the hands of Mr. Lawley, who carried the job through very successfully in about six months. I went out to Beira to see that everything was properly started, and remained with Lawley for about a month.

XXXV

Big Game Stories

THERE are several islands in the Pungwe River, some miles above Beira, which we called Hippo Islands from the fact that we had seen at times as many as thirty hippos disporting themselves in the river near them. Crocodiles, too, were plentiful and lions numerous. One day we saw a lion sticking in the mud on the river bank, and two natives in a dugout went close up to him and beat him to death with poles.

During the early period of the construction of the Beira Railway, the quantity of game on the Pungwe Flats was enormous. It included thousands of buffaloes, zebras, water buck, hartebeeste, wildbeeste, and practically all other kinds of South African game. On one occasion, when Lawley, Mr. Moore, who was the Company's engineer, and I were going back from the Muda River ballast hole to Fontesvilla, the road was in a bad condition and the engine had left the rails three or four times in a distance of a few miles. It behoved us, therefore, to travel very slowly and with extreme caution. There was one truck behind the engine in which we three were accommodated. We were creeping along at about four miles an hour, taking no particular heed of our surroundings, when suddenly the engine driver discovered ahead a herd of lions, lionesses, and cubs, resting in the side cutting which ran alongside the railway bank. It was an awe-inspiring sight, and the driver was for a moment nonplussed. He knew that he dare not increase speed and run the risk of another derailment. There was not a gun on the train. Few men are valiant in the immediate presence of wild lions, and we three " passengers " deemed it expedient to scramble out of the truck and on to the side of the engine away from the herd. With a view to making as much noise as possible the driver opened his whistle and cylinder cocks and commenced to creep past the place where the lions were resting. The noise was too much for them, for they all bolted with the exception of one stately old lioness, who stood her ground and snarled at us as we passed. Had we remained in the truck it is not improbable that she would have made a jump at one of us, but she funked the engine and its steam and noise. Having reached a position of security we counted in all thirty-two lions, lionesses, and cubs.

The Muda River was also infested with lions. We had a water tank there for supplying engines, and on one occasion when the pump got out of order we sent up a European fitter from Fontesvilla to repair it. There were only natives pumping and they had built for themselves what is called a scherm, and were accustomed to keep a big fire going in front of it to ward off lions. The fitter was unable to complete his work in one day and, as there was no place for him to sleep in, he got the natives to build him a little pondok, a kind of shelter shaped like a " V " upside down, with some grass in it for him for lie on. He was a very tall man, so much so that when he lay down his feet protruded from the end of the pondok. During the night he was awakened by something tugging at his foot. He had not taken his boots off, but, luckily, had unlaced them. He let off such a yell that the niggers were roused and they saw that a lion had got hold of him and was trying to pull him out of the pondok. The boys, however, pluckily seized hold of a lot of firebrands and attacked the lion, who made off, taking with him the fitter's boot and part of his heel, which the animal had lacerated with his claws. If his boots had been done up the probability is that he would have lost his life.

I myself had a narrow escape from running over a lion. One morning I left my hut at Chimoio to travel along the line, on a trolley pushed by four boys. At one stage we were going along merrily downhill, all riding on the trolley, when without any warning the boys jumped off, got hold of the trolley and brought us to a standstill. About twenty yards ahead I saw a big lion coming out of the long grass. Quick as lightning I leapt off the trolley, and did my best to secrete my somewhat corpulent figure partly behind, and partly underneath, it. The lion, however, after gazing at us for a moment or two in a supercilious fashion, evidently concluded that we were unworthy of his attention, or at least would make but an indifferent repast, for he walked across the railway into the long grass on the other side and disappeared. The natives had seen the grass moving and knew it was a lion or some other big animal. If they had not stopped the trolley we should have pitched right into the lion, which would have been bad either for the lion or for the occupants of the trolley.

I resumed my journey and came to a water tank beside which there lived a couple of white men and some natives, employed in keeping the permanent way in order and providing water for the engines. I arrived there about seven in the morning, and was surprised to find nobody about. I therefore shouted, and in response one of the white men emerged timidly from the tent. I spoke severely to him, because the man ought to have been at his work at daybreak. Then I noticed the Kafirs beginning to descend from the water tank. I asked what it meant. It appeared that the noise of my trolley and the shouting of my boys had driven away two lions which had been besieging the men in the tent, and the Kafirs had escaped into the tank to get out of the way. The white men showed me where one of the lions had been sweeping under the tent, with one of his paws, trying to reach them. They had been dodging from one part of the tent to another to avoid the lions' claws. The marks were quite plain on the floor of the tent, so I refrained from reprimanding these men for not being at their work as early as they ought to have been under normal conditions. In one month the lions "scoffed" two of our white employees—a yard foreman and a Frenchman.

In addition to the other wild animals there were great herds of zebras in the region through which the Beira Railway passed. My cousin Harry entertained an idea which, had he lived, would have been carried out. It was to collect and tame a few thousand zebras. To do this several hundred miles of fencing wire would have been required, with which there would have been no difficulty in enclosing, on the Pungwe Flats, thousands of head of game, including the zebras. This would have meant fencing about five miles in each direction. This completed, the area would then have been divided, and subdivided, by further fencing until the zebras could have been captured. The zebra is an animal not at all difficult to tame; and Zeedeburg, the coach contractor in Rhodesia and the Transvaal, used to have a span of them running the first stage of his coach from Pretoria.

XXXVI

Lighter Moments

ALTHOUGH life on the Beira Railway was no picnic for white men, still, in our leisure moments, we had some excellent times together. Dr. Williams, whom the reader will remember as our medico at Crocodile Poort, was still our medical officer, and was stationed at Fontesvilla, where there was an hotel with a billiard table. The doctor was very fond of a game, and he and I were great rivals. I could, however, relieve him of a "fiver" whenever I really had the inclination, but he never would realize that I was a slightly better player than he, and he was therefore always anxious for a tussle with me at the table. It was a case of playing under difficulties, because the climate was so hot and the insects were so numerous that every five minutes the game had to be stopped in order that the table might be swept clear of them. Attracted by the oil lamps over the table, these unwelcome spectators came in immense numbers and gave us no end of trouble.

The doctor occasionally drank sufficient to upset his physical equilibrium. I have never known his head to be affected, but there were times when his legs proved incapable of bearing their appointed burden. His residence was a nice little hut situated about 200 yards from the hotel. To get to it one had to pass over a swamp of black mud through which a pathway had been constructed; and as long as one did not deviate from the path one was free from trouble. Once off it, however, meant up to the knees or the middle in black mud. It was often pitch dark when we finished billiards, and on these occasions the doctor carried a lantern of the ordinary stable pattern, with a candle inside. It frequently happened that as soon as he struck the swamp path he went down on his hands and knees, hung the lantern round his neck, and proceeded home in such an undignified manner rather than risk a midnight bath in the black mud.

Amongst Lawley's assistants was " Charlie " Buchan, whose brother Frank was our paymaster and general office superintendent. Old Dr. Williams was subject to very serious attacks of fever, and there was a time when we thought we were going to lose him. One morning, as they were walking up the line, Messrs. Lawley and Buchan went to pay the old man what they thought would be a farewell visit. The doctor was almost *in extremis* and appeared to be unconscious. They were both very fond of him, and Buchan tearfully suggested to Lawley that it was the last occasion on which they should see him alive. Lawley did not think so. The result was a callous bet between them of £10 that the doctor would or would not be dead before they returned. They took a last pathetic look at their old friend, who had just strength enough to wink with one eye, and Lawley bent over him in case he wished to impart a dying message. The patient could just audibly whisper: " I heard you. Bet another £10 for me." The offer was made and accepted. In the afternoon when they got back, the doctor, though still desperately ill, was better, and I am sure the prospect of winning the £10 was a dominant factor in restoring him to health.

My appetite, both for liquids and solids, has always been a source of amusement, and sometimes of concern, to my friends. I had a particular partiality for German beer, which was, in a minor degree, shared by Messrs. Lawley and Moore. On one trip of forty-eight hours up the Beira Railway we drank, between us, three hundred bottles of this excellent refreshment. On another occasion, about the same time, I had a memorable breakfast at Delagoa Bay. Three of us—I refrain from mentioning the names of my companions—had a thousand oysters with about eight bottles of champagne. The oysters were small, but of very delicate flavour. There is much virtue in a good appetite, so long as one is able to foot the bill.

XXXVII

Days of Hustle

IN October 1893 I left Beira, proceeded down the coast and, after doing all I could to send supplies to Lawley, I went on to Vryburg, where I found that my cousin Harold was making good progress with the Vryburg-Mafeking Railway. I spent Christmas at Cape Town, and while there opened negotiations with Mr. Rhodes for the construction of a railway from Sterkstroom to the Indwe coal mines in Cape Colony. The contract for this line, which is over sixty miles in length, was executed in the following year, and the work of construction, which was of a very heavy character, was completed in 1896. Then I returned to England, and while at home arranged the contract for the first extension of the Beira Railway. My brother and I had come to the conclusion that it would be advisable to turn ourselves into a limited liability company, and to enter into partnership with a financial house of good standing. We had had such friendly and profitable business relations with the house of Erlanger that we proposed to the old Baron that he should join us. This he agreed to do and we have never had occasion to regret the alliance. We formed the firm of Pauling and Company, Limited, which was registered in September 1894. The original capital of the company was £80,000, but in 1899 it was increased to £300,000. Erlangers continued to take a hand in the finance of the various railway projects which we afterwards carried out, as they had done in the case of the railway from Beira to Fontesvilla, for which they and Messrs. Ochs Brothers found the necessary funds.

In view of the strenuous life I was then leading I thought it desirable to take a little holiday and made a trip to Paris, Venice, Milan, Rome, and back to England. On my return to London, at the request of Baron d'Erlanger, who was the chairman of the Channel Tunnel Company, I went to Dover, and after an inspection there made a report to him on the preparatory work that had been done for that scheme.

This project has suffered many vicissitudes, but in view of the unflagging interest of the Barons Erlanger, father and son, the latter having succeeded the old Baron as chairman of the company, I am confident that ere long the work will be commenced and it would satisfy my ambition if I were to help carry out the work.

Shortly afterwards—in September 1894—I left again for South Africa. I had many and long talks with Mr. Rhodes whom, of course, I had frequently met and with whom I had constantly kept in touch for some years previously. I had heard that he was considering the idea of offering me an appointment in Rhodesia, and when, on my arrival in Cape Town, he asked me if I would be willing to help him by becoming a member of the first Rhodesian Council, and by taking charge of the departments of mines and public works for a few years, I readily acquiesced, subject to obtaining the approval and consent of my partners. Mr. Rhodes promised me that, provided we would work reasonably and at a fair profit, he would see that the construction of Rhodesian railways was entrusted to my firm. I pressed my partners to allow me to oblige Mr. Rhodes. They agreed, and I told him I would get to Salisbury by the end of the year and take up my position on the Council. I proceeded *via* Durban and Delagoa Bay to Beira, and helped Lawley for a month or two on his work.

XXXVIII

Civil Service

THE Beira Railway had by that time reached Chimoio. From there I started for Salisbury, a distance of some two hundred and thirty or two hundred and forty miles, partly on horseback, and partly by coach with mules which had been sent to take me up. In fulfilment of my promise to Mr. Rhodes I arrived at Salisbury in December 1894 and at once reported myself to Dr. (afterwards Sir Starr) Jameson, who was the Administrator. The first council of Rhodesia consisted of the doctor, Mr. Duncan, Surveyor-General, Judge Vincent, nominated by the Imperial Government, and myself; and later on, Sir Thomas Scanlen, Legal Adviser, and Colonel Frank Rhodes, who acted as Administrator in the absence of Dr. Jameson. Early in 1895 I was gazetted Commissioner of Public Works, in which capacity I was placed in charge of all roads, public buildings, and also of railways, as, and when, they should be constructed. In the following April Mr. Rhodes placed the Department of Mines under my control. I organized both these departments as well as I could. After a time Mr. Duncan, who had been acting as Postmaster-General, became too busy with survey work to give proper attention to the postal department, so I was asked if I would take over that department in addition to my other duties, and, being always keen to get as much work as I could, I had no objection to undertaking this extra work.

A rather amusing incident occurred during the time I was Postmaster-General. It was in the rainy season, and the English mail for Salisbury, which had to be

WORK IN PROGRESS AT BEIRA ON THE CONVERSION OF THE 2 FT. GAUGE TO 3 FT. 6 INS. GAUGE ON THE BEIRA-UMTALI LINE.

OPENING OF THE BROAD GAUGE INTO BEIRA, 10TH JULY, 1900. BACK ROW, RIGHT: D. LIVINGSTONE, F. SMITH, JEFFRIES, HEATH. CENTRE ROW: C. MORGAN, DR. H. H. LOVELL, J. MAYER, R. H. DEAN, D. O. E. LEE, R. J. HULLNECK, H. NEWMAN, F. E. BUCHAN, SIR C. METCALFE, A. L. LAWLEY, A. T. IRON, C. F. HYLAND, COL. R. BEAL, A. T. RAWLING, G. M. CHARLTON AND A. HAINS. FRONT ROW, RIGHT: A. N. PRESTON, CAPT. G. W. DICKEY AND B. EVANS.

THE "PAULINGTON", NAMED AFTER MR. GEORGE PAULING, WAS BOUGHT FROM THE CAPE TOWN (MONUMENT STATION) TO SEA POINT RAILWAY. IT CAME INTO SERVICE WITH THE MASHONALAND RAILWAY IN 1901. THE NAME "PAULINGTON" WAS ALSO GIVEN TO AN HOTEL AND A SUBURB NEAR THE RAILWAY STATION IN UMTALI.

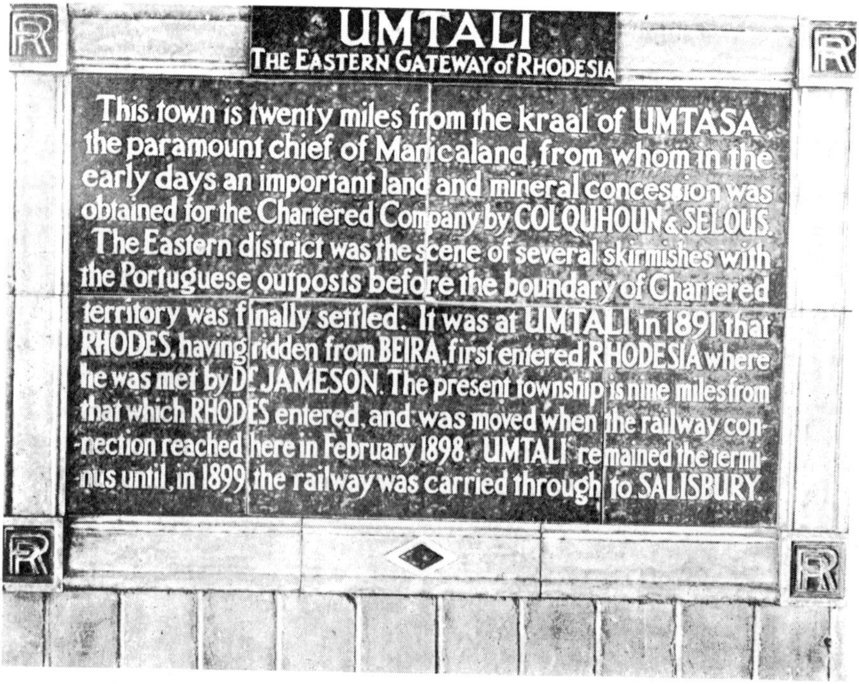

PLAQUE ON THE UMTALI RAILWAY STATION.

IN THE AMATONGAS FOREST. THE LINE CLIMBS 3,500 FT. BETWEEN BEIRA AND UMTALI.

THE DEEP-WATER WHARF UNDER CONSTRUCTION AT BEIRA IN 1927.

CAPE TO CAIRO RAILWAY

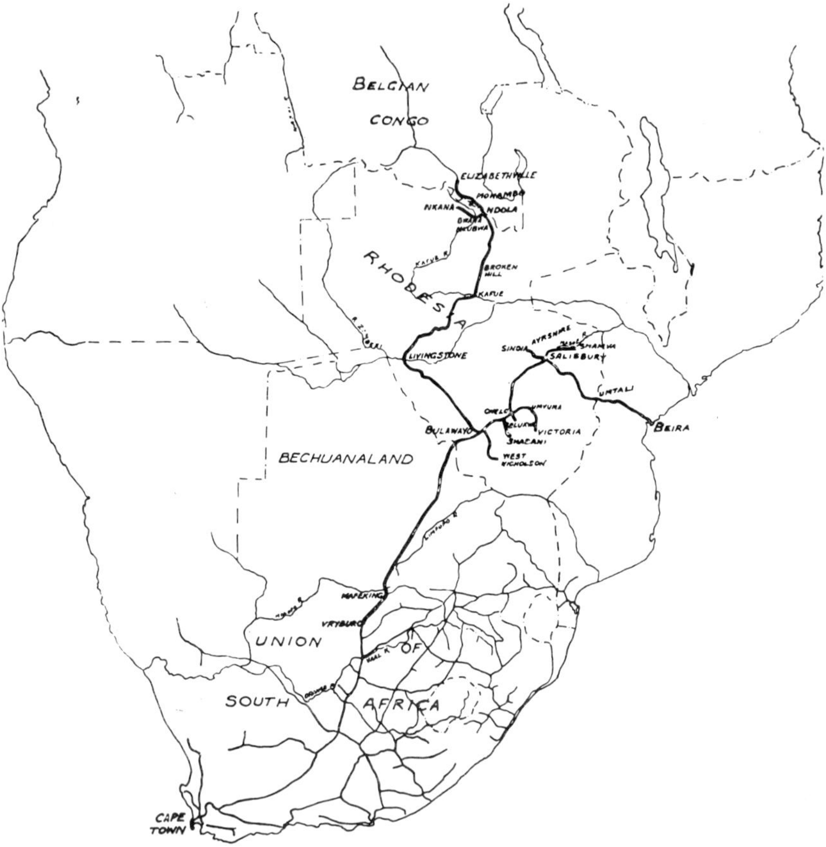

MAP OF THAT PART OF THE CAPE TO CAIRO RAILWAY BUILT BY PAULINGS.

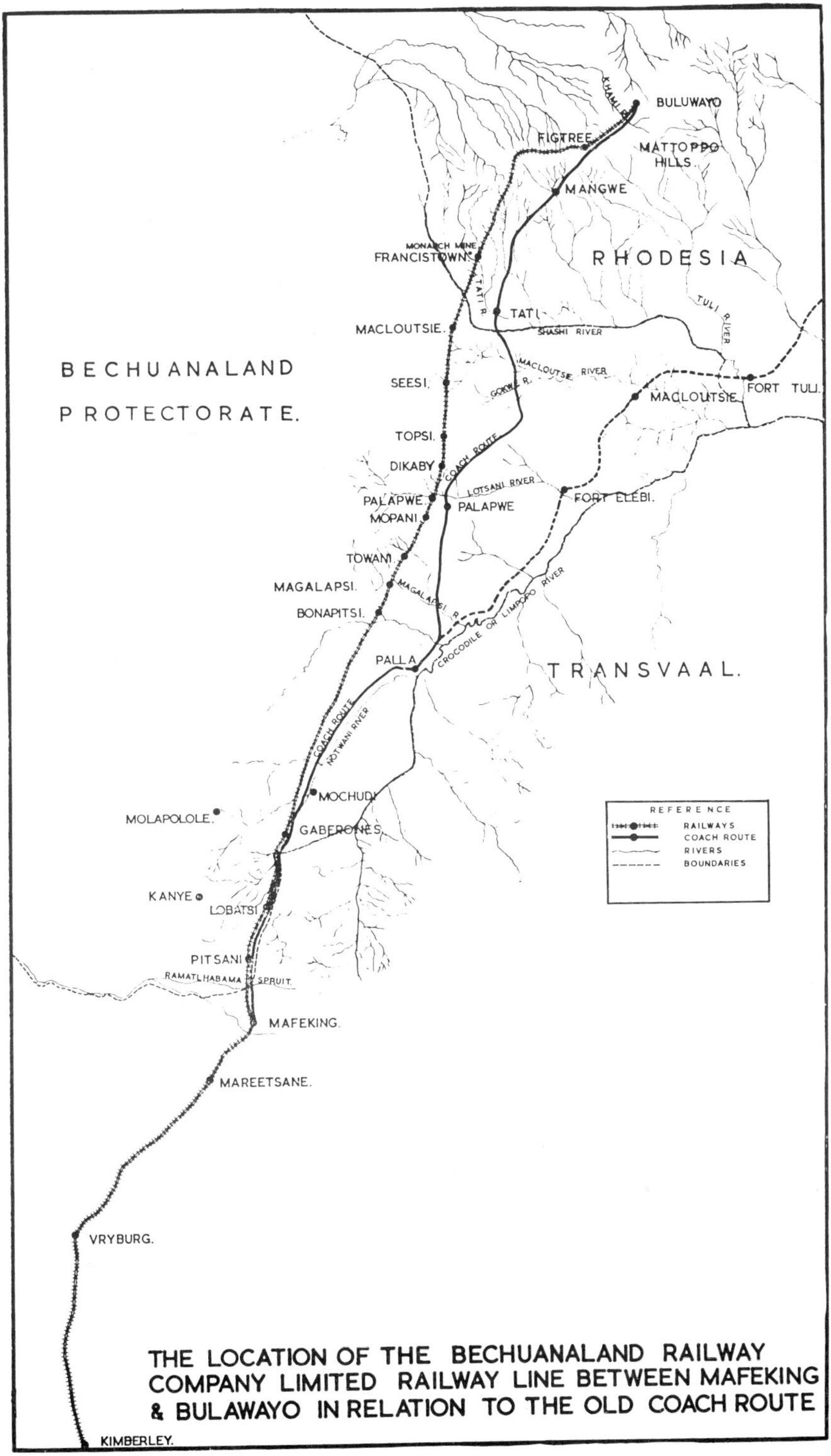

THE LOCATION OF THE BECHUANALAND RAILWAY COMPANY LIMITED RAILWAY LINE BETWEEN MAFEKING & BULAWAYO IN RELATION TO THE OLD COACH ROUTE

A PASSENGER TRAIN CROSSING THE TATI RIVER-BED NEAR FRANCISTOWN IN 1897. BRIDGING FOLLOWED LATER.

TYPICAL PLATELAYING SCENE IN RHODESIA. PAULING AND COMPANY WAS ENTRUSTED WITH THE CONSTRUCTION OF THE FIRST 1,531 MILES OF THE CAPE TO CAIRO RAILWAY. THE WORK EXTENDED UNDER SUCCESSIVE CONTRACTS FROM 1893 TO 1910.

THE SHASHI RIVER BRIDGE IN BECHUANALAND (BOTSWANA).

WAYSIDE STATION IN BECHUANALAND (BOTSWANA) ON THE MAFEKING–BULAWAYO LINE SOON AFTER ITS CONSTRUCTION.

COVER OF THE OFFICIAL PROGRAMME FOR THE OPENING OF THE MAFEKING–BULAWAYO LINE BY SIR ALFRED MILNER ON 4TH NOVEMBER, 1897, IN THE 60TH YEAR OF THE REIGN OF QUEEN VICTORIA.

brought up by coach all the way from Mafeking, a distance of about eight hundred miles, was seriously delayed, in fact, six weeks had elapsed since we had received any English letters in Salisbury. Merchants and other business men of the place were very angry and blamed the Chartered Company for the bad mail service. This was no novelty, as we were always getting blamed for something. The company were not overburdened with popularity, and it was well known that many members of the community were only too anxious to get us into trouble and thereby to induce the Imperial Government to cancel the charter and to take the country over themselves. Hence we had to be careful to use every endeavour to keep the public in as sweet a temper as possible. The firebrand in Salisbury at that time was a man who controlled the "Rhodesia Herald." The Chamber of Commerce met, and a deputation was appointed to interview the Postmaster-General on the subject of the late delivery of mails. This deputation presented itself at my office. I was very sympathetic, but pointed out that the delay was caused through the wet season having flooded the rivers and seriously damaged the roads. The deputation then raised the question as to why the roads were not kept in better order, and why the rivers had not been provided with wire ropes so that when they were in flood the mails might be transported across them. I replied that as Postmaster-General these matters were outside my department, but were in that of the Commissioner of Public Works who, I had no doubt, would be prepared to discuss the matter with them. Meantime I suggested we should adjourn to the Avenue Hotel, opposite my office, with the object of having some liquid refreshment, and that they should see the Commissioner of Public Works on the following day. This was agreed to, and, after several rounds of drinks, we parted very good friends.

Next day the same deputation approached me in my capacity as Commissioner of Public Works. At the meeting I endorsed all that the Postmaster-General had told them, and stated that I had done my best with the rivers and roads, having regard to the amount of money at my disposal, and that I could do no more as my funds were exhausted. They asked if I could give them any idea as to the best course they should adopt, and I told them that the only department of the Chartered Company which was revenue-producing was the Mines Department, and that if they wished I would arrange an interview for them with the Minister of Mines. Meanwhile, I proposed another adjournment to the Avenue Hotel, which was carried *nem. con.*, and there we repeated the experience of the previous day. Two days afterwards the members of the deputation, who by that time were beginning to enjoy the fun, came to see me at the Mines Office. There, for the third time, they stated their case. I replied that everything the Postmaster-General and the Commissioner of Public Works had stated I could absolutely corroborate; that it was true the Mines was the revenue-producing department, but unfortunately I had no power to spend any money, or allow the Commissioner of Public Works to do so, unless authorized by the Council; that there would be a meeting of the Council in about a week's time, and that if the Chamber of Commerce would memorialize the Council I, as one of its members, would see that their memorial received every consideration; and I suggested that for the present we should adjourn to the Avenue Hotel, which we did. Perhaps I should add that I had no financial interest in that establishment.

I had every reason to believe that by the time the memorial was ready the mail would have arrived. This it did, and although the "Rhodesia Herald" tried to keep the indignation of the public and of the Chamber of Commerce at boiling point, it failed to do so. With the arrival of the letters the grievances vanished into thin air, and they accepted my assurance that it should not occur again, which I repeated to them—at the Avenue Hotel—after they had brought me the memorial for the Council.

XXXIX

Rhodes, the Raid, Rinderpest, and Rebellion

DURING 1895 I visited Cape Colony and saw my cousin while he was superintending the construction of the Indwe Railway. I had been sent for by Mr. Rhodes, and in company with Colonel Frank Rhodes went down to his historical residence at Groot Schur about the end of October of that year.

For some little time previously I had, as Commissioner of Public Works, been receiving through Beira and forwarding to Salisbury considerable quantities of munitions of war for the British South African police. On arrival at Groot Schur I had various conversations with Mr. Rhodes, who wanted me to arrange for the extension to Bulawayo of the railway beyond Mafeking. I informed my partners in England about this, and asked them to see to what extent and on what terms the extension could be financed, and left it at that. Mr. Rhodes took advantage of these interviews to talk to me in general terms about the position of Johannesburg, and solicited my opinion of the prospects of a revolution in the Transvaal. I expressed the opinion that it would be very difficult, if not impossible, to have a successful revolution in such a country, unless the bulk of the working population were in favour of it, and that, so long as the white men, or artisans, were earning thirty shillings a day in a country where they could live comfortably at £6 a month, it would be difficult to persuade level-headed men of that description to make an effort to upset the Government. Mr. Rhodes replied to the effect that I knew a lot about railways and other business matters, but "damned little about politics." I was shrewd enough to guess what was in his mind, and told him that I would go back to Rhodesia and carry out my duties in that country. To this he agreed and shortly afterwards I left for Salisbury. The story of the Raid is of too recent occurrence to call for much repetition here. As everyone knows, a very bad mess was made of it. On the 29th of December 1895 Dr. Jameson, with between five and six hundred men, set out from a point near Mafeking to capture Johannesburg and to overthrow Kruger. In less than a week they were forced to surrender at Krugersdorp, some twenty miles from Johannesburg. We in Salisbury knew nothing of what was occurring, and only heard of the occurrence through cables from England. The London directors disassociated themselves from Jameson's action, and I cabled to them that the Raid had taken place without the knowledge or approval of the Council or ministers of the Chartered Government. I sent this telegram in case any of our enemies in England might seek to implicate the Chartered Company in that inglorious fiasco. Unfortunately, as I thought, Lawley was an active participant in the Raid and, while on his way back to Beira, was made prisoner at Johannesburg. This I learned a few days after the occurrence, and within a week I heard that he was in prison in Pretoria. I immediately made an unsuccessful effort to bail him out for £2,000 on condition that he should proceed to Beira to resume his work on the railway.

In the following May I had another trip south and ascertained that the Transvaal Government meant to keep their captives in "durance vile" until such time as they saw what attitude was to be taken up by the Imperial Government. During a brief visit to Pretoria I made several attempts to see Lawley, but all without avail. However, by the end of the month he was released and returned to his duties.

The year 1896 proved a very eventful one for Rhodesia. Mr. Rhodes had been called home to attend the first inquiry about the Raid. The Matabele rebellion had broken out, and his presence in Rhodesia was urgently required. He left England and travelled *via* the east coast. In Egypt he chartered an Austrian Lloyd boat to bring him to Beira. I was asked to meet him there. On my arrival I heard, through Lawley, who was very friendly with Colonel Machado, at that time the Portuguese Governor, that Paul Kruger had been pulling the strings to get the Portuguese Government to arrest Mr. Rhodes and to hand him over to the Transvaal authorities. The intention was to take him to Melsetter, about a hundred miles south of Umtali, where there was a big Dutch farm colony, and where the Transvaal authorities would be ready to take charge of him. Lawley and I pointed out to Colonel Machado that if such a thing were attempted the whole of the railway men would rise up and take Beira, and that there would be no end of trouble for the Portuguese authorities. Colonel Machado, however, had anticipated our representations by telegraphing to Lisbon begging his government to have nothing to do with President Kruger's scheme, and he assured me that Mr. Rhodes could land with perfect safety. When the steamer arrived I went on board and found Mr. Rhodes in a very excitable state. I told him all I knew, and amongst other things I had to tell him that rinderpest had broken out amongst the cattle in Mashonaland and that the Matabele rebellion was a very serious matter. My information only served to calm his temper, for he loved to meet and to overcome difficulties, and he landed in first-class spirits. We went by rail to Chimoio, where we saw the first cases of rinderpest. Owing to insufficient knowledge of it nothing could be done to eradicate the disease, although all kinds of remedies were tried. Ultimately it practically wiped out the cattle and most of the game in Mashonaland, Matabeleland, and Bechuanaland; and although, as it got further south, it decreased in violence, and more effective remedies were applied, at least 2,000,000 head of cattle must have died in these three territories alone from the disease.

About the same time it was decided to send a column to the relief of Bulawayo, as that part of Matabeleland was being hard pressed by the rebels. The column, on my recommendation to Mr. Rhodes, was put in charge of "Bobbie" Beal, who had been my inspector of public works, and who had previously been in the Bechuanaland police. Sir Charles Metcalfe, who had come to Beira with Mr. Rhodes, and whose advice had been taken on all matters, left with the column. To add to the difficulties of administration rebellion had also broken out in the adjoining territory of Mashonaland. Lord Grey, who had succeeded Dr. Jameson as Administrator of Rhodesia, was in Bulawayo, and Council meetings were held every morning, at which Sir Frederic Carrington, representing the military of the Imperial Government, was present. Lieut.-Col. Baden Powell acted as secretary, and to introduce a welcome note of levity among those serious times, he occasionally amused us in many ways, particularly by his ability to draw two different sketches at the same time, one with his right and the other with his left hand.

Matters had become very serious in Mashonaland, particularly for the Chartered Company. Colonel Alderson was coming up from Beira with imperial troops, and his idea was to map out the country into sections and to build an enormous number of blockhouses. Luckily, Sir Frederick Carrington, who was an old Kafir fighter and a good friend of mine, agreed with me that this would be unnecessary, and the Chartered Company were saved the enormous expense that such an undertaking would have entailed. In order, however, to attain this end we had to resort to strategy. It was realized that as soon as Colonel Alderson reached Salisbury he would be the superior officer, because Judge Vincent, the only member of our council left there, had no military rank. Sir Frederic suggested a solution of the problem, and we asked Judge Vincent whether, if the former were made a commandant general he would occupy a rank superior to that of Colonel Alderson. The judge thought so, and the necessary permission having been obtained by telegram from the High Commissioner at Cape Town, Sir Frederic was made commandant-general before Colonel Alderson reached Salisbury, and I heard afterwards that he evolved from his own mind a uniform befitting his new rank.

XL

Mining Laws and Relaxations

NATURALLY in my official capacity I visited nearly every part of Rhodesia for the purpose of supervising the work of my various departments. I had been but a few months in office when I made my initial visit to Bulawayo. The journey occupied about three days and four nights each way, and the monotony of the excursion was relieved by a capsize which, happily, had no serious results. My first impression of Bulawayo was that it was a really wonderful place, and I found it generally accepted that there were many good and rich things in the country. I took a specially great interest in the Mines department, as I had had considerable experience in that business, and although I did not hold any university or other degree, I considered myself little less competent than any mining engineer that I had met. I had a great deal of trouble with Mr. Rhodes about the Rhodesian mining laws. Under the influence of American mining engineers he insisted that the Rhodesian mining law should not be the same as that of the Transvaal, and Rhodesia to-day has a mining law which has already given rise to one of the most expensive lawsuits ever heard by the English law courts, viz., that between the Globe and Phoenix Mine and the Amalgamated Properties of Rhodesia, and the future has, I feel confident, many more suits of a similar nature, all caused by the advice of the American mining engineers which Mr. Rhodes followed.

As it was invariably my custom to mix freely with all sorts and conditions of men, I played billiards in almost any billiard saloon where I could get a good game. On one occasion I was playing at the Kopje, Salisbury, when a prospector named M'Loughlin, who was inclined for a spree, caught hold of me as I was about to make a stroke. He did not know who I was, but I turned round and threw him on the floor with a backheel, putting my knee into his stomach as he fell, and thus squeezing all the breath out of him. He looked horrified and astonished, but when he recovered breath enough to get up, he shook hands with me, and said I was the only man who had thrown him. He was a very well-known prospector, renowned for his strength, and this little wrestling match did me more good with the rougher class of prospectors and others than anything else in my official experience.

On another occasion, during my first official visit to Bulawayo, while I was playing black pool in the Charter Hotel, I noticed two young fellows who lost rather heavily. It was obvious that they were not people of sufficient means to justify them playing as they did. They did not know that I was Postmaster-General, although I was aware that they were connected with the Post Office. When I returned to Salisbury it occurred to me to have an audit of the stamps in the various post offices. At that time both revenue and postage stamps were kept in the Postmaster-General's department. The revenue stamps varied in value from £5 to £150 and were used on title deeds, land transfers, and similar documents. There was no real record of these stamps, and my postmaster at Salisbury, thinking the idea of stocktaking a good one, carried it out there to my satisfaction, and the results were almost as they should have been. I determined then to go to Gwelo and Bulawayo, and left Salisbury in my coach to visit some of the mines and ultimately to reach Bulawayo with the object of taking stock of the stamps in that Post Office. Whether my object became known in

Bulawayo or not, or whether there was anything to be covered up or not I do not know, but when I was within two days of Bulawayo the Post Office was burned to the ground and stamps to the declared value of £30,000 were supposed to have been destroyed. Anyhow, the fire had precluded the possibility of obtaining any satisfaction in my mission.

XLI

A Transplanted Township

SHORTLY after Mr. Rhodes left the Austrian Lloyd boat he and I had occasion to pay a visit to Umtali, where the people were very excited because I had surveyed the route of the railway and had recommended that Old Umtali should be put on a branch line and that the main line should pass direct *via* the Odzi River to Salisbury. This was absolutely necessary, because the line to Old Umtali would have necessitated very heavy and very costly work, including a tunnel under Christmas Pass. A public meeting was convened, and I told Mr. Rhodes that a solution of the difficulty would be to shift the township of Old Umtali and to lay out an exactly similar township on the site where New Umtali now stands. At the public meeting Mr. Rhodes, as had been arranged, asked me, in my capacity as Commissioner of Public Works, to state my views. I pointed out to the meeting that an exactly similar township could be laid out and that I had Mr. Rhodes's sanction to offer the owners of sites and buildings in Old Umtali corresponding sites in the new township and either to pay them for the buildings they had erected at Old Umtali or to put up, free of cost to them, similar buildings in the new township. They objected that this might put some of them at a disadvantage with regard to proximity to the railway station, but, as I pointed out, no site for the railway station in Old Umtali had then been decided upon, consequently no one could claim a grievance on that score. After a short meeting it was unanimously agreed that our ideas of a new township should be adopted. I got Mr. Duncan, the Surveyor-General, to send down surveyors, and with the local surveyor I selected the present site of the township.

This problem having been satisfactorily disposed of, Mr. Rhodes and I left Umtali and proceeded to Salisbury, where he became my guest in the building then known as Government House. I had selected the site of this house shortly after my arrival in Salisbury, and it was constructed according to my fancy. We found it very comfortable; a huge verandah, thirteen feet in width, ran round it, on which my wife used to give a dance five or six times a year. My salary from all my various posts was £600 a year, not sufficient to entertain very lavishly, but luckily I was not then wholly dependent on my official position for my income.

The Civil Service, therefore, did not prove to me a remunerative occupation. In those days prices were awful. While my house was being built the price of galvanized iron was about £60 a ton. Beer was six shillings and sixpence a bottle. I have written elsewhere in these pages of my capacity in that direction. It is a matter of mere calculation to arrive at the amount available out of my salary for tobacco and other necessities after my thirst was satiated. But the life was pleasant, and although I felt to some extent divorced from my appointed vocation, time never hung heavily on my hands.

XLII

Mafeking to Bulawayo

MR. RHODES had requested me to visit Beira, to do some business for him there, and then to go round *via* Cape Colony and up to Bulawayo, where I was to meet him. It was his idea that I should proceed to England to arrange for the finance and construction of the line northwards from Mafeking to Bulawayo. The finance for the first hundred miles having been arranged, work was started at the end of 1895. Shortly afterwards the outbreak of rinderpest amongst the cattle of the country created great difficulty in transporting into Matabeleland even the necessaries of life, and the extension of the railway to Bulawayo was urgently wanted. The total rail distance from Mafeking to Bulawayo is about five hundred miles, and I had told Mr. Rhodes that, given a free hand, I would undertake to get the rails through for the last four hundred miles of the distance within four hundred days. I went as far as Mafeking by rail, and from there had a special coach to take me to Bulawayo. The journey, which took us nine days to accomplish, was a terrible one. At every coach station and frequently along the road the stench from the unburied bodies of cattle, which had died from the rinderpest, was awful, and two or three times I was physically sick from the nauseating odour which one seemed not only to smell, but to inhale.

As the coach approached the Matopo Hills, the stronghold of the Matabele, the Matabele rebellion having broken out, we travelled during the night as quietly as we possibly could in order to avoid being attacked by the rebels. We could see their fires on the hills, but although the prospect was disquieting, no attempt was made to stop us. On our arrival in Bulawayo, I found that Mr. Rhodes had gone out with Plummer's column. While he was away, as I subsequently heard, he received a cable to proceed to England to attend the resumed meeting of the Raid Inquiry, which had been adjourned while he returned to Africa. During his absence public opinion in England had grown very strong in favour of bringing him home to face the resumption of the inquiry. His reply to the summons is, I think, well known. It was to the effect that he could not go as his presence was absolutely necessary in Rhodesia, and that on the morning after the despatch of his reply he was going out to fight the Matabele.

During 1895 Mr. Rhodes had mentioned to me that it might give rise to adverse comment if I continued to be an active member of my firm, which was then constructing railways in Rhodesia, and at the same time retained the office of Commissioner of Public Works. I therefore, at his request, resigned from the directorate of my firm. Unfortunately, the health of my brother, who had taken my place in the firm, became a source of considerable anxiety to me and, for that and other reasons, before I had been in the Rhodesian public service for a year, I would gladly have relinquished my position had it not been for the possibility of offending Mr. Rhodes. It was not until early in 1897 that at an interview with him in Bulawayo I stated that I would not be able to remain much longer with the Chartered Company, as the firm wished me to return to them in order to take charge of the business because of my brother's illness. Mr. Rhodes pressed me very hard to remain, and said that if it was a question of money he would undertake that I should make as much money by remaining with him as I could by going back to my firm, and he also promised that if I remained in Rhodesia he would give me the highest position in the country. This was an instance—and I do not think it was an isolated one—of Mr. Rhodes being ready to promise anything to attain his end. Whether he would afterwards be able or willing to carry out his promise would, I knew, be a matter controlled by expediency. As a point of fact, he had already asked me, when I went to Cape Town, to see Mr. Milton, who was then in the Cape Civil Service, and to offer him on his behalf the position of Administrator in Rhodesia. I also told Mr. Rhodes that in addition to the firm requiring my services, I preferred to be my own master, as I had always been from the time I started work in Africa until I accepted an official appointment, and although my position with the Chartered Company left me practically in that position, still my status was in reality that of a servant. Notwithstanding his representations I was insistent, and after two and a quarter years of service in Rhodesia I tendered my resignation. Early in April 1897 I left Salisbury and proceeded *via* Cape Town to England.

By this time arrangements had been made for financing and supplying materials for the railway from Mafeking to Bulawayo. The finance was principally done by Messrs. Erlangers who, in fact, have been instrumental in finding the great bulk of the money required for the Rhodesian railways since their commencement. Having made all necessary arrangements at home, I returned once more to Africa. On arrival at Cape Town I went up and saw the work started beyond Mafeking. The contract was placed in charge of my cousin, Harold Pauling, who carried out my promise to Mr. Rhodes and built the last four hundred miles of railway within four hundred days. The work from Mafeking was commenced towards the end of 1896 and traffic was open to Bulawayo by the end of 1897.

In view of my many associations with Mr. Rhodes it

MR. HAROLD PAULING'S CONSTRUCTION TRAIN ARRIVING IN BULAWAYO ON 19th OCTOBER, 1897.

THE LOCOMOTIVE, "PRIDE OF THE ROAD", DREW ONE OF THE FOUR SPECIAL TRAINS INTO BULAWAYO FOR THE OFFICIAL OPENING OF THE LINE FROM MAFEKING ON 4th NOVEMBER, 1897.

THE LAST COACH TO LEAVE SALISBURY.

LOCOMOTIVE NO. 1, THE CECIL J. RHODES, DREW THE FIRST OFFICIAL TRAIN INTO SALISBURY FROM UMTALI ON 22ND MAY, 1899. THE LEGEND ON THE LOCOMOTIVE HEADBOARD READS: "NOW WE SHAN'T BE LONG TO CAIRO".

THE GOURITZ RIVER BRIDGE ON THE CAPE CENTRAL RAILWAY BETWEEN RIVERSDALE AND MOSSEL BAY. A NEW RAILWAY BRIDGE, BUILT IN 1931, IS SEEN UNDER CONSTRUCTION IN THE FOREGROUND.

HEAVY EARTHWORKS IN PROGRESS THROUGH HOUW HOEK PASS IN THE CAPE.

THE MAZOE DAM UNDER CONSTRUCTION IN 1920. THE WALL IS OVER 100 FEET HIGH AND WAS BUILT OF CONCRETE BLOCKS, THEREBY OBVIATING THE USE OF SHUTTERING.

might seem churlish to attempt any serious criticism of his character. While recognizing his many great qualities, which history will endorse, I cannot refrain from suggesting that, probably in common with all other great personalities, he had his weaknesses. He was particularly susceptible to the plaudits of the public, which made him bumptious; and at times he seemed utterly heartless. But no criticism, however much it may be justified, can challenge his right to the title of " Colossus," so far as the development of South Africa is concerned. As indicative of the peculiarities of great men I prefer to limit my observations to two more or less amusing incidents which came within my own knowledge.

Whenever Mr. Rhodes became excited or intensely interested in anything he was apt to talk in a peculiarly high-pitched voice. On the occasion of his first meeting with Lawley, which occurred during the building of the railway from Beira to Umtali, the coach which conveyed Mr. Rhodes and his party, including Dr. Jameson, from Rhodesia arrived about three days later than had been expected, and whether the delay had affected the temper of Mr. Rhodes I cannot say, but, without warning, he proceeded to swear and to abuse Lawley in the presence of the whole railway camp, until by a gradual crescendo of unparliamentary language he reached his high falsetto tone. Lawley, who is usually able to provide a *quid pro quo* when it is a question of language, realizing that, without any apparent reason, he was being stultified in the eyes of his subordinates, invited Mr. Rhodes to say who the h— he thought he was, and told him, in a flood of railway vernacular, that there was no necessity for him to squeal like a damned rabbit. Mr. Rhodes, obviously astonished at Lawley's unexpected daring, walked off to a neighbouring clump of trees. Lawley, acting on the instructions which had been telegraphed to him, gave orders for the luggage from the coach to be put on the waiting train, and then notified all concerned that the train would leave in five minutes, and that all those who were not aboard within that time could reach their destinations as they chose. Mr. Rhodes entered the train just at the last moment—so much so that his carriage door was not closed when it moved off. On the journey a stoppage was made to take in water and Mr. Rhodes sent Dr. Jameson to Lawley with an invitation to join him in his compartment. Lawley did so, and Mr. Rhodes, who had calmed down, resumed his natural method of speech, expressed his deep regret at the occurrence, and asked Lawley to shake hands with him.

From that day Mr. Rhodes and Lawley remained the best of friends. During his periodic visits to the railways, Mr. Rhodes invariably accepted Lawley's hospitality which was on several occasions reciprocated at Groot Schuur.

On another occasion he came to me in a similarly excited condition, and in the same falsetto voice shouted "Pauling, I won't be bullied by your cousin Harold. He bullies me every time I see him." I replied: "All right, Mr. Rhodes, I have plenty of other work for my cousin and I will send him elsewhere, so that you need never see him again."

Now, Mr. Rhodes knew the value of my cousin's work in Rhodesia on the railways and at once assumed his natural manner and said, "I don't want that, Pauling. Your cousin has many good points. I was a little excited. All I want you to do is to ask him to be a little more careful in the way he speaks to me."

I replied: "I am sure that if you are civil to my cousin he will be civil to you as there is no one in the world towards whom he entertains so great admiration and respect."

After that they were always good friends.

XLIII

A Great Bereavement

BEING satisfied that everything was going well with the Mafeking-Bulawayo job, I proceeded *via* Johannesburg and Delagoa Bay to Beira. Lawley was then, with his usual untiring energy, pushing forward with the inland extension of the Beira Railway. I went over the work with him, and after discussing all matters pertaining to his contract, he and I went through to Salisbury. It was while there that I received very alarming news from England as to the state of my brother's health, and I determined to return home without delay. I left Africa *via* Beira and arrived in England in May 1897. The information I had received about my brother had not been exaggerated. I found him so ill that I at once had him examined by a specialist, who pronounced that he was suffering from cancer. Within two days of my arrival he underwent an operation which disclosed the fact that the disease had so far advanced that there was no hope of recovery. He accepted the inevitable with that indomitable courage which was ever one of his greatest attributes, and which never failed him during the few months that elapsed before the end came. During that period his malady did not altogether prevent him from taking an interest in our affairs, and all arrangements were made for me to resume control of the firm's interests.

Harry's death, which took place in London on the 16th November 1897, was the hardest blow I have ever had. To each other we had been more than brothers. Our friendship amounted almost to a mutual devotion, and from the days of our childhood never an angry word had passed between us. Although I was but three years his senior, he invariably did everything he could to meet my wishes, and it seemed to be a pleasure to him to try to please me; and I always endeavoured to do my utmost to reciprocate the kindness of his disposition towards me.

While in England during his illness I had determined to make for myself a home in that country. I looked at no end of properties within a distance of from twenty to thirty miles from London, but could not make up my mind as to any of them. One day Lawley, while home on a short holiday, told me that he had discovered the very place to suit me. I was so tired of looking around and so busy with the firm's business that on his recommendation and without having seen the place myself, I purchased a small estate at Effingham, where I still reside. The house was then comparatively small, but I have stupidly spent a large sum of money in adding to it and spoiling it.

After Harry's death I spent some time at home, and it was not until August 1898 that I paid another visit to South Africa. This was a particularly hurried visit, for after going up to see the Beira work I left Cape Town in the following November, and having returned to England, I spent my second Christmas at Effingham. In May 1899 I again left for Cape Town. We had arranged with Mr. Rhodes and the Chartered Company to extend the railway from Bulawayo *via* Gwelo to the Globe and Phoenix Mine, a distance of rather more than one hundred and fifty miles. I was present at the cutting of the first sod in Bulawayo on the 30th May 1899, and the contract, which was carried out under the charge of Mr. Harold Pauling, was completed in November 1902. I then went on to Beira, and remained there a few weeks with Lawley to see how he was getting on. On my return to Cape Town we tendered to the

Cape Government for the construction of a railway over Sir Lowry's Pass to Caledon. We proved the successful competitors. I only visited the job twice, once to see it properly started and once during its construction. The work was very heavy and included the making of the largest tunnel in the Cape Province and several large bridges and viaducts. Of a total length of fifty-six miles, sixteen of them have a gradient of one in forty. This railway was completed in October 1902.

XLIV

The New Cape Central Railway

ALTHOUGH I had originally negotiated for a contract for the New Cape Central Railway, I had been unable to carry it through, and it passed into the hands of Mr. John Walker, a very capable, hard-headed Scotchman. For several years he gave the Cape Government a considerable amount of trouble and, I think, made money. His connection with the railway was, however, severed about the time the rails reached Ashton, a distance of some forty miles from Worcester, and the extension came into the hands of my firm. The Cape Government subsidized this railway on the same principle as they had done the Kowie Railway. The extension from Ashton to Swellendam, forty-four miles, was commenced early in January 1896. I was present at the cutting of the first sod and left Mr. H. H. Myburgh, one of Harold Pauling's lieutenants, in charge of the contract. This section contained much very heavy work, and was not completed until 1898. I was particularly anxious that the line should be continued as soon as possible beyond Swellendam to Riversdale, another sixty-five miles, because I was afraid that if the New Cape Central Railway did not provide this extension, the Cape Government would eventually build a line from Sir Lowry's Pass through Caledon *via* Swellendam to Riversdale, which would, of course, seriously prejudice the line from Worcester to Ashton. With the financial assistance of Messrs. Erlangers the Company were able, in 1899, to arrange for the additional mileage which, however, owing partly to the very heavy work involved, was not completed until 1903.

While this was in course of construction I had an

idea of putting through a scheme by which the line would have been extended, not only to Mossel Bay, but on to Oudtshoorn through George. The full scheme, however, did not materialize, and the New Cape Central Railway system ends at Mossel Bay, the extension to which we completed early in 1906. The total length of the system is just over two hundred miles. It is owned by a private company, in which my firm and my partners hold a considerable interest. The line passes through a fertile country, and the local industries, which consist chiefly of the production of wine and brandy, agriculture, and the rearing of ostriches, are capable of great development. Mossel Bay itself is one of the most charming seaside resorts in the country, and when it was linked up with the line to Oudtshoorn the New Cape Central Railway became a portion of the most direct railway artery from Cape Town to Port Elizabeth.

The consulting engineer for the railway was Mr. (now Sir) Robert Elliott Cooper, with whom I had previously come into contact when he was consulting engineer for the Kowie Railway. Sir Robert has been for some years past the chairman of the New Cape Central Railway Company, Limited. On my suggestion Mr. Fred Dawson, who was formerly the general manager of the Londonderry and Lough Swilly Railway Company, Limited, was sent out, a number of years ago, to take up the general managership of the New Cape Central Railway, and under the wise direction of Sir Robert, supported by the able management of Mr. Dawson, the line which, for some considerable time was unprofitable, has prospered greatly. It is one of the few remaining privately owned lines in the Union of South Africa, and, as the Colonial Government have the right[1] to purchase it on certain terms, I should not be surprised if, ere long, that right is exercised, when it will become an important section of the State railways of the country.

[1] This right has now been exercised.—Ed.

XLV

Home Work

PREVIOUS to 1894 any contracts with which I was connected in this country were carried out in the name of Pauling and Elliott. Such contracts included work for the Great Western Railway Company at Bristol and Reading, for the London and South Western Railway Company on the Lee and Solent Light Railway, and for the Neath Highway Board at Neath.

In September of that year the firm of Pauling and Elliott was dissolved, and Pauling and Company, Limited, was registered, as I mentioned before, with a capital of £80,000, which in 1899, owing to the development of the business, was increased to £300,000. Both before and after the creation of Pauling and Company, Limited, the work in this country was carried out under the supervision of Mr. Edwin Elliott. We did not make much money out of our early contracts, but I had hopes that we should ultimately make good in England, for I had great confidence in Mr. Elliott who, as we have seen, had been Firbank's agent for many years, and who had as much experience of English contractors' business as any other contractors' agent in the country. He had got into touch with an Irish engineer, and I was persuaded to tender for two light railways in County Donegal, one from Carndonagh to Buncrana—nineteen miles—and the other from Letterkenny to Burtonport—forty-nine miles. We got these contracts, and if we had been treated fairly and allowed to make deviations, without the severe conditions imposed upon us, which would have improved the

THE ASSOPOS VIADUCT ON THE PIRAEUS–TAPAPOULI RAILWAY IN GREECE. THE CENTRAL ARCH HAS AN 80 METRE SPAN. THE 388 MILES OF RAILWAY INVOLVED VERY HEAVY WORKS AND A NUMBER OF STEEL AND MASONRY VIADUCTS.

THE CONCEICAO BRIDGE ON THE SOUTHERN SAN PAULO RAILWAY IN SOUTH AMERICA.

railway whilst greatly reducing the cost, we should have made money. We were, however, held to the absolute letter of the contract, specifications, and surveys, and the result, I am sorry to say, was the purchase of experience at very heavy cost. We also had a bit of ill-luck on the Burtonport line. About half a mile of railway, after it had been laid and while it was being ballasted, suddenly disappeared into an underground lake, the crust of bog overlying the lake having given way. As we could not build a railway over a bottomless bog it was necessary to provide for a detour to skirt the edge of the morass, and to link up farther on with the line as originally surveyed. We found that it was a much more difficult matter to arrange a deviation in Ireland than in Africa. It took us a long time to get permission from the competent authority to make this deviation and the delay was to us costly. When ultimately we did obtain the necessary authority we had, at our expense, to make the line through very heavy and very hard rock which, of course, added greatly to the loss we sustained on the contract. Whilst these railways were being built, I made several trips to Ireland. The work was originally under the supervision of Mr. Elliott, and, later on, in the hands of my old partner, Mr. James Butler. All our united experience and advice was of no avail, and, owing to the exacting terms of the contracts and the extremely literal interpretation placed upon them by the authorities concerned, both jobs resulted in very considerable loss to the firm.

In England we did a lot of work, partly for the South Eastern and South Western Railways, but chiefly for the Great Western Railway. Amongst these I may mention the widening of the line from Hungerford to Savernake, and then from Savernake to Stert, and the construction of the railway from Stert to Westbury. We also built electric tramways in Coventry and in Norwich, as well as many other minor works. The largest contract, however, which we undertook in this country was for the building of a railway for the joint committee of the Great Central and Great Western Railways from Northolt to High Wycombe. Although only twenty-three miles in length, it involved extremely heavy work, including a tunnel at Londwater, and at Gerrard's Cross one of the largest cuttings in England. From the latter we had to remove on a long lead about a million and a quarter cubic yards of material.

To all these works I gave from time to time what attention I could, and for a month or two I even took charge of the High Wycombe job, but it was impossible for me to do everything, and I had to leave to others more than I ought to have done. The net result was that, on the whole, work in this country proved unprofitable to the firm and caused me much anxiety and worry.

XLVI

Greece

DURING the year 1899 Messrs. Erlangers had been, together with their friends the Batignolles Company of Paris, negotiating for the construction of a railway from Piraeus to Larissa, in Greece. This railway, which exceeds three hundred miles in length, was intended to link up ultimately with the other European railways so as to provide a route whereby passengers could travel direct from any part of Europe to Athens. Some years previously a concession for this line had been given to an English company which, after carrying out a small portion of the work, had failed. When it came into the hands of the group represented by Messrs. Erlangers and the French company, my firm was offered participation, and in March 1900 I went to Greece with a view to determining whether it would be worth while for my firm to accept any interest in the contract. I visited Lamia and other parts of the proposed route, came to the conclusion that the job would be quite a nice one, although I was of opinion that the terms proposed were not so good as they should have been, having regard to the extremely heavy nature of the work and the risks involved. It was, however, arranged that we should get on with the very heavy work on the line and that the Batignolles Company, who are railway and public works contractors as well as builders of locomotives and steel work of every description, should start from the Piraeus end and work northwards. I saw the work started. My previous experience had taught me much about Greek methods and customs, so I did not feel strange to the country. The engineering staff, representing my firm, consisted of Messrs. Henry Guarracino, C. F. Tristram, A. E. Cooper, and C. H. Southwell. The two first-named had had a great deal of experience of railways in Turkey and Roumania, and were in a position to secure the services of good sub-contractors, accustomed to work in Greece and experienced in tunnel work. In these circumstances, after seeing the work started, I left with an easy mind, satisfied that good progress would be made. I had miscalculated the Greek. Whether it was that both we and our French partners consistently refused to resort to bribery, or whether it was jealousy on the part of the Greeks against foreign intervention in the construction of their railway, I do not know, but we were subjected to deliberate and systematic obstruction. It became so bad that after consultation with my colleague, the representative in Athens of the Batignolles Company, we determined to appeal to our respective ambassadors, put our case before them, and ask for their support. We went in the first instance to the French ambassador who, after listening to our story, agreed without hesitation that we were being treated unfairly, and assured us that he would take steps to ensure that the conditions would be altered. We then proceeded to invoke the assistance of the British ambassador. In view of my previous experience in Turkey I was not brimful of hope that we should receive much support from that quarter, and, as a matter of fact, such was the attitude of the British plenipotentiary towards us that he did not even have the courtesy to invite us to a seat. We, however, took the liberty of pulling chairs up to his table and sitting down, and I then commenced to put our case before him. I had scarcely commenced speaking before he interrupted me to observe that as the English Government had no official knowledge of our position, he could not help us. To this I replied, without any excessive display of politeness, that I had scarcely expected any assistance from him; that I had previously had unfortunate experience of English ambassadors elsewhere; that he appeared to be much the same as the others; and I concluded with the muttered prayer, "God help England!"

Having thus given vent to my feelings I took up my hat and in company with my colleague walked out of the room. I am inclined to think my harangue was not without some effect, for the conditions slightly improved, and the obstructive tactics of the engineers were to an extent modified. Right up to the end, however, we had trouble with the Greek Government and the engineers, and what ought to have been a splendid contract for us turned out to be but a moderately good one.

Some years later we, in conjunction with the same partners, were interested in the construction of the railway from Papapouli to Topsin—a distance of sixty miles.

XLVII

A Grand Tour

THE Boer War broke out in October 1899. During the whole period of this war I did not visit Africa. It was then that I made my trip round the world, and in any case the war, for a time, put an end to serious African activities on my part. I think, however, I may fairly claim that my firm, in an unostentatious fashion, contributed to the ultimate success of Great Britain. We did not suspend our operations on the Beira Railway and Mr. Lawley did much useful work for the Carrington expeditionary force, sent to the relief of Mafeking, in landing troops, horses, and munitions of war at Beira for that force, and in forwarding them up the line. Mr. Harold Pauling and his staff in Rhodesia also gave much help in the same direction.

Early in 1900 we obtained from the British North Borneo Company a contract to build a railway from Jesselton to Beaufort—a distance of some sixty miles—in Borneo and to construct a deep sea pier at Jesselton. In the following November I set out to see the new work and travelled *via* the United States. I remained a few days in New York, where I experienced all the discomforts of one of its leading hotels. After visiting Niagara and spending a few days in Chicago, I proceeded by the Southern Pacific express to San Francisco. One afternoon I was sitting in what was called the observation car, at the rear of the train. About eight or ten other passengers, all Americans, were in the same car, and some of them, observing that I was a stranger, sought to interrogate me as to my views regarding their country. I told them that if they would promise in no circumstances to take offence and really wanted me to tell the truth, the whole truth, and nothing but the truth, I would tell them candidly what my experience led me to think about the United States. The condition was accepted and we commenced to talk. I started by describing my difficulties in getting my cigars through the customs. I had not attempted any smuggling, but the delay was awful. I then told them of my experience at the hotel in New York. Whilst there I had invited some friends, English and others, whom I had met in New York, to dinner. After dinner I naturally suggested coffee and cigars, and as we were a large party I concluded that we might have these things without getting up from the dinner-table. I started to light up a cigar, but was immediately stopped in a very brusque manner by one of the waiters and told that no smoking was allowed. I pointed out that there was no notice to that effect, but the waiter, in insolent terms, said that that had nothing to do with the matter, and that we could not smoke there. There was no alternative but to go to another room. There were some ladies amongst the party and one or two of them lit cigarettes. Another waiter then came up and peremptorily informed us that women were not allowed to smoke in public in America, so that was stopped. I began to think that the chief end of an American waiter was to be offensive to the guests. I then went on to tell my travelling companions that the hotel, it being the winter season, was heated up to a very high temperature and it was naturally extremely stuffy. I complained, and, in the haughty manner to which I had become accustomed, was told to turn off the radiator in my bedroom. This I did, but the heat still came under the door from the corridor, and the room remained as stuffy as before. In the ordinary way I should have opened the window to get fresh air, but this was impracticable because there was a blizzard blowing outside.

In my room there was a dial with a pointer on it, and round the dial were marked the names of a number of necessaries and luxuries, including drinks. The idea was to set the dial to whatever was wanted and to ring the bell. I did this several times, varying my requirements, but on every occasion all I got brought to me was the same thing—iced water. Iced water has never been a favourite beverage with me. By this time I had learned to be patient; the soft answer that turneth away wrath would have been lost on an American waiter; and to have complained would have invited another storm of insolence. So I cooled my brow in the iced water. My next story was of an occasion in New York when I was foolish enough to ask a policeman to direct me to a particular place. I thought he was going to hit me with his club, but he only scowled and told me to go to a place warmer even than anywhere in New York and which I am anxious to avoid until I am dead. "That, gentlemen," I said, "has been my experience of your principal city and of one of its principal hotels."

"Now for your railways." We had been on the train for many hours, careering along towards San Francisco. I proceeded to tell my listeners that on the other side we heard much of American railways and of their phenomenal speed. Then I invited them to look at the time-table, according to which the average speed at that time—nearly twenty years ago now—was only twenty-seven miles an hour. I pointed out to them that this was scarcely express speed, and that in South Africa, on a three-feet six-inch gauge line—which they would probably consider a toy railway—we could beat them easily, the train from Cape Town to Johannesburg covering the distance of a thousand miles at an average speed of thirty miles an hour.

We were by this time approaching the country where

I expected to see the Rocky Mountains, and I enquired when we might be prepared to view the wonderful scenery. One of the passengers, who turned out to be a sectional engineer on that part of the line, replied, " We passed the divide half an hour ago."

" There you are," said I, " you advertise your Rocky Mountains all over the world as one of its seven wonders, and I believe one would require a microscope to see them."

There was a roar of laughter at this, and indeed throughout my conversation all the passengers took everything I said quite good-humouredly and seemed to enjoy the recital of my experience in their part of the world. I naturally had appealed to them by asking if they did not consider personal comfort the essence of pleasurable travelling in a foreign country, and that when one went to an hotel one expected a little comfort and some civility on the part of those who waited upon them. They all acknowledged that these were not to be looked for in many of the hotels in America, so I considered I had established my case on that point, and as regards railways I held my argument as to an express train only travelling twenty-seven miles an hour to be unanswerable. Of course, they instanced their fast trains between New York and Chicago, New York and Washington, and other important centres. I admitted that these trains were quick, but that did not alter my contention that a trans-continental train ought to make greater speed than the one we were in.

From railways we passed to the subject of American laws. It so happened that a negro had been lynched a day or two previously at Porterville, one of the stations we had just passed, and the place where he had been lynched was pointed out to me. I remarked: " You have not even got sufficient confidence in your justice to see that your laws are carried out."

A truculent looking individual sitting opposite me,

whom, judging by his appearance, I thought I might be offending, reached out his hand to me and said: " Shake, stranger, you are right."

This gentleman appeared well known to several of the passengers and turned out to be a Pinkerton man on his way to San Francisco. He then took up the conversation and stated that anyone who had money enough could commit murder or any other crime in America and could depend either on getting off completely or on dragging out his defence for a number of years before any legal sentence would be carried out on him. He mentioned a case that was then the subject of much public attention, where a man had been accused of having sent sweetmeats to someone in New York. These sweetmeats had been poisoned, and after eating them the recipient died. From the evidence the case appeared to be quite clear. The Pinkerton man offered to lay—I do not remember how many—dollars that the accused, who was a rich man, would either get off or that the case would last for several years. No one, however, cared to accept the bet, and three years afterwards I saw in the newspapers that the case had not then been settled. To this day I do not know how it ended.

After a tedious ride of five or six days, including a stop of twelve hours at Niagara, we arrived at San Francisco. We had travelled over the most deadly flat country that I have ever seen—hundreds of miles as uninteresting as the South African Karroo. The Rockies, at the point we crossed them, resolved themselves into a low range of hills. The steepest grade between New York and San Francisco was one in sixty-six, and it was therefore little to be wondered at that the trains could carry heavy loads.

I spent a few days in San Francisco and then took passage in the American steamer " China " for Yokohama. Among the passengers there were thirty or forty people, missionaries and their families, who had fled from China at the beginning of the Boxer rising, and who were returning thence as the rising was over. As missionaries they did not appeal to me as being of a very high class, and I got the impression that their chief object was to make money, and that the saving of souls was a minor consideration. This, I know, is a hard thing to write but I cannot help doing so—the more so as they had fled from their posts at a time when decent people would have remained to do all they could to aid their converts.

We called at Honolulu. It is a charmingly beautiful island, the whole of which was then practically under the control of one family. The original emigrant had been a missionary, and had evidently used his position to great personal advantage, as I believe the family have now great power in the sugar world, and have made immense fortunes out of that commodity cultivated in Honolulu. They managed to secure the island for the American Government, and if I had not been on board an American ship I should not have been allowed to land, since neither passengers nor cargo could be taken from one American port to another—and Honolulu is an American port—unless conveyed in American bottoms. The consequence is that the whole of the shipping trade of Honolulu is in American hands.

We had on board a number of Chinese—some alive and others otherwise—who were being returned to China on the expiration of their labour agreements. It is one of the terms of the Chinese labour agreement that, dead or alive, the labourer must be returned to his native country. Gambling was carried on furiously among the Chinese, and many of them lost all they possessed to their more fortunate fellow countrymen. One Chinaman who had lost everything committed suicide. His body was temporarily preserved in some way by the ship's doctor and placed with the other corpses which were being " repatriated."

After arriving at Yokohama I spent a few weeks travelling through Japan. It is a most interesting country and my sojourn there provided a pleasing antidote to the many discomforts and discourtesies I had experienced in America. I visited most of the principal towns, many villages, and saw much of the inland country. I then took passage on a Japanese steamer for Shanghai. The captain and chief engineer were English, but the rest of the officers and all the crew were natives.

About a couple of years previously we had been trying to obtain work in China, and we were then negotiating for a contract to build a railway from Shanghai to Nanking. I had sent Mr. Butler to China to obtain the necessary information to enable us to tender for this work. He had brought full particulars to London, and I had gone into the figures with him and made up our tender. Although we did not ultimately obtain the contract for this work we had opened offices in Shanghai and Hong-Kong with a view to negotiating for Chinese work. Our agents in these places were useful in obtaining Chinese labour to build the Borneo Railway. After a few weeks in China, spent chiefly in acquiring information and local experience, I proceeded by a German steamer, the "Eitel Frederic," to Singapore. While I was there the heat was excessive; perhaps it can best be described as infernal. I generally did my correspondence in the very early morning, and the temperature was frequently over ninety degrees before six o'clock. I had to wait at Singapore about a fortnight before I could obtain a passage by a tramp steamer to Labuan. It was at the latter place that the Governor of British North Borneo resided, and I had to see him *en route*. I remained there a week and then, travelling in a small steamer, I proceeded to Jesselton, the little port from which our railway started.

XLVIII

Borneo

ON arrival at Jesselton early in 1901 I was met by Mr. C. V. Buchan, who, as already stated, had been with us in South Africa, and who had been appointed agent in charge of the Borneo work. The first piece of news I received from him was anything but reassuring. It appeared that a rebellion had broken out amongst the Dyaks or head-hunters, in consequence of which we had been obliged to stop work and go into lager. I considered the number of police in the country quite inadequate for the protection of the inhabitants, so I arranged with the Governor for the supply of a small number of Sikh soldiers. For some time previous to their arrival no attack was made, but we spent an anxious time expecting it nightly. Our residential quarters were situated on a small hill about three hundred yards away from the main railway camp, and when the Sikhs arrived we placed them in that camp and Mr. Buchan, I, and one or two of our white staff slept in the residential quarters. One night we were awakened by heavy firing which was apparently proceeding in our direction from the railway camp. We could hear the bullets whizzing past us, and some of them were so uncomfortably close as to pierce our sleeping huts. Next morning we found that the Sikhs, probably from some imaginary cause, had become alarmed and that they had indulged in an indiscriminating discharge of their rifles. After consultation with Buchan I came to the conclusion that it would be safer to risk the effects of the rebellion than the promiscuous pot-shooting of the Sikhs, and it was therefore decided that we should resume work on the railway and take our chances so far as armed rising was concerned. As it happened, we were not interfered with, and a couple of weeks afterwards the head of the principal rebel, for which a reward had been offered, was brought into camp by a native who had been his first lieutenant, and who claimed pardon and reward. To his untutored mind perfidy, when his own interests were at stake, appeared a virtue, and when, through an interpreter, we endeavoured to ascertain how he had succeeded in obtaining the head of his chief, whom the natives believed to be invulnerable by blade or bullet, he told us he had remained patiently in hiding until his victim slept and had then adopted the primitive, but effective, method of bashing his head in with a big stone. I am not disposed to be squeamish, but I shall never forget the moment when he brought his trophy into our office wrapped in a dirty loin-cloth, and when he rolled out of the cloth the hirsute and bleeding head on to the floor at our feet. Even now, as I think of it, I am frail enough to feel " creepy."

I spent some time with Buchan, and during that period a curious incident occurred which is illustrative of the character of the Chinese. On going through the job one day we came to a very heavy cutting, the work on which had been sub-contracted to Chinese navvies. There were several hundreds of them, and the great majority appeared to me to be in a very low state of health. I asked Buchan what price they were getting for their work, and from the low figure he mentioned I concluded it was unreasonable to expect them to do it for the money. He agreed that the terms on which they had accepted their contracts were such as to prevent them from earning enough to keep themselves in good food. Hence their physical condition. I found that each of the Chinamen had a share in the contract, but that the management of it was deputed to two of them. I therefore sent for these managers and told them that the work they were doing was turning out much harder than had been expected either by them or by us, when they took the contract, and that I proposed to raise their price. They replied that they must consult their brothers, and they did so. The next day they came to me and, to my astonishment, declined to take the higher, or any, price different from that which had been agreed to. They informed me at the same time that they had previously communicated with their guild in China and that money was being sent to them to enable them to fulfil their contract. Meantime, all I could get them to agree to was to accept my offer to give them a good supply of food, for which they could pay us after they had received their expected money from China. This settled the matter for the time being, but I was curious to know why they had refused the alteration to a higher price, and some time afterwards, when I became more intimately acquainted with the deputies, they told me that they could not understand a proposal to alter a bargain after it had once been made, and they were candid enough to add that they had not much confidence in me for suggesting such a thing. It seemed to strike them that if the work had turned out easier than had been expected I should have made an effort to lower their price. It was futile for me to attempt to persuade them that this was not my custom, and that all I had tried to do was to help them because they were good men and were applying themselves to their work under adverse conditions. I felt quite sure that this incident had undermined their confidence in us.

Another little incident, which was more amusing to the rest of us than to the leading figure in it, occurred on the survey. While one of our engineers, Mr. M'Inerny, was running a traverse through the jungle he wanted to get a sight on a certain line, and to do this a tree had to be removed. This tree chanced to contain at the time a bees' nest. The Java axemen whom we had employed to cut down jungle pointed out to the engineer that if the tree were cut down the bees would get angry and probably offensive. M'Inerny, however, insisted, so they went on working to cut the tree down. When they saw it was just about to fall the natives cleared out as fast as their feet could carry them. M'Inerny, however, stood by his theodolite about thirty yards from the tree. The bees at once made for him in battle formation, and had he not jumped into a waterhole in the swamp through which the line was passing he would have been stung to death. Once in the hole he had to keep ducking his head under the water to keep away the bees, which were unremitting in their efforts to sting him. The natives, seeing his position, lit some big smoke fires, which in time drove the bees away. Meanwhile M'Inerny was being rendered bloodless by the leeches in the swamp hole. The district swarmed with leeches, and one could not pass through the swamps without collecting a host of them, no matter what protection might have been invoked. M'Inerny was pulled out nearly dead and, having lost so much blood, it was several weeks before he was fit to resume work.

Another feature of the part of Borneo through which the line was being built was the sago swamps. The stench from these swamps was worse than any other stench that can possibly exist in this world or, I fondly hope, in the next. Compared with it the smell of Kipling's "Oont" must have been as the odour of roses, and it was anything but a pleasant experience to build a railway through them.

I went to the other end of the line where Mr. C. F. Tristram was in charge, and where I found him occupied in making the survey through dense jungle and very heavy country. On returning to Jesselton I spent a little more time with Buchan, arranging to overcome various difficulties we had been forced to face through shortage of rolling stock. Then I made a trip to the north of the island to a place called Kudat, where I found that the rebellion had been much worse than at Jesselton. About a fortnight previous to my arrival the whole of the white inhabitants had narrowly escaped being massacred. Fortunately, the forces of law and order had just been able to drive off the rebels and the outbreak was then practically extinguished. My object in going to Kudat was to look at some forest country in the vicinity as we had obtained the right to peg out a timber concession. I had to make a dangerous sea journey in a small launch to get to the forests. This I did, pegged out the concession, got some saw mill machinery, which I had purchased in Singapore, set up and put to work. The timber consisted principally of camphor wood. Many of the trees were over one hundred and thirty feet in height, and shot up from sixty to a hundred feet without throwing a branch. They were from five to six feet in diameter for a good distance up the trunk and the timber was splendid. We also found a large quantity of wood known as bilian. It is a kind of ironwood—very long and straight, and most suitable for piles. It resists the sea-worm and we supplied large quantities of it to Hong-Kong and other Chinese ports. This concession was afterwards amalgamated with an existing timber company working on the Sandakan side of Borneo, and under the name of the China Borneo Timber Company has since been very successful. On my way back I called at Jesselton and got a tramp steamer to Singapore *via* Labuan where, in conjunction with a Chinaman named Wang Li, I formed a syndicate to make ice. This was very necessary for our Borneo work, and under the management of Mr. Wang Li regular supplies were sent there. Thence I obtained passage by a German steamer for Genoa, and arrived in England about April 1901.

XLIX

A Coal Venture

FOR about two years, apart from an occasional visit to Greece, varied with a detour on one occasion to Belgrade in connection with some prospective Servian work, and on another to Malta to collect information to enable us to tender for the St. Elmo breakwater and some dock work there, I remained in England, supervising generally the affairs of the firm, and it was not until the spring of 1903 that I paid another visit to South Africa. I went up to Johannesburg, and in view of subsequent events the impression which I then gained of the place and which I recorded in a letter sent home at the time, may be of interest:

" This place is at present in a very bad state and has to go through a bad crisis. I think many merchants and speculators will go under, and it will, as usual, end in the big houses swallowing up a lot of good things and clearing the atmosphere to their own advantage; then I think good times will come, as the gold is here and, anyhow, for a good many years to come can be gained at payable prices."

About three years previously I had made an arrangement with a Mr. Stone to take up an option, which he had secured before the Boer War, to purchase a farm from a Dutchman. This farm was situated not far from Johannesburg and we bought it for considerably less than £20,000. Messrs. Erlangers and I advanced the necessary money and Mr. Stone had a one-third interest in the venture. We sold the property at a large profit to the Johannesburg municipality, who acquired it for use as a sewage farm. Mr. Stone then presented a scheme to me for acquiring some farms which were situated in the Middleburg district and on which there was a large quantity of very good coal. Having conferred with Messrs. Erlangers, we agreed to take up the scheme, and—to cut a long story short—we lost on the Middleburg business all the money we had made out of the sewage farm. Intrinsically the proposition was an excellent one, but what we had not sufficiently provided against was the tremendous competition we had to face on the part of other Transvaal coal mine owners. Some of our competitors were interested in the control of the various gold mines to which, naturally, they sold their coal, and they were also able to exercise great influence in connection with the Government railways, with the result that we were seriously handicapped in our efforts to obtain contracts for departmental suppliers. We were allowed to open and equip thoroughly our mine and then the price of coal at the pit's mouth fell all over the Transvaal to 3*s*. 6*d*. and in some cases 2*s*. 6*d*. per ton. We could not afford to sell at these prices with any hope of profit, and, after holding on for a year or more, during which we lost several thousand pounds, I withdrew from the venture, and I believe that Mr. Stone had ultimately to sell the whole property to the National Bank for a very small sum. Messrs. Erlangers and I succeeded in recovering only a very small portion of the money we had sunk in the scheme. Although I have frequently burnt my fingers in such outside fires, I sometimes feel that I have yet to learn my lesson. In my own business I have made few mistakes, but instead of restricting my efforts, I have constantly been persuaded to participate in all kinds of extraneous ventures. Naturally, gold mining has always attracted me, and I have lost a lot of money in such schemes.

L

Africa in London

ONE of these outside schemes, in which I took a large interest, was the running of an entertainment in London which was called "Savage South Africa." The fundamental idea of this show was to bring Rhodesia to the active notice of the British public. About twelve months before the commencement of the Boer War Dr. Rutherfoord Harris had suggested to me the formation of a syndicate with the object of sending to England, under the charge of my old friend Mr. Frank Fillis, of Fillis's Circus, some Rhodesian and Dutch white men, who should take with them a number of Matabele and other South African natives, specimens of Rhodesian game, and various other attractions. The syndicate was formed and its object received the approval of Lord Grey and the Chartered Company. Lord Grey joined the board and I was appointed chairman. We chartered a "Castle" steamer and loaded it in Cape Town with about fifty white men and a hundred and fifty native warriors, together with some women and children; all the paraphernalia for their huts and domestic life; about eighty Basuto ponies and some Cape horses; and the actual coach which had been attacked by the Mashonas in their rebellion while it was on its way from Mazoe to Salisbury. We had intended to include trek oxen in the outfit but were informed that these would not be allowed to land in England. We had several South African antelopes, a lion, and a number of other beasts making up a small menagerie.

All arrived safely in London and, an agreement having been entered into with Mr. Imre Kiralfy, we opened at Earl's Court. One of our great attractions was the Kafir kraal, where the natives were to be seen practically in their savage state and where the conditions of their domestic life were reproduced as faithfully as the surroundings would permit. This attraction attained great popularity, and it frequently happened that in one day as many as sixteen thousand people paid sixpence each to view the kraal. Some prurient people commenced an agitation against the exhibition of the kraal on the ground that the sight of lusty savages, scantily attired, tended to demoralize the good people of London. Other allegations which, if not unfounded, were greatly exaggerated, were made as to undesirable occurrences when the savages were allowed outside the exhibition. As a matter of fact we made it a rule not to allow any Kafirs outside the exhibition unless they were accompanied by some of our white staff. Questions were, however, asked in the Houses of Parliament and the newspapers were full of references to the kraal. For a time the agitation had an effect, the very reverse of what its promoters desired. It gave us a magnificent advertisement with the result that tremendous crowds were anxious to visit the entertainment. By and by, however, the exaggerations of the agitators began to have their effect. Lord Grey, together with other prominent people connected with the Chartered Company, resigned from the Board, and Dr. Harris and I were left to carry on the show. Our original syndicate had put up, I think, about £60,000, and it became increasingly evident that if we remained at Earl's Court we should soon get on the wrong side of the financial stream. We accordingly took an early opportunity of terminating our agreement with Mr. Kiralfy, and succeeded in hiring Olympia on more advantageous terms. By the time the show was transferred to Olympia the Boer War had broken out and the outlook was very glum. People had no heart to patronize places of amusement and we realized, when it was too late, that our proper course would have been to close down the entertainment and to repatriate all the people we had brought to England. During the progress of the exhibition I had become satisfied that a change of management would be desirable, so I got a great friend of mine, Mr. Edwin Cleary, who had had considerable experience as an impresario, to run the show at Olympia. The arena there was so huge that it gave us a splendid opportunity for putting up some remarkable scenes. One of these was the native attack on the Mazoe coach. Two of the white men on the coach, as well as some of the natives, had been at the real attack. It was a very realistic piece of work. Natives, more than half hid among the long grass, threw assegais, and fired rifles; the white men lying on top of the coach returned the fire, blank of course, and the driver whipped up his horses, the whole thing being magnificently done.

Another outstanding feature of the exhibition consisted of a representation of the last stand of Major Wilson and his little band of heroes who were outnumbered and killed on the banks of the Shangani River in December 1893. This scene was most realistically reproduced. Not only did the white men know the business thoroughly, but the natives infused into their attacks such a force of enthusiasm that there were times when several of their adversaries had narrow escapes from being wounded by their assegais.

While the show was in progress news reached England concerning the armoured trains which the British were employing on the South Africa railways against the Boers. We applied the idea to the show and I arranged for a locomotive, and a truck, filled up with sheet iron to resemble as closely as possible the armoured trains actually in use, to be sent from one of our English contracts to Olympia. In the truck we placed a maxim gun with several white men, some of whom were to work the gun and the others to fire the rifles with which they had been armed. We laid about a hundred and fifty feet of railway track and made a huge proscenium on the side of the building opposite to the auditorium. All of a sudden the whistle of the train sounded shrilly in the distance, and it was evident that the train was approaching from among the South African scenery which had been very faithfully portrayed along, and in front of, the whole length of one side of the building. Presently the engine came in sight and, with gradually increasing speed, reached the open where, according to plan, it was attacked by the enemy, some of whom were genuine Boers, but the majority had been engaged as supers in London. By the time the engine appeared the noise of the firing of the maxim gun and the rifles had become intense and the whole scene was excessively thrilling. Before the train reached the other side of the proscenium it had attained such a speed that the most strenuous efforts had to be used by applying brakes both to the locomotive and to the truck, in order to prevent the end of the building from being knocked out. But the whole scheme was carried out with such consistent efficiency that we never had an accident.

Another of our star attractions was a great hunting scene. Two Dutchmen, armed with rifles, and obviously out for big game, appeared in the arena. For a brief period they kept the attention of the audience engaged by adopting the usual tactics of the hunters. Presently a lion, which had been secretly uncaged, could be seen making his way among the long grass. Night after night he played his part with almost human intelligence. Seemingly the monarch of his surroundings, he surveyed the scene with that indifferent composure which is characteristic of his kind under normal conditions. Roaring now and then, as the applause of the people appeared to gratify or annoy him, he commenced to climb a pathway among the scenic rocks. Just as he reached the summit and was about to disappear behind a boulder, the Boers fired, the lion was shot dead, and his body fell into that part of the arena where he had first appeared. At least, so it appeared to the public, who paid to be deceived and were recompensed accordingly. It would have been difficult to define adequately at the time how the scene was arranged, but the war has found us an apt description in the word "camouflage." Cleary had arranged the scene very cleverly. A ring round the lion's neck was connected by a wire to the lion's cage, which was secreted behind the boulder at the summit of the scenery. Both the ring and the wire had been painted so as to be indistinguishable by the audience. The lion was fed but once a day, and his feeding had been arranged to synchronize with the conclusion of the performance. Being hungry by the time his "turn" arrived, his one object was to reach his food with the least possible delay, and with Cleary's training he never made a mistake. Simultaneously with the shooting and the lion's disappearance behind the boulder a stuffed counterpart kept ready for the purpose fell from the summit, and the excellence of the effect was reflected in the acclamations of the public.

It is a melancholy indication of the spirit of these times that all this splendid show failed to attract large audiences. People were too much down in the dumps. While the historic sieges of Kimberley and Mafeking were in progress, few people were disposed to seek enjoyment. Consequently, after a time, the syndicate, having fulfilled its obligations to repatriate the people imported from Africa, was wound up at considerable loss to its promoters and to those who had supported them.

Mr. Fillis took over a part of the show and resumed his business as a travelling circus proprietor, while the

THE VICTORIA FALLS STATION AS GEORGE PAULING KNEW IT.

A TEMPORARY TRESTLE BRIDGE NEAR THE MATETSI RIVER BETWEEN BULAWAYO AND THE VICTORIA FALLS.

MR. AND MRS. GEORGE PAULING PHOTOGRAPHED AT THE ORIGINAL VICTORIA FALLS HOTEL.

THE VICTORIA FALLS HOTEL IN THE EARLY 1900's.

PAULINGS WERE UNSUCCESSFUL IN THEIR TENDER FOR THE CONSTRUCTION OF THE VICTORIA FALLS BRIDGE WHICH WAS BUILT BY THE CLEVELAND BRIDGEBUILDING AND ENGINEERING COMPANY LIMITED OF DARLINGTON.

OFFICIAL OPENING OF THE VICTORIA FALLS BRIDGE BY PROFESSOR FRANCES DARWIN, SON OF CHARLES DARWIN, ON 12TH SEPTEMBER, 1905.

BEFORE THE ARRIVAL OF LOCOMOTIVES NORTH OF THE KAFUE RIVER BRIDGE. OX-DRAWN TRUCKS WERE USED FOR PLATELAYING.

TYPICAL CONSTRUCTION ENGINEERS' CAMP.

fertile mind of Cleary had also evolved another scheme. It was to take over a section of the wreck with which to assist him in opening a show in Paris. At that time the Paris Exhibition, including one of the first automobile displays, was about to be inaugurated, and I warned Cleary that he would be sure to lose our money by seeking to run a show which would not be patronized, because I foresaw that all who went to Paris would spend their money at the big exhibition. However, my friend thought differently and in my folly I agreed to join him. We both lost our money, but were to some extent repaid by many amusing episodes which had better remain unrelated.

LI

More Ventures with Mr. Cleary

IT will be remembered that a considerable number of years ago great things were expected of gold production in West Africa. Mr. Lawley, several others, and I formed a syndicate with the object of obtaining gold-bearing properties in that part of the world, and we sent out a mission for prospecting purposes. Mr. Cleary was in charge, and he was accompanied by one of our engineers, a Mr. Frame, who had had some experience in the particular work for which he was engaged. Arrived at his objective, Ashanti, Cleary obtained concessions for very large properties and in due season he forwarded the necessary titles and relative documents home for us to negotiate in this country.

When the deeds arrived I came to the conclusion that we had quite enough property to form a large company and I was anxious that Cleary should come to England to assist in the promotion. He, however, was not of my opinion, and from the correspondence that took place between us by telegraph, it was apparent that there remained one particular concession to the acquisition of which he attached especial importance. One of his cables contained a mysterious request to send out a phonograph machine with the necessary discs for taking records. While at a loss to understand his intention we complied with the request and awaited information as to the purpose for which the machine was required. It ultimately transpired that the particular area which had been enjoying Cleary's exceptional attention was reputed to contain many gold-bearing reefs, but that, as it contained the burial ground of many Ashanti chiefs, the natives had refused to grant a concession over it, even to him, although from his natural and gifted disposition he had readily acquired the friendship and goodwill of all the natives with whom he had come in contact, irrespective of their standing. He had got all the land he wanted, except the burial ground, concerning which the chiefs of the tribe remained resolute. Cleary—one of the most genial men I have ever met—had also secured the friendship of the native commissioner of the district, who was familiar with the local language, and who, at Cleary's request, consented to talk certain words into the phonograph. All this having been completed, Cleary called for an indaba with the chiefs, which took place one night around a fire in front of his hut. Secreted behind a curtain in the hut lay the phonograph. The native commissioner was there—ostensibly as an interpreter—and a trusted native had been deputed at a given signal to turn on the machine. After some general conversation reference was made to the burial ground, and the natives repeated that in the absence of a message from the spirits of their departed chiefs, nothing would induce them to give the concession for the burial ground to anyone. This, of course, proved Cleary's opportunity, and, through the interpreter, he informed them that he had just been in communication with the spirits of their dead chiefs who had a message to deliver to the indaba. Thereupon, in the native tongue, the phonograph declared that it was the desire of the departed fathers that the concession was to be given to the white man who was beloved by the spirits and who was the best friend the natives ever had, or were ever likely to have. Great was the astonishment of the assembled natives, but such a message could not be ignored. Cleary got the concession, which in due season was delivered in London.

When I found that he would not take my advice and

return home, I went to work with other members of the syndicate who had influence in the City to float the original concession—that is all the acquired property minus the cemetery. We had virtually secured an offer of £150,000 cash and many thousands of vendor's shares from one of the largest West African Gold companies existing at that time. I did my utmost to ensure that the offer should be accepted, but a spirit of greed seemed to obsess the other members of the syndicate and unfortunately it was refused. The ultimate result of this West African speculation was that none of us made any money and that Cleary, through, I think, his own obstinacy in remaining away too long and in seeking to obtain too much, just missed a fortune.

Another venture in which I was interested with "Mike" Cleary was a flying proposition. He had arrived in England at the time when Paulhan, the aviator, was giving his first aeronautic exhibitions in this country. Cleary, while travelling from Southampton to London, chanced to see Paulhan in the air near Sandown Park. As an illustration of the aptitude with which "Mike" was accustomed to grasp the potentialities of a chance prospect, I may say that on the following day he told me he wanted to proceed to Paris the same evening, his idea being to come to an agreement with Paulhan, who was also returning to Paris, and to get the latter to go to the United States and give flying exhibitions there. Ned—as he is known to his intimate associates [1]—is a native of the United States, and said he was sure he could get contracts in various American cities to pay large sums of money for such exhibitions. He went to Paris, I having agreed that if he succeeded in making arrangements with Paulhan, and if it should be necessary, I would put up £5,000. He moved to and fro between London and Paris several times during the following fortnight, and in the meantime he had

[1] Mr. Cleary has died since these Memoirs were written.—Ed.

got one or two of his American friends in Paris to help him, and contracts had been fixed up to give flying exhibitions in St. Louis, San Francisco, Los Angeles, Buffalo, and other American cities. The aggregate amount of these contracts extended to something over £100,000, and it was considered that the total time necessary to give the exhibitions should not exceed six weeks. It must be borne in mind that flying was then only in its infancy, that it was winter time, and that aeroplanes were not so successful then in bad weather as they have since become. The weather in most of the places in respect of which Cleary had made contracts was good in the winter time and that was one of his principal reasons for the selection he had made. He obtained from America an advance on the strength of the contracts he made with Paulhan, so that I did not have to put up my £5,000.

Within three weeks of his having seen the flying at Sandown, Cleary and M. Paulhan were on a steamer with two aeroplanes and two mechanics *en route* for New York. They landed there and gave exhibitions at one of the cities for which Cleary received about £10,000. He then moved on to another city, the contract for which was £20,000 for about a week's flying. Meanwhile the Wright Brothers had been moving the courts in America to restrain him from having any further flying done, their contentions being that they had a master patent for flying and that no one could go into the air in America without their permission and consent. They were successful in obtaining an injunction against Cleary, with the result that a stop was put to his venture. M. Paulhan returned to France and Cleary, instead of making, as he would have done, £60,000 or £80,000 out of his idea, only made a few thousand pounds.

LII

The Argentine

A PROPOSAL had been made to us to establish a connection with the Argentine, and for the purpose of carrying out work there we formed a subsidiary company called "La Compania de Obras Publicas del Rio de la Plata, Ltd." This company was to be worked jointly by Mr. Philip Lander, an engineer with whom I had been acquainted and who had had considerable South American experience, and a South American engineer named Calastreme. I called the latter Mr. Catastrophe and, as it happened, the soubriquet proved to be prophetic, because the company did not prove a financial success. During the few years we continued work there we carried out about a dozen contracts, some of them of considerable magnitude. In 1904, while I was returning from one of my periodical excursions to South Africa, I transferred at Madeira into a Royal Mail steamer bound for Buenos Aires, where I arrived in June of that year. The Obras Publicas Company was then engaged in carrying out several railway and other contracts in different provinces of the Argentine. Pauling and Company, Limited, were at the same time engaged in preparing a scheme for a port at Rosario, one of the largest cities of the Republic, situated on the Parana, about two hundred miles from Buenos Aires. The project was a very large one, and, much to my regret, we were not successful in obtaining the work. We were, however, paid a premium which more than covered our expenses, as our design was considered one of the best that had been presented to the authorities. A Mr. Saturnino Unzue, one of the largest landed proprietors of the Argentine, had also asked us to prepare a scheme for a port on his property. I met him in Buenos Aires, and the excessive hospitality which he extended towards me made my visit to South America especially enjoyable. He took me to his home estancia, as he called it, which was the smallest of his properties and was situated about seventy miles from Buenos Aires. There I saw in one camp over one thousand slaughter oxen, nearly a thousand horses, and, in one building, seventy pedigree bulls all of the best English blood. Mr. Unzue was reputed to have an income of a thousand pounds a day, and some idea of his wealth may be gathered from the fact that he bred and sold yearly about one hundred and twenty racing colts for which he obtained an average price of about £400. He had, on the one estate I saw, two thousand cows in milk. All the milk was sent to Buenos Aires, and I was informed that for a certain period during each year, at one of the big dairy establishments there, the milk of fifty thousand cows a day was turned into butter and cheese. At the time of my visit he owned altogether something like three hundred thousand head of cattle and over twenty thousand horses, besides unnumbered sheep, and I learned that there were many others in the country nearly as rich as he.

My trip to the Argentine was a revelation, and I formed the most favourable impression of a wonderful country. I had, by reading, made myself slightly acquainted with Buenos Aires and the Argentine, but no book could give any idea of the reality. The population of Buenos Aires was then over a million, and its increase during the preceding ten or twelve years had been something like five hundred thousand; the docks were magnificent, and had been built at a cost of eleven millions sterling. The whole trade of the country consisted of cattle, wool, butter, grain, and the like;

and I found that at one cold storage place alone five thousand head of cattle were slaughtered daily; at one skin, hide, and wool market building there was a covered floor space of two hundred thousand square feet which, during the working season, was constantly full, sales taking place twice a week. The tramway systems, partly electric and partly horse, were principally in the hands of English companies, as were also the railways, but the majority of the merchants of Buenos Aires were of other nationalities—Spanish, French, Belgian, Italian, and German. Spanish was the language invariably spoken and written. There were many English and Irish landowners. Most of these were fairly rich, some of them very much so. They consisted generally of families who had settled in the country from forty to eighty years previously. Vast areas, extending to thousands of square miles, were under grain cultivation, and in one year eighty thousand ploughs were sold in Buenos Aires.

There was one other big Argentine scheme in which Pauling and Company, Limited, became interested. It was for inundation canal works in the province of Buenos Aires. We obtained a definitive contract for the work, amounting to a million and a half sterling, but, for some reason or other, the government of the province decided to cancel the contract, and in consideration of the cancellation we were paid the handsome sum of £150,000.

DONNYBROOK, TERMINUS OF THE 98 MILE 2 FT. GAUGE STUARTSTOWN RAILWAY IN NATAL. IT CLIMBS FROM SEA LEVEL TO 3,000 FT. IN 41 MILES. AT THE TERMINUS THE 2 FT. GAUGE JOINS THE 3 FT. 6 INS. GAUGE.

GUESTS AT THE OPENING OF THE OLIFANTS RIVER BRIDGE ON THE SELATI RAILWAY WHICH LINKS KOMATI POORT AND ZOEKMAKAAR IN THE NORTH EASTERN TRANSVAAL.

LIII

THE TRANSVAAL ENGINEERING AND CONTRACTING COMPANY, LIMITED

IN the year 1903 a company was formed in the Transvaal, called The Transvaal Engineering and Contracting Company, Limited. Pauling and Company, Limited, were its largest shareholders, and with them there were associated in the new company Mr. W. S. Royce, who had carried out a considerable number of contracts for public works construction in South Africa; Mr. James Butler, who has sometimes been my competitor, but more frequently my partner; and the firm of A. L. Secretan and Company, Limited. This company lasted for six or seven years, during which period it executed various contracts, amounting in value to about three-quarters of a million sterling. These included sewage works for the Johannesburg municipality, and the diversion of a river at Bloemfontein to cope with the periodical inundations that had been occurring there. The diversion involved the construction of a number of bridges, all large-span arches of solid dressed stone, which remain a lasting monument to the credit of all who were connected with their design and construction. The company also built a railway from Modderpoort to Bethlehem, just over a hundred miles, and completed various minor contracts in connection with railway and other work in the Free State and in the Transvaal. The largest work, however, for which the company was responsible was the Stuartstown Railway in Natal, which, although only about the same length as the Modderpoort-Bethlehem line and of a smaller gauge, contained much heavier work and cost nearly £300,000. The contract for building that line, which was obtained in open competition, was taken in the name of Pauling and Company, Limited, but the actual work was carried out under the aegis of the Transvaal Engineering and Contracting Company, Limited, which had a very successful career and which was liquidated only when we thought it would be better to resume any work we could get in the name of Pauling and Company, Limited.

LIV

The Development of Southern Rhodesia

WHILE the interests of my firm had been developing in so many directions in different parts of the world we had not been idle in Rhodesia. In 1899 the extension of the Beira Railway from Umtali to Salisbury had been completed. The terminus of the line northwards from Cape Colony had for a time remained at Bulawayo, but early in the present century construction was resumed between the two points with the result that before the end of 1902 the connection was linked up, and the main line from Cape Town to Beira—a distance of two thousand and thirty-five miles—became an accomplished fact. In the meantime the discovery of mineral wealth in various districts induced the authorities to construct branch lines, and in the same year we completed the construction of a two-feet gauge line from Salisbury to the Ayrshire mine, a distance of seventy-five miles. Some years later we were entrusted with the conversion of the Ayrshire line to the standard South African gauge, and an extension was made to the Eldorado mine, and, later, to Sinoia, whence I believe that ere long a railway will be built *via* the Khariba Gorge on the Zambesi to a point on the existing line near the Kafue River, which will have the effect of reducing the distance from North-Western Rhodesia to Beira by several hundred miles. As a matter of fact the preliminary surveys were made some time ago and, in my opinion, had it not been for the war, the work would now have been completed.

Amongst other branch lines which my firm built

between the year 1900 and the commencement of the European war, were those from Gwelo to Selukwe (twenty-five miles); Bulawayo to Gwanda (a hundred miles); a small branch to the Eldorado mine; Gwelo to Blinkwater (fifty miles); the Mazoe line (twenty-two miles); the Shamva line (fifty miles); and the line from Umvuma to Victoria (seventy-five miles). All these branches were built primarily with a view to exploiting gold discoveries and incidentally to develop the agricultural resources of the areas which they were destined to open up; and most of them were visited by me at one time or another while the construction operations were in progress.

About the same time that the through railway connection was established between Cape Town and Beira, arrangements were being made for building the continuation of the line in a north-western direction from Bulawayo towards the Victoria Falls *via* Wankies, where extensive coal deposits had been discovered. The section to Wankies was completed in 1903, and to Victoria Falls in the following year. While this was under construction, Sir Charles Metcalfe, the eminent engineer who, in conjunction with Sir Douglas Fox and Partners, has been charged with the supervision of all Rhodesian railway development, and I went on to the Falls to choose the route of the railway and also to pick out a suitable site for the bridge across the Zambesi. That bridge, in accordance with the expressed desire of Mr. Rhodes, has been erected at a spot where, when the wind is in a certain direction, it is washed by the spray from the Falls. Built on the cantilever principle it is, I believe, the highest in the world, and its central span extends to some five hundred feet in length. For purposes of comparison I have heard it stated that the distance from the bed of the river to the rail level is somewhat greater than that of the top of the dome of St. Paul's Cathedral from the ground. It was built by the Cleveland Bridgebuilding and Engineering Company, Limited, of Darlington. My firm had sent in a tender but it was too high; their tender, on the other hand, was too low, and I hardly think they made a profit on the work. I had had so great a connection with railway work in Rhodesia that I was sorry we had not the honour of building the bridge, but honour of that kind can be purchased at too heavy a price.

LV

A Grand Trek

SOME time previously a contract had been entered into for the extension of the railway north of Victoria Falls in the direction of the Congo border, for a distance of about a hundred miles, to a place named Kalomo, and while this work was in progress another contract for an additional two hundred and fifty miles to Brokenhill mine had been executed. We had not waited for the bridge over the Zambesi to be finished, but had conveyed all our railway material over the gorge by a cableway propelled by electric power, and under the untiring and inspiring supervision of Mr. Lawley we made almost as much progress as we could have done if we had had the use of the bridge. Thousands of tons of materials were conveyed across the river by means of the cableway, which was capable of carrying a load of ten tons at a time. Locomotives, taken to pieces on the south bank of the river, were borne across by this means, and re-erected on the north bank. Before many months, however, we did get the use of the bridge which, of course, helped us to some extent in proceeding more expeditiously with the work.

Accompanied again by Sir Charles Metcalfe I proceeded to Rhodesia and found that the rails had practically reached Kalomo. Sir Charles Metcalfe and I decided to go on beyond the railhead as far as the Congo border, our object being to select a suitable route for the railway. We were able to drive or ride for nearly two hundred miles to a point beyond the Kafue River, but from there had to tramp a similar distance to a place called N'dola, which is not far beyond the Bwana M'Kuba copper mines, and almost on the borderland between Rhodesia and the Belgian Congo. It proved a most interesting trek. Our *entourage* included the Native Commissioner for North-West Rhodesia, an excellent shot, who had also the advantage of being familiar with several Kafir lingos; my secretary, Mr. H. E. Pooley; a French chef whom we had engaged in Cape Town; my personal servant Edouardo, who had been with me for about ten years and who is still in my service and accompanies me on all my travels; and about three hundred native carriers. When we reached a place beyond which it was not considered safe to continue the use of horses, with or without carts, we commenced our long trail, and the order of our going was somewhat after the following fashion:

As had been my invariable custom on the veldt, I was always astir before daybreak, preferring to rely on my own resources to see the due commencement of our daily task. Each morning I sent off an advance party consisting of our European manager and about a dozen natives. The former had considerable knowledge of the country and proved an excellent guide. His duty was similar to that of the advance agent of a touring theatrical party. By his skill as a marksman he also provided game and birds to contribute to our maintenance, and he selected spots where water was available to arrange our encampments for breakfast and midday meals. We travelled by the compass, and although we occasionally came across Kafir footpaths, or paths made by big game, there was no regular road. When we struck camp Edouardo, the cook, and the great majority of the carriers were sent ahead, Sir Charles, the Native Commissioner, Mr. Pooley, and I following almost immediately afterwards. We retained a few boys with us to carry water and other immediate necessaries, and a machela, or slung hammock, to be used in case any of us should become ill or too footsore to walk. We then trudged along at a set pace for about three or four hours, making about nine or ten miles until, about ten o'clock in the morning, we reached the place where the camp had been made for breakfast. By that time it had become warm, almost beyond conception, for we were in the season of the year just before the rains when everything was burnt up.

About two o'clock each afternoon camp was struck and the carriers, with Edouardo and other impedimenta, were sent on to a place to be selected by our white guide for the night's encampment. About an hour later Sir Charles and the rest of us commenced the last stage of the day's journey. This generally took us until about six o'clock, when we reached the camp, where everything was found ready, tents pitched, and all in order for our evening meal and the night's rest. Our chef, who turned out to be a regular treasure, provided magnificent dinners. How he did it none of us could conjecture. Of course, we had plenty of tinned goods and a sufficiency of fresh game, but day after day he furnished us with a dinner equal to anything I have ever had in any of the big hotels of England or any other part of Europe. We had not neglected to include in our baggage plenty of champagne and other liquors, and this was made cold by the method which is familiar to all travellers in tropical countries. After a hot dinner and a good glass of wine we occasionally played a rubber at bridge, but we were generally tired enough to lie down, indulge in a somnolent smoke, and go to rest.

On the trip we were much annoyed by lions. The weather was so hot that it would have meant suffocation to have kept the ends of the small tents we occupied tied up, so at the entrance to each tent we made a barricade consisting of tins, portmanteaux, bundles, and other articles that would make sufficient noise to awaken us if an inquisitive lion chanced to knock them over.

LOCOMOTIVE BEING FLOATED ACROSS THE KAFUE RIVER.

THE NINTH OF THE KAFUE RIVER'S THIRTEEN SPANS BEING FLOATED INTO POSITION.

VICTORIA FALLS BRIDGE ACROSS THE ZAMBESI RIVER.

RHODES' DREAM

Up from the Cape where the wild seas thunder,
Over the Falls, where a haze of spray
Keeps the North and the South asunder,
Swings she swift on her headlong way—
Speeding tireless, night and day,
Past the Lakes in their magic chain,
Waking the Desert to wide-eyed wonder,
Racketing, rocketing, roars the Train.

A silver wedge in the bushland spaces
Cleaving North through a heathen land,
Stamping the wild with the White Man's traces,
Trimming the rough for the Master Hand,
Girdling earth with a magic band,
Lighting the night with a steady gleam,
Meeting dawn in the far-off places,
These are the fruits of Rhodes' Dream!

Beasts scared off from the pools at dawning
Grunt and growl as she rumbles by,
Forest-folk in the misty morning
Gaze aghast ere they turn to fly—
Trim and true is each bolt and tie,
Trestle and culvert snugly laid,
(Now and again at the whistle's warning
Elephants trumpet down the glade).

"Cape to Cairo! — Steamer to Steamer!
Rail and wire from South to North . . ."
Men guffawed at the Master Schemer,
Fools waxed loud in their foolish wrath . . .
But the project held, and the words went forth,
Sister-nations hurried to aid,
Stung by the dream of a dumb, dear Dreamer,
Men toiled on till the rails were laid.

Out of the South where the ships are plying,
Into the clutch of the parched Karroo,
Past the crags where his bones are lying
Under their slab on the World's wide View . . .
'Tis none so long since the world was new
And the mammoth moved in eternal snows,
But the dream he dreamed when he lay a-dying
Bids to come true. And perhaps — he knows.

—Cullen Gouldsbury

WITH A TOTAL LENGTH OF 1,398 FEET THE KAFUE RIVER BRIDGE WAS, FOR MANY YEARS, THE LONGEST OF ITS TYPE IN SOUTHERN AFRICA.

PAULING'S CONTRACTOR'S TRAIN WAS THE FIRST TO CROSS THE COMPLETED KAFUE BRIDGE IN 1906.

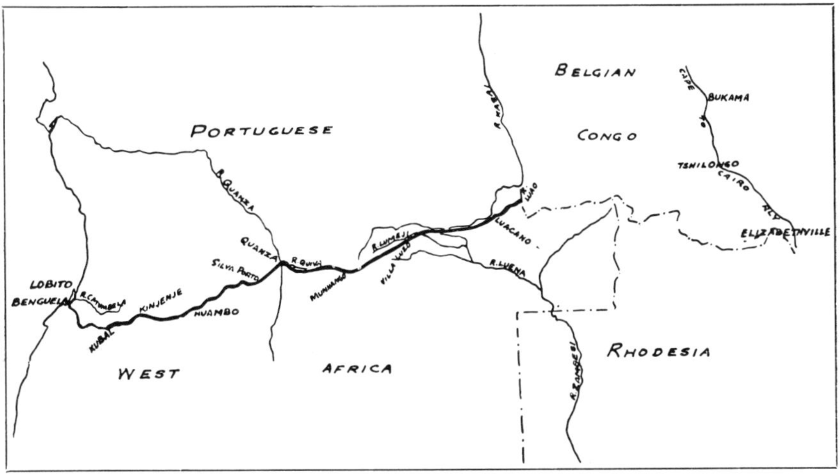

SKETCH MAP OF THE BENGUELA RAILWAY LINE.

TEMPORARY BRIDGE OVER AN ARCH CULVERT UNDER CONSTRUCTION ON THE BENGUELA LINE.

CONCRETE DAM UNDER CONSTRUCTION ON THE CUANDO HYDRO–ELECTRIC PROJECT.

MASS CONCRETE WELLS UNDER CONSTRUCTION AS PART OF THE DEEP–SEA WHARF AT LOBITO BAY.

We did not, however, prove sufficiently attractive for a leonine invasion. Our only casualty was one of the natives who, while sleeping with his fellows at a spot where they had allowed their fire to burn low was carried off by one of the lords of the forest. The natives always slept in the open, but kept roaring fires going so as to keep off the lions.

We remained a day or two at Broken Hill to inquire into the condition of the lead and zinc deposits there. From Broken Hill we went on to N'dola. In picking out the railway route we had followed as closely as possible the main direction to Broken Hill and N'dola, and we found there were very little physical difficulties to overcome. When the line came to be staked out the surveying engineers were able to avoid places of any great difficulty, but, generally speaking, they followed the route which Sir Charles Metcalfe and I had taken.

We remained a couple of days at N'dola and then started to walk back to railhead. This we reached without adventure, and I remember that on the day we arrived there Lawley, to show us what he could do, laid in five and three-quarter miles of permanent way materials in that one day. To do this a special effort was necessary, but it served to show what could be done with organized gangs under experienced supervision. The rails were, of course, only laid on what is called the formation, but engines and trucks were able to pass over them and the roadbed was made good afterwards.

Our three hundred carriers were recruited from various races. The Native Commissioner told us that of them about thirty belonged to a cannibal tribe, and from these Sir Charles had chosen a very intelligent boy whom he called Jim, and whom he made his body servant. One night we encamped at a spot close to one of the few native kraals that we passed during our journey. The following morning, after we had been walking about half an hour, Edouardo came to me and in his peculiar English said that Jim had a baby. At first I was unable to comprehend this alarming information, but after some cross-examination it appeared that Jim had in his possession a little picaninny about two months old. We brought the trek to a halt and sent for Jim, who had discreetly assumed a position some distance behind his fellows. Sure enough, he was carrying a fine little native child. The Native Commissioner was requested to inquire where he got it and why he was bringing it with him. Jim replied with charming *sang froid* that he had stolen it from the kraal, near which we had spent the night, and that he and his brothers were looking forward to the luxury of a cooked baby for a meal that night. I really believe this was seriously intended. Jim was severely reprimanded and the picaninny was returned to its kraal at once.

Soon afterwards we had occasion to learn that Jim's vices were not restricted to cannibalism. One morning, after we had been walking for an hour or two, we noticed that we had camp followers in the form of two Kafir women. The Native Commissioner sent for them and it was discovered that Jim was responsible for the unauthorized additions to our staff. It appeared that one of the native women came from among the élite of a kraal near N'dola, while her companion occupied a position similar to that of a maid-servant. Jim had induced the lady to take advantage of the absence of her husband from home to run away from the kraal. The Native Commissioner at once instituted a kind of court and Jim was arrested and brought before him. It was explained to the culprit that it was not only sinful but illegal for one man to steal another man's wife. He was also told that such an offence against the moral and statutory laws sometimes occurred, even amongst white people, but that the transgressor was liable to heavy fines. Having delivered a serious lecture, the Commissioner suggested that in this instance the delinquent should be mulcted in a fine of ten shillings. Although the moral aspect had little or no influence on Jim, he was very much alive to the material side and at once repudiated the idea of paying anything. Ten shillings was about as high an amount as he could understand. Ten is the highest numeral provided for in many of the Kafir languages, and is about the maximum the Kafir intellect can comprehend. Jim's great anxiety was that the wandering women might be immediately returned to their own tribe. His wish was complied with and the local legal records were thereby deprived of what might have become a *cause célèbre* in Northern Rhodesia.

I returned to England by the East Coast route. We travelled from Beira in an Austrian Lloyd steamer, and spent a couple of days at Zanzibar. I had been negotiating to build the tramways on that island and was anxious to see the place. On reaching Egypt I remained there for a month, most of which was spent in a dahabeah or houseboat on the Nile. It was a peaceful and unexciting experience, too much so, perhaps, for my temperament, and I did not greatly regret my return to England.

LVI

Northern Rhodesia and the Belgian Congo

REFERENCE has already been made to the line from Victoria Falls to Kalomo, which was completed in 1905. In the following year it was extended nearly three hundred miles to Broken Hill, which is situated in an area where extensive deposits of lead and zinc have been discovered. On this section the Kafue River, a very large tributary of the Zambesi, had to be negotiated. Lawley was in charge and, in the construction of the bridge over the Kafue, he had a task of considerable difficulty. It consisted of fourteen spans, each one hundred feet long. The necessary piers, which were of solid masonry and concrete, were built at regular intervals across the river in water about ten feet deep. The spans were erected one by one on the bank and slid, by means of rails, on to a steel pontoon which had been sent from this country for the special purpose of being used in connection with the erection of the bridge. As each span was shipped the pontoon was pulled into the bed of the river and guided between a pair of the piers, where it was made fast until the span was fixed in its proper position. Lawley completed the erection of the bridge within six months which, I should think, is almost a record for a structure of its size and description.

Construction thence to the Congo Border, another hundred and thirty-five miles, was not completed until 1909 when, without interruption, the railway was continued into Belgian territory as far as Elizabethville, a hundred and sixty-five miles beyond, which was reached in 1910. This section was under the supervision of Mr. H. C. Carter, who for many years has been one of my chief agents. When the contract to Elizabethville was finished, Belgian interests decided to continue the construction under the aegis of a Belgian firm, and for that purpose there was formed the Société Coloniale de Construction. Recognizing, however, the experience of my firm in railway construction and the value of our personnel we were offered and accepted a material interest in the new company, and a number of our former employees are still in its service. The first work of that company was to extend the line to Kambove, which was reached in 1913. Kambove is the headquarters of the Union Minière Company and the centre of a great copper-bearing area. Three years later the line was extended to T'schilonga, and a connection has since been established with Bukama on the Upper Congo. This has rendered possible a combined rail and river journey from Boma, at the mouth of the River Congo, to Cape Town, a distance of between four thousand five hundred and five thousand miles. The Belgian Congo is a country full of promise, and within its confines great railway development is inevitable.

LVII

The Benguella Railway

EARLY in 1903 I was approached by my old friend Mr. Robert Williams, whom I had known since the early Kimberley days, with regard to commencing the construction of a railway from Lobito Bay in Portuguese West Africa, which would have for its ultimate object the development of the Province of Angola and the tapping of the inestimable mineral wealth of the Belgian Congo. Lobito Bay, which is less than five thousand miles from England, is reputed to possess the finest natural harbour on the west coast of Africa. Situated as it is, only about eleven hundred miles from the Katanga copperfields, the wisdom of selecting such an outlet for the mineral wealth of the richest area in Central Africa is obvious. At present there are but two other outlets—Cape Town, which is over two thousand miles distant from Katanga and about six thousand miles from England; and Beira, about one thousand six hundred miles from Katanga, and so far distant from England that competition with Lobito Bay is out of the question. No finance had then been provided for the work, but, after seeing Sir Charles Metcalfe on the subject, I agreed to send out an expedition to start the work. It was under the charge of Mr. Frank Grove, who had previously been in Tasmania for my firm. This party carried out a certain amount of work on the railway, and later on we built a very handsome bridge over the Catumbella River, about eight miles along the coast in the direction of Benguella. The bridge consists of a single span about two hundred and forty feet in length. After a time financial difficulties intervened and the work had to be stopped. My friends did not then see their way to undertake the financing of the project on a large scale, and Mr. Williams made an arrangement with a group in the City of London to find some money in return for which they obtained a contract to build a portion of the contemplated line on the basis of actual cost plus a percentage. Work was thus resumed, and although I had for the moment no personal interest in it, the real supervision was, I believe, in the hands of former members of my staff. When the contractor had built something less than a hundred miles the railway company had apparently come to the conclusion that the cost was excessive, for Mr. Williams came to see me on the subject and as the result of our conversation, the contract was shortly afterwards determined. The resumption of the work was then offered to me and I accepted it on terms more favourable to the company than those of the contractor whose services had been terminated. Since then, subject to intermissions owing to financial difficulties, we have continued to build the railway and were engaged on it until after the commencement of the War, by which time the railhead had reached a point five hundred and twenty kilometres from Lobito. When the War is over I have every confidence that the finance will be arranged, and that the extension to the border of the Belgian Congo, about five hundred miles, will soon be built.[1] Meanwhile, the Belgians will doubtless make a strong effort to carry a branch from their main line to link up with the Benguella line as soon as it reaches their territory.

The Angola Province is well worth opening up by railways. There is a large area of very fertile land, thickly populated in places, and quite enough traffic in the Province itself to warrant the construction of the Benguella Railway, and when the Belgian Congo portion

[1] This has since been arranged.—ED.

of the line is built, thus bringing Lobito Bay into railway communication with the great mineral wealth of Katanga, the Benguella Railway should prove as paying a concern as any other in Africa. It should also have the effect of reducing the cost of copper production by many pounds per ton. Moreover, it will provide the shortest route from England to Rhodesia and Johannesburg, and although I do not think it will become a favourite route for general traffic, it will certainly carry considerable quantities of high-class goods, where the matter of a slight increase in freight will not be of so much importance as speedy transit. A large number of passengers, too, who have leisure and may be desirous of seeing much of Africa, including the Victoria Falls, will, in all probability, avail themselves of the Lobito Bay route.

LVIII

Wasted Efforts

IN such a business as mine it is constantly necessary to be expending time and money in examining projects which, from competition or for other reasons, do not fructify. In my time I have had submitted to me schemes for work in nearly every country in the world—from Alaska to New Zealand, from Manchuria to Peru. In practice only a very small percentage of such schemes materialize, and I am satisfied that if I had at my disposal the aggregate expenditure that my firm, during the quarter of a century that it has been in existence, has incurred in the process of inquiry into the propositions that have been submitted to it, I should be enjoying not merely a comfortable, but an opulent, income. To illustrate my point it is necessary to refer to only one or two examples.

As the first I may mention the Great Western Railway of Tasmania. It was, as far as I can remember, a proposition for a line of about a hundred and fifty miles in length. I sent out Mr. Frank Grove, an engineer in whom I had the utmost confidence, to make the necessary surveys. This was duly accomplished and for a time there appeared excellent prospects of the scheme being adopted. It could not, however, be financed and we ultimately lost the money we had spent, and I sacrificed the time and trouble I had taken in looking into it. Had this railway been built it would have involved an expenditure of several millions sterling, and would have proved of very great benefit to Tasmania. Some day I hope it will be built, as the country is in great need of it, and it will provide the Mount Lyell copper mines and a huge tract of country in the northern half of the island with access to Hobart Town, which is the best port in the island.

As another indication of misdirected effort I should like to cite the case of the Uganda Railway, particularly because it brings into prominence the relative merits, as applied to Government work, of departmental methods compared with the system of letting out work to contractors. At a very early period in the history of British East Africa I had approached the British Government for a concession to build the railway from Mombasa to Lake Victoria Nyanza. On the 8th of April 1895, in conjunction with our bankers, Messrs. Erlangers, we made an offer to construct and equip a line of six hundred and fifty-seven miles in accordance with a report, which had been submitted to both Houses of Parliament in 1893, against a cash payment of £2,240,000, equal to an average of £3,409 per mile, and we undertook to complete the work within four years. To this offer we received no official reply. In August of the same year there was published as a Parliamentary paper the report of a committee who had been appointed to consider the question of railway communication with Uganda. The net result of the report was that modifications were suggested which, it was anticipated, would reduce the cost of the railway from £2,240,000 to £1,755,000, or £2,700 per mile. This pious effort towards economy does not appear to have been effective, for on the 25th of June 1900 an Act to provide further money for the Uganda Railway was promulgated and included the following provision:

"The Uganda Railway Act 1896 shall have effect as if four million nine hundred and thirty thousand pounds were substituted for three million pounds."

The net result was that the line cost about £10,000 a mile against the £3,409 for which my firm had offered to build it, and the actual work took several more years than the period within which we had undertaken to complete it.

The only conclusion I can come to is that the engineering advisers to the Government were against us and, unfortunately for the interests of the British Empire in general, and British East Africa in particular, the advice of the engineers was taken. Instead of building a railway of three-feet six-inch gauge (the same as the railways of British South Africa), a metre gauge was decided upon. The work was placed in charge of engineers who had little or no experience of Africa, but who had acquired an engineering reputation in India; and British East Africa was saddled with a railway of metre gauge, which cost nearly three times as much as it ought to have done. It must also be borne in mind that when we offered to do this work we volunteered to put up any security that might be demanded to ensure that we would carry out the contract.

We had a somewhat similar experience in connection with West Africa. In 1901 I sent out to the Gold Coast two very capable engineers, and on the information obtained through their investigation we made a firm offer to the Colonial Office to build the line from Tarkwa to Kumassi—an estimated distance of about a hundred and forty miles—for the sum of £6,650 per mile, complete, including survey and rolling stock. Our offer was refused on the ground that the arrangements for the construction of the railway by the Gold Coast Government were so far advanced that it was not possible to consider any alternative proposal. The Gold Coast Railways have, I believe, cost at least £10,000 a mile.

Reference was made in Parliament to our offer and my firm had the honour of being mentioned in a Blue Book issued in 1904 and entitled " Papers relating to the Construction of Railways in Sierra Leone, Lagos, and the Gold Coast." This book constituted in reality an attempt to justify the departmental as against the contract method of carrying out public works. I do not intend to refute its specious arguments here, preferring to point out that inefficiency on the part of an employee under the contract system is generally punished with what is known in plebeian circles as "the sack," while similar inefficiency under the departmental system is not infrequently rewarded with a knighthood or a baronetcy. On one occasion I went to see the late Mr. Joseph Chamberlain regarding some of these railways, and he promised to do what he could to get any offer I might make fair consideration, but his permanent officials were, I think, too strong for him.

In all my experience, whenever I have tried to obtain work from any office connected with the British Government, I have always been blocked by the same departmental system. I do not for a moment insinuate that there exists anything in the nature of corruption. It is, in my opinion, simply a form of jealousy on the part of the officials and a desire to have at their disposal a large amount of patronage in the shape of dispensing appointments and placing orders.

There was one other work, which I have always regretted was not entrusted to us, and for our failure to obtain it I am entirely to blame. That was the construction of the Simonstown Docks in the Cape Peninsula. The tender was prepared in 1901 while my cousin Harold was still alive. Its preparation had been entrusted to him and, of course, he had the assistance of several capable and trusted servants of the company. When it was completed and referred to me I was apparently in a "funky" mood, for I added a very considerable sum to its amount. The effect of my action was to increase our price above that of Sir John Jackson's firm, whose tender was in consequence accepted. It was an unfortunate mistake on my part, because with our exceptional knowledge of the Cape I am confident that we should have carried out the work cheaper than any other contractor could have done, and the experience thus gained would, in all probability, have provided us with a favourable opening for obtaining other maritime work for the Imperial Government.

LIX

China

THERE is no country in connection with which Pauling and Company, Limited, have devoted so much time and spent so much money with less return than China. For twenty years we have been struggling to obtain an opening in that country. From time to time we have obtained contracts more or less definitive, but with one exception these have all fallen through, chiefly because of international complications, and the jealousy with which some other powers have regarded the prospects of British contractors obtaining a footing in the land of the celestials. And, even in the case of the exception, as the contract was executed only the month before the War broke out, years may elapse before it becomes operative.

So far back as 1898 we were in negotiation for a contract for the construction of a railway from Shanghai to Nanking. Mr. James Butler was then sent out to China to investigate local conditions, obtain prices, and make all the usual preliminary enquiries. At one time we were very sanguine about obtaining the work, but, notwithstanding great efforts on our part, it was not entrusted to us. We had a somewhat similar experience in regard to the lines from Hankow to Canton and from Canton to Kowloon.

Other engineers followed Mr. Butler. Lawley was on his way to China, travelling by the Trans-Siberia Railway, when the Russo-Japanese war broke out, but, after getting as far on his journey as Lake Baikal, he was forced to return.

After seven or eight years of fruitless effort we came to the conclusion that, in addition to our engineering staff, we ought to be represented in the Far East by a diplomatic agent and, on my recommendation, the post was offered to the Right Honourable Lord ffrench, with whom, years previously, I had become acquainted in South Africa, and of whose capabilities I had formed a high opinion. The appointment was soon justified, for in a comparatively short period we obtained contracts for railway extensions in North China. These, however, were never ratified owing, I believe, to the attitude taken up by Japan who, in certain parts of China, has consistently opposed the introduction of any foreign interests other than her own.

We carried out some survey work in the province of Anhui, and also in that of Kwangsi. The object of these surveys was really to obtain sufficient information to enable us to submit definitive offers for construction; and the Anhui survey is of unique interest to us, inasmuch as it is the only work we have carried out in China for which, up to the present, we have been paid.

For some time several of the larger nations of the world had been vying with each other in seeking to obtain commercial, if not territorial, supremacy in different parts of the Chinese Empire. About the year 1909 Lord ffrench got into touch with the late Mr. Willard D. Straight, who represented a very large and influential group of American financiers, and between them they succeeded in securing a contract for a line from Chinchowfu, on the line from Pekin to Hsinminfu, in a northern direction *via* Tsitsihar to Aigun, which is situated on the Amur River, not far from Blagoveschensk—a total distance of about seven hundred miles. The preliminary agreement, which was signed by the Viceroy of Manchuria and the Governor of Fiengtien on behalf of the Manchurian Administration, was ratified by Imperial edict in January 1910. In April of the same year Mr. Straight, on behalf of his group, accepted the loan agreement, and in the following month we concluded our construction contract with the Manchurian Administration. The Russian Government, however, intervened and informed the Chinese Government that they objected to the construction of such a railway. Japan also notified China that if the line was to be built she would want such participation as might be agreed upon by the interested parties, and also that she would require China to construct a branch line between the Chinchow-Aigun Railway and the South Manchurian Railway, which is under Japanese control. In the end, after much international negotiation, the opposition was apparently so strong that the Chinese Imperial Government failed to ratify the detailed loan and construction contracts.

When Dr. Sun Yat Sen became interested in the railway development of China he was very actively supported by Mr. George Bronson Rea, who is, I believe, proprietor and publisher of the "Far Eastern Review." Mr. Rea spent much of his time in Europe and in the United States, and I had many interviews with him when he was in this country. The net result was that Lord ffrench, on our behalf, entered into a preliminary agreement with the China International Railway Corporation for the finance and construction of a line of railway from Canton to Chun King with an extension to Lanchow. This was one of the chief arteries in Mr. Rea's grand project for the opening up of China by railway development. After we had obtained our preliminary agreement the revolution broke out in China, and the powers which had been given to Dr. Sun Yat Sen were revoked by the Chinese Government. Negotiations with them were continued by Lord ffrench with a view to obtaining the ratification of the Canton-Chun King contract, but the Chinese, for some reason, proposed to substitute for that contract one for building

THE FRONT HALL, THE LODGE, AT EFFINGHAM, SURREY, BUILT BY GEORGE PAULING IN THE EARLY 1900's.

MR. AND MRS. PAULING AND ELDER DAUGHTER DOLORES IN 1910.

Lonavla Jany 24/13

I am going back to Mummy Saturday

My darling Dolores

Just a short note for you & Jane; I know Mummy writes the long ones. Mummy came up here with me last Monday & went back to Bombay today Thursday. This is the place where we are doing a lot of work, building very big Masonry dams or walls to hold up immense lakes of water behind them; then the water is let out thro' very large pipes falling down almost perpendicularly for nearly 2000 ft. this gives an enormous power, which is turned into Electric power, & taken along wires 80 miles to the Cotton mills in Bombay where it works the machinery to spin the cotton into

LETTER WRITTEN BY GEORGE PAULING TO HIS YOUNG DAUGHTERS DOLORES AND JANE WHILST ON CONSTRUCTION IN INDIA.

x x x x x x x x x x x x x x x x x x x x x x x x x x x

all kinds of cotton goods; when
you grow a bit more you will
understand all this & I am sure
be very interested. Yesterday we
went to a place called Shiranta
about 15 miles away where we
are building another big dam. There
are about 8000 men & 2000 women
& children working; all black
people; the women & children carry
earth & stones in baskets on their
heads, very hard work but they
are accustomed to it — & it does
not hurt them, but enables them
to earn money & buy food. I
am busy here with Mr Ormsby & the
Engineers; looking into every thing so
I may be satisfied that all is going
well, & that I may make also some
money to keep things going at Sydney home.
I want you to give Jane a good kiss
for me & when I come back I will repay

it to you. I know you will have been a good girl. Many Ronnie Hilda & Dolly from me
& give Jason lots of love. Best love to you & Jane from Daddy x x x x x x x x x x x x x x x x x x x x x

WALWHAN DAM WITH TEMPORARY BUND AT VALVE CHAMBERS ON THE TATA HYDRO-ELECTRIC POWER SCHEME IN INDIA

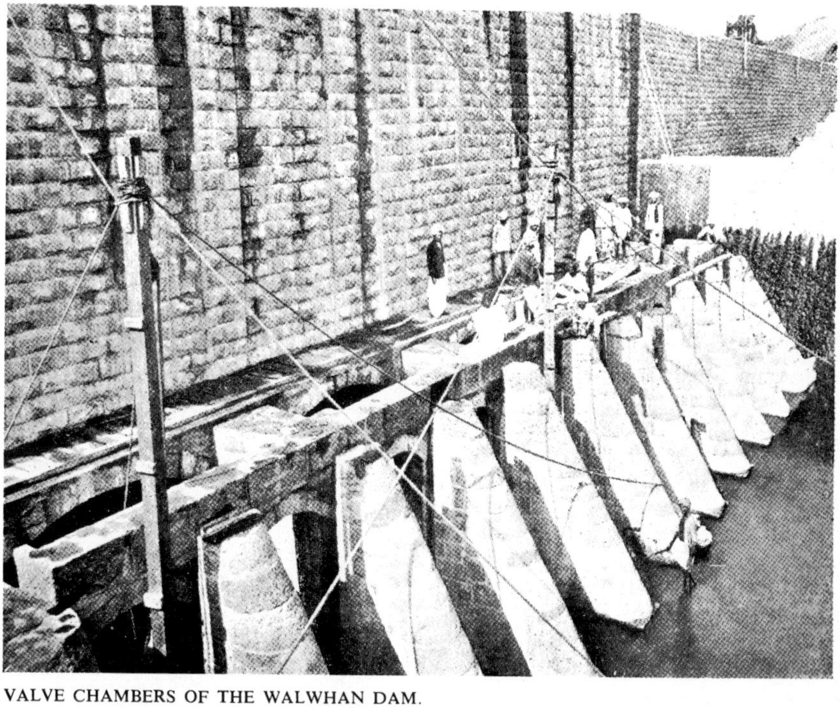

VALVE CHAMBERS OF THE WALWHAN DAM.

a line from a point on the Yangtsze River opposite Shasi, in the province of Hupeh, *via* Changteh and Yuanchow in the province of Hunan, and Kweiyang in the province of Kweichow to Singyifu in the same province. In addition to this main line there was to be a branch from Changteh to Changsha, the capital of the Hunan Province. Such a railway, when, sooner or later, it must be constructed, will extend to over eight hundred miles and will open up a vast track of country, the wealth of which has so far remained untold and untapped. I arranged to send out, under the charge of Mr. H. C. Carter, a survey party which, frequently under conditions of extreme difficulty, traversed the whole distance. From the many excellent photographs taken by Mr. Carter the line, when it is built, will pass through scenery which can hardly be surpassed in its beauty and magnificence. The country is little known to Europeans, and with the advent of the railway new fields will be opened up to British enterprise.

Before the reconnaissance survey was completed we had obtained our definitive contract, duly ratified by the Chinese Government and recognized by the British Foreign Office. It was a hard fight, so much so that Sir John Jordan, who was then the British minister at Peking, wrote to Lord ffrench on the 27th of July 1914 as follows:

"Let me congratulate you very heartily on the completion of your very arduous task. It must be a great relief to have it all behind you and to have really reached a practical agreement at last. Let us hope that in years to come the Shasi-Singyi Railway will prove a success proportionate to the efforts which it has cost to obtain the concession."

A week later the Great War broke out, and the contract, in all its oriental splendour of massive seals and many-coloured ribbons, has since reposed in our office safe.

Q

During the twenty years we have been striving to get work in China it has cost us something like £60,000 with practically no return. But contractors are patient people, and we still wait, even if we do not see.

LX

INDIA

ALTHOUGH in preceding years I had made several minor excursions outside the realms of railway construction, it is only within the last decade that my firm have been carrying out extraneous work on a very large scale. I refer particularly to the Tata Hydro-Electric project in the Bombay Presidency.

The first conception of the idea of conserving water among the Western Ghats during the monsoons so that it might be used for the purpose of generating electricity to create driving power for the numerous industrial concerns in Bombay has been claimed by several people, but I believe it is generally attributed to a Bombay architect, the late Mr. David Gosling. That gentleman appears to have realized the enormous potentialities of the natural conditions existing in the Ghats for the development of his grand idea. The peculiar formation of the mountains is of such a character that there exist at a very considerable altitude several valleys, each with a large catchment area, and Mr. Gosling's basic idea was to construct dams at the outlets of these valleys and thereby to create enormous artificial lakes, the waters of which could be conveyed through pipes on a steep gradient to a much lower level at which the necessary generating station would be provided. Mr. Gosling prepared a preliminary scheme, and efforts were made to finance the project in England. These efforts were not altogether successful, and ultimately the business passed into the hands of one of the wealthiest and most enterprising firms in India, Messrs. Tata.

They invited Messrs. Alfred Dickinson and Company, the well-known engineers, to look into Mr. Gosling's scheme. Messrs. Dickinson engaged the late Mr. R. B. Joyner, a distinguished engineer with extensive Indian experience, who specialized in the particular class of work for which he had been engaged, and who went out in 1905 to investigate the matter. The result of his visit was that a much larger project than had been contemplated by Mr. Gosling was devised.

It was some time in the year 1906 that the possibility of obtaining contracts for the construction of these dams was first suggested to me, and in the following year I deputed one of our engineers, Mr. O. C. Ormsby, to visit the site of the proposed works, so that he might make himself acquainted with the local conditions, ascertain the cost of labour, and gain such other information as might be requisite to enable us to submit a reasonable tender for the work. The project, as developed, included the creation and harnessing of three lakes, viz., Lonavla, Walwhan, and Shirawta. The usual delays, inevitable in the exploitation of any outstanding idea, occurred, and it was not till the year 1911 that we entered into our first contract with the Tata Hydro Electric Power Company, Limited. That contract was for the erection of dams necessary to create the Lonavla and Walwhan lakes, with an infinite variety of subsidiary works. It also included a provision, by which we secured an option on the construction of the Shirawta Dam, which we duly exercised, and which was embodied in a second contract entered into in 1913. The works under the first contract are now finished, while those under the second are approaching completion.[1]

I appointed Mr. O. C. Ormsby to the office of our resident agent on the works; and my cousin, Mr. Percy Pauling, has on several occasions made extended

[1] These have since been completed.—ED.

visits to Bombay. I have been there but once while the construction has been in progress. This was early in 1913, and although at that time relatively little work had been done, I saw enough, with the knowledge I had previously acquired through studying the subject, to be greatly impressed with the magnitude and importance of the idea. The whole scheme has been conceived in a commanding and daring fashion and reflects the greatest credit on all who have been connected with its authorship and, if I may so suggest, its execution.

In a paper which Mr. Dickinson read before the Institution of Electrical Engineers in April 1915, he gave, amongst much other interesting information, the following particulars relating to the three lakes:

Name of Lake.	Height of dams in feet.	Length of dams in feet.	Surface acreage of lakes.	Water stored, millions of cubic feet.
Lonavla	19	5,500	986	361
Walwhan . . .	54	4,500	1,535	2,560
Shirawta . . .	74	8,000	3,174	6,963

The details of this interesting work are sufficient to fill a volume by themselves, and indeed much has already been written of them, but it may not be out of place to reiterate some of the salient features as set forth by the consulting engineers. From the lakes where the water is collected, and which, when all are completed, will hold 6,580,000,000,000 gallons, it is conveyed by means of canals to the forebay, which is of the nature of a reservoir. From the forebay to the generation station is a distance of some thirteen thousand feet, within which the variation in altitude extends to seventeen hundred and twenty-five feet. Although we were not concerned with the electrical section of the scheme, it is interesting to note that after the electricity is generated at the power station, it is conveyed by an overhead transmission line to the receiving station at Bombay, between forty and fifty miles away. At the receiving station it is distributed and transmitted to the consumers, which consist for the most part of cotton mills.

In addition to these dams we have had to construct ducts, tunnels, weirs, pipe lines, and all the other necessary work involved in such a gigantic undertaking. The figures quoted can scarcely be expected to convey, particularly to the lay mind, any adequate idea of the volume of the work. Shirawta Dam alone, if it does not dwarf the Assouan Dam, which in its day was so much advertised as an outstanding engineering feat, makes it small by comparison. More than three hundred yards longer and quite twenty feet higher, if it were possible to superimpose the Shirawta Dam over that of Assouan the latter would be completely lost to view.

When the work is completed and the three lakes are full the combined surface of water will extend to about five thousand seven hundred acres, or about the equivalent of a lake nine miles long by one mile wide. The total quantity of rubble masonry in the three dams and in subsidiary works, is considerably over a million cubic yards. It is scarcely to be wondered that before the last stone is laid the work will have been in progress for something like nine years.

While these works were being carried out, Mr. Ormsby learned that in connection with the quadrupling of a portion of the Great Indian Peninsula Railway between Bombay and Kalyan, the engineers had decided to make a cut off by constructing a tunnel through the mountains about twenty miles from Bombay. Mr. Ormsby sent home all the particulars and we obtained the contract. The tunnel is nearly a mile in length, and its construction involved the removal of over five hundred cubic feet of material, chiefly rock, per lineal foot. The work was commenced in 1913 and completed in 1916.

I am not quite certain whether our first Indian

exploits will be remunerative, but they certainly have made great additions to our education and experience, which I have no doubt will prove of advantage to us in the future, not only in India, but in other parts of the world.

LXI

East and Central Africa

As an illustration of the lack of British enterprise in speedily developing one of the world's great natural resources within the boundaries of the Empire, I cannot think of any better example than that of the Magadi Soda Lake in East Africa. It will soon be twenty years since that lake was discovered by the great scout and explorer, the late Major Burnham, and for at least ten years such a valuable property lay untapped. One cannot help reflecting that if the lake had been within, instead of a few miles outside, German territory, its produce would have been placed on the markets of the world within a few years. Situated less than a hundred miles from the nearest point on the Uganda Railway, it has a superficial area of over thirty square miles. It has been estimated to contain from forty to fifty millions of tons of crude soda, and, although I have never visited it, I am given to understand that as the crust containing the soda is removed, fresh soda forms rapidly like ice on the surface of the lake, so that the supply may be regarded as practically unlimited. Major Burnham was sent out by an exploring company called the East African Syndicate, Limited, in which I had a financial interest. Shortly after the discovery was made, other representatives of the same syndicate were despatched to survey the country, particularly with the object of ascertaining a feasible route over which a railway might be constructed from the lake to the Uganda main line. The Government were approached to provide financial assistance, it having been recognized that the marketing of such a valuable product as soda would be instrumental in benefiting the East African Protectorate, and in bringing very needful grist to swell the receipts of the Uganda Railway. But the mills of Government, except when they are grinding taxpayers, grind slowly, and the representations of the East African Syndicate were pigeon-holed. To record the history of the Magadi Soda Lake and of its opening up as a commercial proposition would waste more space and take up more of my time than I can well afford. Suffice it to say that so far as my firm are concerned we sent out two expeditions to survey and report. The first, under one of my most trusted henchmen, Mr. H. C. Carter, supported by Mr. Walter Sweetman, reached East Africa in 1905. Then, as now, big game was probably more abundant there than in any other country in the world. There is a tradition that after the Uganda Railway was built it was no uncommon occurrence for a stationmaster at one station to telephone instructions to his colleague at the next to make the next train a non-stop as several lions had taken possession of his platforms, and the staff, for self-preservation, had been forced to go into hiding. In such circumstances it was, of course, necessary that our engineers should be well armed. Mr. Carter, usually the most level-headed of men, apparently suffered from a lapse of shrewdness, for he entrusted a native with a loaded rifle. This is a primitive way of courting disaster, and Mr. Carter promptly got the contents of a double-barrelled .500 cordite express rifle—which, by the way, was intended for a rhinoceros close at hand—just above the ankle, and, instead of going over the ground between the Uganda Railway and the Soda Lake, he enjoyed a forced retirement for several months in the Nairobi hospital. Mr. Sweetman deputized and reported in due course. A year or more afterwards I sent out Mr. O. C. Ormsby, who made an independent investigation which confirmed that the most serious matter to be contended with in the construction of the railway would be the absence of permanent water along the line of route.

From these investigations nothing resulted. For a few years the matter remained more or less dormant until, in the year 1911, the Magadi Soda Company, Limited, was formed and acquired a ninety-nine years' lease of the area containing the soda deposit. That company also obtained power to build the connecting railway and to construct a pier at Kilindini to facilitate the export of the product. By that time the Government had realized the importance of Major Burnham's discovery; surveys were made on behalf of the Crown Agents for the Colonies; and competitive tenders were invited to build the railway and to carry out the other essential works. Possibly because of the knowledge we had gained through our previous missions to East Africa we were successful in obtaining the contract. I placed Mr. E. W. Hickes in charge of the work which, owing to landing and transport difficulties, scarcity of water, and other circumstances, took longer to complete than we had expected. All the materials for nearly a hundred miles of railway had to be landed at Kilindini and conveyed over the Uganda Railway to a point about two hundred and eighty miles from the sea; and so serious was the water problem that we had to send out no less than ninety miles of piping. The War had broken out before we were able to hand over the line, which was done in sections, the last of which was not delivered up until towards the end of 1915. As Lake Magadi is in close proximity to German East Africa the new railway is well within the war zone, and special precautions had to be taken to protect the works. Numerous attempts to damage them were made by the Germans, both during and since the period of construction, but with no great degree of success; and I fancy that the existence of the line has been of great assistance to our military authorities.

The War has naturally hindered the exploitation of the lake, but the existence of the soda in almost incalculable quantities, and the fact that it can be placed on the markets of the world at competitive figures, have been established. It cannot be long before Magadi becomes one of the greatest assets of the colony.

With regard to Central Africa, I had hopes at one time that the construction of the Shiré Highlands Railway from Port Herold to Blantyre might be entrusted to my firm. It was, however, built departmentally. After it had been in existence for some years it was realized that owing to the extreme difficulty with which in the dry season river steamers were able to get up the Shiré as far as Port Herold it would be advisable to extend the line to a point on the River Zambesi, where the latter was easily navigable to the sea. The whole cotton and tobacco exports of the country were being held up at Port Herold and a fresh outlet became imperative. The necessary concessions were obtained, partly from the Portuguese Government, and partly from the Government of Nyassaland Protectorate—as the route passes through both territories—by the Central African Railway Company, Limited, and in the year 1913 we entered into a contract with them to build the line from Chindio, the point which had been selected on the Zambesi, to Port Herold. The length of the line was only about sixty miles, but the construction took nearly two years to complete, chiefly owing to the difficulty of transport up the Zambesi River and the necessity of re-handling the railway material when the Ziwe Ziwe River, an important tributary of the Zambesi, was in flood. Mr. Lawley was the agent in charge of this work, and his chief assistants were Messrs. E. R. Marsland and W. H. Fretton. To indicate the difficulties we have to contend with in opening up new territories through the civilizing influence of the "iron horse," I might mention that in this case all the materials, rails, sleepers, bridgework, plant, and the multifarious other things essential to the completion of a railway were shipped from England to Beira, where they had to be transhipped into sea-going barges. These were towed to Chinde, at the mouth of the Zambesi, a distance of a hundred and fifty miles. At Chinde everything had to be reloaded into river barges and conveyed to Chindio, which is about a hundred miles up the river. Discharged there, they were loaded into trucks and taken on to the "end of steel" as the construction proceeded. Twenty-three miles north of Chindio the line reached the Ziwe Ziwe River, which had to be negotiated by a steel screw pile bridge, consisting of thirty-three spans of fifty-six feet each. The erection of the bridge took about twelve months to complete, and during that period Lawley was pushing on with the work on the north side of the river. In the dry season a temporary line was laid across its bed for the purpose of transporting material, but during the rainy season double re-handling had to take place, inasmuch as such materials had again to be placed in barges by which they were taken across the river, where they were transferred to trucks so that they might be taken to railhead. The construction of this bridge was of an exceptionally difficult character because of the sandy nature of the river bed.

The railway was completed in 1915, when a through connection was established between Port Herold and Blantyre. This, however, is only a section of a main artery which, before the whole of the Nyassaland Protectorate can be properly exploited, will involve the linking up of Beira with the Zambesi at a point somewhere opposite Chindio[1]; the construction of a bridge across the river, which, in itself, will be no mean engineering undertaking; and the extension of the existing line beyond Blantyre to the southern extremity of Lake Nyassa. When these works materialize I hope

[1] This section has now been completed.—Ed.

that Pauling and Company, Limited, will be there to continue their pioneer work in that part of the world.

Another East African project in which my firm are interested has for its object the linking up of Lake Nyassa by railway to a point on the Indian Ocean. In this case the proposed outlet is at Port Amelia on Pemba Bay in Portuguese East Africa. The bay consists of a land-locked area extending to some forty square miles, and is reputed to be not only one of the finest shipping havens in Africa, but amongst the largest natural harbours in the world.

In 1912 we entered into an agreement with the Compagnia do Nyassa, by whom a large territory in Portuguese East Africa is administered, to make a survey of the suggested line. A party under the charge of Mr. C. F. Tristram was sent out, and it took them about six months to do the work. When the railway is constructed it will be well over five hundred miles in length, and although the country through which it will pass is somewhat handicapped owing to the scarcity of water, it is, in parts, very fertile. There are few areas in Africa where so little development work has been done, but from the little exploration that has already taken place the country is believed to have enormous potentialities from a mineral as well as from an agricultural point of view. As in so many other cases, the War has hindered its exploitation by nearly a decade, but I have every confidence that ere many years have passed, as has been so rapidly accomplished in many other parts of Africa, the civilizing influence of railway construction will render the term "dark" no longer applicable to that part of the continent.

LXII

Au Revoir

HERE—for a time at least—I must bring my story to an end. In 1915, the War having put a stop to other forms of contract, I contracted appendicitis. The surgeons of to-day assure us that the removal of the appendix is simplicity itself. With some people it may be so, but in my case it was a deep level proposition, so much so that eighteen months elapsed before the wound healed. During the greater part of that period an effective brake was applied to my industrious disposition, while the War itself had a similar influence on the affairs of Pauling and Company, Limited. Apart from exercising a supervision over the construction of several magazines and other war buildings at home, and being associated with others in building a portion of the Murman Railway in Northern Russia, we have done little or no work of military importance. Most of our men are earning, if they do not win, distinction in some or other of the theatres of war. A few will never come back, but I hope that the majority will be spared, and that when the awful carnage comes to an end, they may be restored to us unbroken, when, united once more, we may resume where we left off, and continue to be of some use in opening up the unexplored parts of the earth.

Although I commenced the writing of this book with much misgiving, it has proved such a real pleasure, that I am loth to end it. I think it was Gibbon who, when he completed his "Decline and Fall of the Roman Empire," said that he felt he had parted with an old friend. So, in a smaller degree, is it with me. Through a kindly memory I have lived again in a few brief months all those laborious years, with their triumphs and their failures, revelling in the former, and all but oblivious to the latter.

As I began, so should I like to end. In such a career as mine it is in the nature of things that my interests must often have conflicted with those of others, and conflicting interests not infrequently beget enmity. If I have set down anything in these pages that may appear to savour of animosity, it has been unintentional. Possibly, having throughout my life been a man of action, with few pretensions to literary ability, I may not have expressed myself with sufficient or appropriate emphasis on that point. But, so far as I am concerned, the dead past has long since buried its dead, and I trust that the obsequies have been respected by my quondam foes as by myself.

It would be false modesty to assume that, judged by human standards, I have not attained to some degree of success in life. That I attribute to a great extent to a powerful physique combined with an inordinate capacity for hard work. For such gifts I hope I have been sufficiently grateful. But such success as has come my way could never have been achieved without the fidelity and the loyalty of so many people who, at one time or other, have supported me in my many interests, of which the greatest has been that of Pauling and Company, Limited. Chief amongst these I must account my only brother. Our lives were so wrapt up in each other, our interests were so common, and our mutual affection—I might almost say devotion—was so intense, that we might have been the literal incarnation of the poet's idea:

> Two souls with but a single thought.

Harry's death robbed me of a large slice of the joy of life. Many others, too, of whom I would particularly mention my cousin Harold, have crossed the bourne, but happily there still remains a considerable number of the old brigade. Amongst these are Mr. Edwin Elliott, one of my earliest contracting mentors, who continues to carry on business for himself[1]; Mr. James Butler who, in disagreement as in unison, has always remained amongst my greatest friends; Mr. A. L. Lawley, one of the most forceful personalities I have met, ever ready at a moment's notice to proceed to any accessible part of the globe; and Mr. John Scott, a faithful friend and servant, who has long exercised a supervising eye over my material and moral welfare. Of a slightly later generation I might mention Mr. C. V. Buchan, Mr. H. C. Carter, Mr. O. C. Ormsby, Mr. F. O. Stephens, Mr. P. W. Hull, Mr. E. W. Hickes, Mr. C. F. Tristram, and my cousins, Messrs. Willie and Percy Pauling, all of whom have been active helpers in furthering the affairs of Pauling and Company, Limited.

Without the consistent and able co-operation and support of these and many others I might have reached some degree of prosperity, but my firm could never have attained to its present high standard of success.

Nor can I conclude without reiterating the value of my connection with the house of Erlanger. I can never forget the kindness and the sympathy of the late Baron. A man amongst men, he helped me greatly to lay the foundations of my ultimate fortune, and since his death his sons have constantly held out to me a guiding hand along the pathway to financial success.

To all these I desire to express my deep sense of gratitude. In my friends, as in my servants, I have been particularly fortunate, and to such of them as may take the trouble to read these reminiscences I wave a cheerful and a genial *au revoir*.

[1] Mr. Elliott has died since these Memoirs were written.—Ed.

CHISWICK PRESS: CHARLES WHITTINGHAM AND GRIGGS (PRINTERS), LTD.
TOOKS COURT, CHANCERY LANE, LONDON.

SURVEY CAMP AT YUANCHOW ON CHINA'S SHASI–SINGYIFU RAILWAY.

MAGADI PIER IN KILINDINI HARBOUR UNDER CONSTRUCTION.

DREDGING THE FOUNDATIONS FOR THE WALL OF THE EXTENSIVE WORKS UNDER-TAKEN AT KILINDINI HARBOUR.

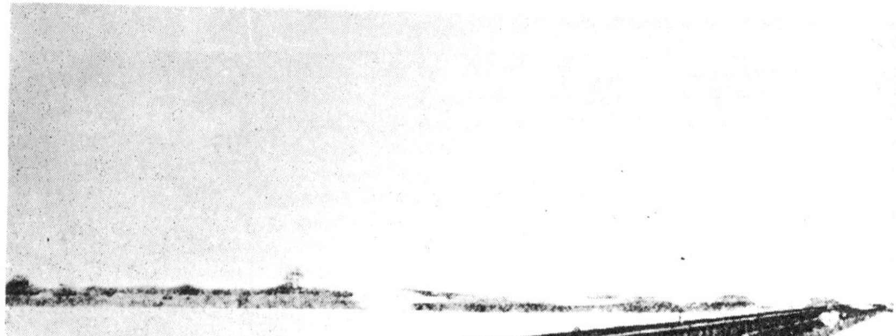

THE ZIWE ZIWE BRIDGE OVER A TRIBUTARY OF THE ZAMBESI RIVER ON THE CENTRAL AFRICAN RAILWAY. A SCREW-PILE STRUCTURE OF 33–56 FT. SPANS.

APPENDIXES

TO THE

RHODESIANA REPRINT LIBRARY

EDITION

Bulawayo
April, 1969.

APPENDIX 1

Minutes of Meeting of Directors held at 19. St. Swithin's Lane, London. E.C. on Friday, the 28th July, 1893 at 4. p.m.

Present

Alfred Beit. Esq (in the Chair).
Rochfort Maguire. Esq M.P.
Thomas Shiels. Esq.

Mr Hawksley
Mr Canning

Registration of Company.

Mr Hawksley reported the Incorporation of the Company on the 24th May, 1893, with registered address 19, St Swithin's Lane E.C, and submitted a copy of the Memorandum and Articles of Association

Directors

The appointment of the following Directors by the signatories to the Memorandum of Association was reported:—

Honourable C.J. Rhodes. M.L.A
Alfred Beit, Esq.
Rochfort Maguire, Esq. M.P.
Thomas Shiels. Esq.

Minutes —— 28th July 1893 —— continued

Appointment of Officers.

The following appointments were now made:-

Secretary in England

Herbert Canning. Esq.

Secretary in South Africa

Dr. F. Rutherfoord Harris.

Bankers.

The Standard Bank of South Africa Ltd

Solicitors

Messrs. Hollams, Sons, Coward & Hawksley.

Agreement

The Agreement between the British South Africa Company and the Bechuanaland Railway Company Limited was submitted, approved and ordered to be sealed.

The Agreement with Mr. George Pauling of 26th May 1893 for the construction of the Railway to Mafeking, which had been signed by Mr. Rhodes on behalf of the Railway Company in Cape Town, was submitted and approved, and it was agreed that the guarantee by Messrs. Erlanger & Co. that Mr. Pauling would carry out his Contract should be accepted, their liability to be limited to £10,000 which was to run off as the — Retention Fund under the Contract was formed.

It was resolved that the British South Africa Company be requested to guarantee the performance by the Railway Company of its Contract with Mr. George Pauling; any sums paid under this guarantee to be deemed a payment pro tanto under Clause 4 of the Agreement between this Company and the British South Africa Company.

P.T.O

Minutes ——— 28th July 1893 ——— continued

Seal

The Secretary was authorised to obtain an Official Seal for the Company as well as the necessary books and papers.

Banking Account.

It was resolved that the Company's Bankers, the Standard Bank of South Africa, Limited, be requested to honour drafts upon the Company's account when signed by any two Directors & countersigned by the Secretary.

The Secretary was instructed to hand a copy of this Resolution to the Bankers, together with specimens of the Directors' signatures.

[illegible]

Facsimile from the Minute Book of
The Bechuanaland Railway Co. Ltd.

APPENDIX 2

Minutes of a Board Meeting held at 120 Bishopsgate Street E.C., on Friday the 7th August 1896 at 3 p.m.

Present

Alfred Beit Esq }
Rochfort Maguire Esq } Directors
Mr Canning Secretary

74 Extension of Railway to Bulawayo

With regard to the Extension of the Railway to Bulawayo it was resolved to accept the terms of Mr. H.C. Pauling's letter of the 7th August, the Contract not to be known until a reply had been received from the Cape Government to the Company's cable of even date: In accepting the terms of the said letter the Secretary was to point out to Mr Pauling that the present Debentures issued so far are not sufficient to pay for the whole contract but in case the additional funds required should not be raised in time to effect its completion, the Contractors are to have the right of stopping the ordering and supply of material as also the construction of the earth works for such portion of the line as the Company may not have sufficient funds to complete.

A Beit

Facsimile from the Minute Book of
The Bechuanaland Railway Co. Ltd.

APPENDIX 3

Minutes of a Special Board Meeting held at 15 St. Swithin's Lane. E.C. on Wednesday the 21st July 1897

Present.

George Cawston Esq. — In the Chair.
The Lord Lurgan.
F. Baring Gould Esq.
Major F. I. Ricarde Seaver, F.R.S. (Edin.)

Mr Hawksley — Solicitor
Mr Jones — Secretary.

Alfred Beit. Esq. and Sir Charles Metcalfe. Bart. also attended the Board.

13. **Minutes.**
The Minutes of a Board Meeting held on Monday the 17th May 1897 were read and confirmed.

14. **Proposal for Construction of Line from Umtali to Salisbury.**
The Secretary submitted a letter from the British South Africa Company enclosing letter from Messrs Pauling & Co. Ld. dated 20th July 1897 setting forth the terms and conditions on which they were prepared to construct the Railway from Umtali to Salisbury. The proposals contained in this letter were

Minutes 21st July 1897 Continued

discussed and it was decided not to consent to any alteration in the Share Capital of the Company. Subject to this it was — determined to inform the Chartered Company that this Company was prepared to accept in principle the proposals of Messrs Pauling & Co. Ld provided such consents as were necessary were obtained from the Beira Railway Company Limited and the Beira Junction Railway Company Limited, and that Messrs Pauling & Co Ld would come under terms to pay One hundred pounds (£100) per day penalty if the work was not completed within two years. All requisite documents to carry out these arrangements to be submitted to this Board.

Chairman

Facsimile from the Minute Book of
The Mashonaland Railway Co. Ltd.

APPENDIX 4

Umtali. 16th July 1900.

Mr Rhodes and Sir Charles Metcalfe recommend taking over from Messrs Pauling & Company, Limited, on behalf of the Mashonaland Railway Company, Limited, the ten stands at Umtali with the residence erected thereon for the sum of Five thousand pounds. which cost £9000

I recommend above.

C. J. Rhodes.

I agree to the above on behalf of Pauling & Co Ltd

A L Lawley

APPENDIX 5

AN INTERVIEW WITH MR. JOSEPH CHAMBERLAIN

(Unpublished chapter from Mr. George Pauling's original manuscript).

When Mr. Rhodes reached Bulawayo he went to stay with Lord Grey and Sir Charles Metcalfe at Government House, and I joined them there. The morning after my arrival I was up at about five o'clock and had a talk with Mr. Rhodes. During our conversation, as we walked up and down the verandah, he said very seriously:

"Now, Pauling, when you reach England, I would like you to go at once to Mr. Hawkesley (who was then Solicitor for the British South Africa Company). He will take you to see Mr. Chamberlain and the Duke of Devonshire, and I want you to tell them in your most emphatic language that if I am made to go to England now, whilst I am so absolutely necessary here for the welfare of Rhodesia, I shall open my mouth and tell all I know."

I said that I would do exactly as he had told me and that morning I left by special coach via Mafeking *en route* for England.

On my arrival in London my first visit was to Mr. Hawkesley. He made an appointment with Mr. Chamberlain and took me to the door of that Minister's private room in the House of Commons. When I entered the room Mr. Chamberlain was sitting at a small table and asked me to sit down opposite him. He then said:

"I understand you have a message to me from Mr. Rhodes." I replied:

"Yes, with your permission I will give you the message as nearly as possible in the words that Mr. Rhodes told it to me."

This I did, and Mr. Chamberlain, who was playing with a pen on a piece of blank paper, looked up at me and said very quietly:

"I wonder what he means."

I replied:

"If you do not know what he means it is not for me to suggest it to you, but I can tell you that he means what he says."

Mr. Chamberlain was silent for a few moments and then, looking towards me again, he continued:

"You can let Mr. Rhodes know that I will do all I can."

He then asked me some questions about South Africa generally, and amongst them he inquired whether I thought the Boers could be supplying rifles to the Matabele, since several rifles which had been captured were marked with the Transvaal Government stamp of Z.A.R.

I replied that he must not believe anything of that nature, as I was absolutely certain from my knowledge of the Boers, and my long residence in South Africa, that it was contrary to the principles of any Boer to arm the natives to fight against white people, or indeed to let them have guns at all.

Mr. Chamberlain did not appear satisfied. He banged his fist on the table and said:

"If I could only prove the Transvaal people were supplying arms to natives, I would have war with them tomorrow."

He then bade me "Good afternoon" and I left the room.

I may say that when I went in to deliver my message I had a sort of idea that it was possible I might get into trouble and be handed over to the police, although, of course, I could not quite see on what grounds this could be done.

Mr. Hawkesley was waiting for me in the corridor and the first thing he did was to ask me to repeat, as nearly as possible, the words of my interview. I did so and he took them down in a notebook. About two or three years afterwards Mr. Hawkesley came to me one day in my office in Westminster and said:

"Pauling, do you recollect the gist of your interview with Chamberlain, and will you repeat it to me?"

As I was complying with his request he compared what I said with what he had taken down at the time in the notebook, and informed me that the words were substantially the same. He then went on to say:

"Would you repeat this conversation in a law court if I asked you to?"

I replied:

"Certainly, I was not bound to any secrecy about it and if you think it necessary, I will repeat it."

He told me that Mr. Chamberlain had been very troublesome and that it might be necessary to take some action against him, in which event my evidence, as above, would be of service to him.

The day after I saw Mr. Chamberlain I went by appointment to meet the Duke of Devonshire at Devonshire House, Piccadilly, and, as requested by Mr. Rhodes, I repeated my message in practically the same words that I had used to Mr. Chamberlain. The Duke heard me, pondered for a few moments, and then said:

"Good morning, Mr. Pauling."

I returned the salutation and walked out, and shortly afterwards gave Mr. Hawkesley an account of the interview, the same as I had done in the case of Mr. Chamberlain.

Not long after my meeting with the latter, he made a speech in the House of Commons, very much in favour of Mr. Rhodes, which practically put a stop to the clamour to send him home at that particular time. What occurred at the ultimate inquiry about the Raid is a matter of public knowledge, but my reason for writing down what I have done here is that I consider both Mr. Rhodes and Dr. Jameson took upon their shoulders blame which others deserved, and I maintain that neither of them was responsible for the attempt to take the Transvaal in 1895.

Some time afterwards I travelled to England with Barney Barnato. I was very frank with him, and as he had rubbed me up the wrong way, I criticised him somewhat freely. His reply was significant:

"Well, Pauling, I own up to a lot of things, but I am not such a big robber as some of your friends are, because I have never tried to steal a country."

APPENDIX 6

26, VICTORIA STREET,
WESTMINSTER,
LONDON, S.W.

15th December 1925.

Dear Mrs. Booth,

As I, in my official capacity, had to sign a cheque the other day in favour of Constable's people, I gather that the publication of the Memoirs is about to be proceeded with.

I wrote you some little time ago on the subject of the Rhodes - Lawley episode, and in case the matter may mature suddenly I enclose:

A) The record of that episode as set forth in the MSS in Constable's custody.

B) The story as related by Mr. Lawley in a letter to me, but slightly modified by myself.

"B" being longer, seems to me to be more interesting, but I should like to know which you prefer. If Mr. Bland is to write an introduction it might be well to submit both versions to him.

I hope the strike will not prevent the publishers from getting a move on, particularly if it is still intended that the Book should be circulated on the 10th of February.

Trusting you are well, and with kind regards,

Yours sincerely,

David Buchan.

P.S. I hear Mr Lawley has just returned to England. DB.

APPENDIX 7

LAWLEY'S PERSONAL ACCOUNT OF HIS BRUSH WITH RHODES

(Original version "B" referred to in David Buchan's letter to Mrs. Booth—see also pages 161 and 162).

On one occasion during the building of the railway from Beira to Umtali, Lawley received instructions by telegraph to have a train at rail-head, then near Chimoia, on a particular date to convey Mr. Rhodes and Dr. Jameson, together with their party, to Fontes Villa. Platelaying had to be stopped and the train was ready at the appointed time. Mr. Rhodes was expected to arrive by coach from Rhodesia. A day passed, and, notwithstanding that runners were sent out, nothing was heard of the coach and party. On the following day there was still no news of the expected visitors. About nine o'clock in the morning of the third day the coach hove in sight and was drawn up near the train. Lawley was there, and Mr. Rhodes, after a general salutation, said:

"Are you Lawley?"

Lawley replied that he was, whereupon Mr. Rhodes commenced to swear and to abuse him in the presence not only of the visiting party, but of everyone, including about a thousand natives engaged at the platelaying camp. As was usual with Mr. Rhodes when he became excited or lost his temper his remarks were characterised by a gradual crescendo of unparliamentary language until he attained a high falsetto tone. As Lawley's instructions had been carried out to the letter, he was completely astounded, and for some time he listened in the hope of ascertaining the cause of the trouble. No explanation, however, was forthcoming, and, realising that he was being stultified in the presence of his subordinates, he lost his temper and opened fire by saying to Mr. Rhodes:

"Who the H—— are you, and who do you think you are talking to, squealing at me like a damned rabbit. Damn your eyes; I won't allow any man on earth to speak to me like that. Are you mad?" Then followed such a flood of railway vernacular as was the admiration of the assembly with the exception, perhaps, of Mr. Rhodes who was so astonished at Lawley's unexpected daring that he turned on his heels and walked away to a clump of trees about a hundred yards from the train. By this time Lawley was fairly "on his hind legs", and his men were standing around keenly awaiting developments. He gave orders for the luggage from the coach to be put on the train and notified all concerned that it was to leave in five minutes, and that all those who were not aboard could reach their destinations as they chose. Everyone at once boarded the train, except Rhodes and Jameson. The latter went to Lawley and asked what the trouble was between Rhodes and him. Lawley replied that he had not the faintest idea and told Jameson that if he wished Rhodes to travel by the train he had better get him into it immediately as the work had already been stopped for three days and he would not countenance any further delay. Jameson took the hint and Rhodes entered the train just in time—so much so that his carriage door was not closed when it moved off. About 20 miles down the line a stoppage was made to replenish the water supply, and Rhodes sent Jameson to Lawley with his compliments to ask if he would kindly go along to his compartment. Lawley did so, wondering what further trouble might be in store, but he found Mr. Rhodes quite changed. The latter expressed his deep regret at the occurrence, admitted that he was entirely in the wrong and deserved all that he had got, and invited Lawley to shake hands with him. Lawley, in accepting the invitation, explained that if he had not resented the attitude of Mr. Rhodes, his control over his men would have been gone.

From that day Rhodes and Lawley remained the best of friends. During his subsequent visits to the railways while they were under construction, Rhodes invariably accepted Lawley's hospitality, which was on several occasions reciprocated at Groot Schuur. Then the Chimoia incident became a standing joke and the usual salutation of the founder of Rhodesia was—

"Well, Lawley, old man, are we going to have another fight to-day?"

APPENDIX 8

Obituary

(From a contemporary London Newspaper).

Mr. George Pauling

Died 10th February, 1919.

Mr. George Pauling, the senior partner of the well-known contracting firm, Pauling and Co. (Ltd.), died at Effingham, on Monday, after a brief illness.

George Pauling was a very gifted and very lovable personality. He combined immense physical strength with qualities of mind of which perhaps exceptional commonsense, unusual power of penetration, and a keen sense of humour were the most remarkable. With them he was peculiarly well gifted to make his way in the new countries in which his work principally lay, and he made full use of them. He conveyed to all who met him a sense of power, physical and mental, and of abounding life, and the feeling that here indeed was a man. His father, a civil engineer in the service of the Indian Government, became incapacitated through illness when George Pauling was 14 years old; he had therefore to start to earn not only his own livelihood, but that of his mother, brother, and sisters at this very early age. He started at manual labour, and at 15 was apprenticed to the firm of Joseph Firbank and Co., with whom he remained several years.

In 1875 he and his younger brother Harry journeyed to South Africa, where they both entered the service of the Cape Government Railways as junior engineers. George Pauling very shortly afterwards struck out for himself, and entered on his career as contractor on the same railways, with no capital but his brains and magnificent physique with which to combat the tides of varying fortune. His younger brother Harry remained in the railway service for some years, and then joined his brother George, who in the interval had established himself as a well-known contractor.

In 1892 the two brothers became intimately acquainted with Cecil Rhodes and with the firm of Erlangers, and from that time they never looked back. They constructed the whole of the Rhodesian network of railways and many other of the important railways in Africa, which have been such a great factor in facilitating its rapid development. From this time onwards to the death of Cecil Rhodes in 1902, George Pauling was his constant associate. Rhodes consulted him in regard to all his important projects and attached a very high value to his shrewd advice and untiring energy. He was associated with the history of Rhodesia from its earliest days, and from 1894-1896 was its Minister of Mines and Public Works, having been requested by Rhodes to help him by acting in that capacity. He was at the same time member of the Executive Council of Rhodesia. During this period Sir Starr Jameson, Colonel Frank Rhodes, and Earl Grey in succession administered the territory.

Mr. Pauling was a man of simple habits, with no social ambitions. He was one of the biggest of men both mentally and physically, and he had a warm heart and unbounded generosity. He was a staunch Roman Catholic and built a church at Effingham, where his funeral takes place to-day at 11.30.

APPENDIX 9

SCHEDULE OF WORKS CONSTRUCTED BY PAULING AND COMPANY LIMITED/ PAULING PLC

YEAR Completed	DESCRIPTION	LENGTH (Kilometres)
1881	Port Alfred Railway, South Africa	105
1884	Sterkstroom to Aliwal North Railway, South Africa	158
1885	Orange River to Kimberley Railway, South Africa	121
1889	Springs to Krugersdorp Railway, South Africa	90
1890	Crocodile Poort Railway, South Africa	20
1892	Johannesburg to Pretoria Railway, South Africa	58
1892	Haifa to Damascus Railway (uncompleted), Syria	24
1892	Railway works at Bristol, U.K.	
1893	Lee-on-Solent Light Railway, U.K.	10
1893	Road Bridges and Culverts at Neath, U.K.	
1894	Bridges at Reading, U.K.	
1894	Vryburg to Mafeking Railway, South Africa	171
1895	Bridge at Goring, U.K.	
1895	Milford Viaduct and Widening for Somerset and Dorset Joint Railway, U.K.	
1896	Farncombe Station for London & South Western Railway, U.K.	
1896	Hungerford to Savernake Widening for G.W.R., U.K.	14
1896	Siding at Reading for G.W.R., U.K.	
1896	Staff Dwellings for S.E.R., U.K.	
1897	Sterkstroom to Indwe Railway, South Africa	101
1897	Mafeking to Bulawayo Railway, South Africa/Zimbabwe	805
1897	Fratton Bridge for L. & S.W.R., U.K.	
1897	Works at Tunbridge Wells for L.B. & S.C.R., U.K.	
1897	Savernake to Stert Widening, U.K.	18
1897	Stert to Westbury Railway for G.W.R., U.K.	23
1897	Works on Porto Rico Railways, Peurto Rico	
1897	Coventry Tramways, U.K.	10
1898	Beira/Umtali - Narrow Gauge Railway, Mozambique	370
1898	Graff Reinet to Middelburg Railway, South Africa	153
1898	Ashton to Swellendam, being part of the New Cape Central Railways, South Africa	71
1898	Norwich Tramways, U.K.	32
1898	Widening near Ledbury for G.W.R., U.K.	

YEAR Completed	DESCRIPTION	LENGTH (Kilometres)
1899	Umtali to Salisbury Railway, Zimbabwe	282
1899	Piraeus Railway in Greece (in conjuction with the Societe de Construction des Batignolles)	528
1899	Carndonagh Railway, Republic of Ireland	31
1899	Burtonport Railway, Republic of Ireland	79
1899	Widening of Warminster to Wilton Railway, U.K.	26
1899	Hungerford Station, U.K.	
1899	Savernake Station, U.K.	
1900	Beira-Umtali Broad Gauge, Mozambique	370
1900	Patney Station, U.K.	
1900	Goods Shed at Warminster, U.K.	
1900	Andoversford to Cheltenham Railway, U.K.	13
1901	Works at Patney Station, U.K.	
1901	Northolt to High Wycombe Railway, U.K	37
1901	Deep Seawater Pier at Jesselton and Railway from Jesselton to Beaufort, Borneo	97
1901	Perico Ledesma Road, Argentine	
1901	Guachipas Roads, Argentine	
1902	Sir Lowry's Pass to Caledon Railway, South Africa	90
1902	Salisbury/Bulawayo Railway, Zimbabwe	483
1902	Salisbury/Banket/Ayrshire Railway, Zimbabwe	121
1902	Tucuman Dam, Argentine	
1902	Tucuman Irrigation Canals, Argentine	
1903	Swellendam to Riversdale Railways, South Africa	105
1903	French Rand Siding, South Africa	7
1903	De Beers Buildings, South Africa	
1903	La Plata Tramway Ballasting, Argentine	
1903	Bulawayo to Wankie, Zimbabwe	
	Railway No. 1	260
	Railway No. 2	74
1903	High Wycombe Station, U.K.	
1903	Cape Flats Railway, South Africa	15
1903	Gwelo to Selukwe Railway, Zimbabwe	40
1903	Bulawayo to Gwanda, Zimbabwe	161
1903	Roads to Port Unsue, Argentine	
1903	Pichi Mahuida Bridge, Argentine	
1904	Uxbridge New Station, U.K.	
1904	Wankie to Victoria Falls Railway, Zimbabwe	113
1904	Electric Light, Argentine	
1905	Victoria Falls to Kalomo Railway, Zambia	150
1905	Staff Housing at Northolt, U.K.	
1905	Bloemfontein to Modderpoort (platelaying and ballasting), South Africa	82
1905	Tafi Viejo Aquaduct, Argentine	
1905	Arroyo Maciel Bridge, Argentine	

YEAR Completed	DESCRIPTION	LENGTH (Kilometres)
1905	San Nicholas, Argentine	
1906	Riversdale to Mossel Bay Railway, South Africa	93
1906	Kalomo to Broken Hill Railway, Zambia	451
1906	Railway to Eldorado, Zambia	23
1906	Natal Spruit Drainage, South Africa	
1906	Witbank Siding, South Africa	
1906	Uxbridge Viaduct, U.K.	
1906	Uxbridge New Station, U.K.	
1906	Camerton to Limpley Stoke Railway, U.K.	15
1906	Northolt Bridge, U.K.	
1907	Eldorado Mine Railway, Zambia	23
1907	Works at Witbank Station, South Africa	
1907	Valsch River Bridge, South Africa	
1907	Northolt Station, U.K.	
1907	Papa Pouli to Topsin Railway, Greece (in conjunction with the Societe de Construction des Batignolles)	97
1908	Premier Mine Sidings, South Africa	10
1908	Bloem Spruit Training Works, South Africa	
1908	Springs Eastward Railway (platelaying and ballasting), South Africa	193
1908	Stuartstown Railway, South Africa	158
1909	Johannesburg Outfall Sewer, South Africa	
1909	Broken Hill to Ndola, Zambia	217
1909	City Deep Siding, South Africa	4
1909	Vischkuil Siding, South Africa	2
1909	Cullinan Hotel, South Africa	
1909	Gwelo to Umvuma, Zimbabwe	80
1910	Zaire/Zambia Border to Likasi, Zaire	265
1910	Works on Vereeniging Railway, South Africa	
1910	Magazines for de Beers, South Africa	
1910	Benguela Railway K.198 to K.323, Angola	126
1910	Modderpoort Bethlehem Railway, South Africa	164
1911	Benguela Railway K.320 to K.360, Angola	39
1911	Mazoe Railway, Zimbabwe	35
1912	Selati Railway, South Africa	225
1912	Santos Railway, Brazil	161
1913	Benguela Railway, K.360 to K.520, Angola	160
1913	Shamva Railway, Zimbabwe	80
1913	Ayshire Railway Widening, Zimbabwe	132
1914	Likasi-Kambove-Kshilongo Railway (in conjunction with the Society Coloniale de Construction), Zaire	319
1914	Magadi Railway, Kenya	161
1914	Pier at Kilindini, Kenya	
1914	Sinoia Railway, Zimbabwe	6
1914	Umvuma to Victoria Railway, Zimbabwe	121

YEAR Completed	DESCRIPTION	LENGTH (Kilometres)
1914	Zambesi River to Port Herald Railway, Mozambique	101
1914	Tata Hydro-Electric Project, India	
1914	Tunnel on G.I.P. Railway, U.K.	
1917	Hilton Road Tunnel, U.K.	
1916-18	Magazines at Gloucester, U.K.	
	Magazines at Skipton, U.K.	
	Trench Warfare Range, U.K.	
	Explosives Magazines, U.K.	
	The Murman Railway (unfinished) - (in conjunction with the Public Works and Railway Construction Company), U.S.S.R.	
1920	Mazoe Dam, Zimbabwe	
1921	Welgedach Siding, South Africa	
1922	Beira/Zambesi Railway, Mozambique	251
1922	Geduld Siding and Bridge, South Africa	
1922	Transvaal Colliery Siding, South Africa	
1923	Benguela Railway, K. 520 to K. 627, Angola	108
1924	Mogoto Dam, South Africa	
1924	Port Elizabeth Sewerage, South Africa	
1924	Durban Power House Foundations, South Africa	
1925	Benguela Railway, K. 627 to K. 726, Angola	101
1925	Monapa Bridge, South Africa	
1926	Wharf at Kilindini, Kenya	
1926	Benguela Railway, Quanza Bridge, Angola	
1926	Tanganyika Concessions, Tanzania	
1926	Maritzburg Waterworks, South Africa	
1926	Zwartzkopjes Reservoir, South Africa	
1928	Lobito Wharf and Water Supply, Angola	
1928	Shabani Railway, Zimbabwe	102
1928	Benguela Railway, K. 726 to K. 1246, Angola	544
1929	Beira Port Works, Mozambique	
1929	Kilindini Wharf Extension, Kenya	
1929	Benguela Railway, K. 1246 to K. 1347, Angola	105
1929	Luao Bridge, Angola	
1929	Ndola to Roan Antelope Railway, Zambia	37
1929	Mokambo-Mufulira Branch, Zambia	23
1930	Ndola to Nkana Railway, Zambia	64
1930	Ndola Deviation, Zambia	
1930	Benguela Railway-Huambo Workshops and Cuando Hydro-Electric Project, Angola	
1930	Beira Port Works, Mozambique	
1930	Kilindini Wharf - Second Extension, Kenya	

YEAR Completed	DESCRIPTION	LENGTH (Kilometres)
1930	Beira Port Works Extension, Mozambique	
1930	M'Baraki Slipway, Kenya	
1930	Mombasa Oil Jetty, Kenya	
1930	Nkana to Nchanga Railway, Zambia	66
1931	Shimaz Oil Jetty, Kilindini, Kenya	
1934	Dotores Mar Del Plata Road, Argentine	
1935	Power Station, Swansea, U.K.	
1936	Buenos Aires Drainage, Argentine	
1937	Gebel Fulia Dam, Sudan	
1938	Rames Mejia Roadworks, Argentine	
1939	San Felipe Dam, Argentine	
1940	River Rea Scheme, Birmingham, U.K.	
1940	Construction of Army Camps, U.K.	
1942	Construction of 4 No. Ordnance Factories, U.K.	
1942	Track Work, G.S.R., U.K.	
1942	Quay Wall Extension, Glasgow, U.K.	
1943	Tete Railway, Mozambique	85
1943	Phoenix Harbour Units, U.K.	
1944	Dunkwa Railway, Ghana	89
1945-1948	Open Cast Coal Sites	
1945	War Damage Repairs	
1947	St. Saviours Dam, Guernsey, Channel Islands	
1947	Erection of 1,454 B.I.S.S. Houses	
1949	East African Groundnut Scheme, Tanzania	
1950	Mtwara/Rud Railway (Mikandani), Tanzania	129
1953	Queen Elizabeth Quay, Freetown, Sierra Leone	
1953	Kongo Dam, Sierra Leone	
1957	Road Bridges, Sierra Leone	
1957	Port Development, Aden	
1961	U.S. Embassy, London, U.K.	
1961	Avondale Square, London, U.K.	
1961	Blackbush Irrigation, Guyana	
1962	Office Blocks, London Airport, U.K.	
1965	Tapakuma Irrigation, Guyana	
1965	Water Supply Pipeline, Abu Dhabi, U.A.E.	
1966	Roads and Bridges, British Virgin Islands	
1966	Customs Jetties, British Virgin Islands	
1966	Tropospheric Scatter Station, British Virgin Islands	
1967	International Airport, Abu Dhabi, U.A.E.	
1968	Water Supply, Sokoto and Kano, Nigeria	
1968	Abu Dhabi/Al Ain Road, Abu Dhabi, U.A.E	

YEAR Completed	DESCRIPTION	LENGTH (Kilometres)
1970	New Capital, Belize, Central America	
1974	Salalah Power Station, Oman	
1974	Zaria and Katsina Water Supply, Nigeria	
1974	Qabi/Ibri Road, Oman	
1975	Al Ain Town Roads, Abu Dhabi, U.A.E.	
1975	Airstrips, Abu Dhabi, U.A.E.	
1975	Construction of Thumrait Garrison, Oman	
1975	Road from Ibri to Thumrait, Oman	
1975	Asphalt Runway, etc., Oman	
1976	Construction of Service Roads, Oman	
1976	Construction of Thumrait Airbase, Oman	
1976	Bayadat to Hatta Road, Dubai, U.A.E.	
1976	Sweyhan/Al Hair Earthworks, Abu Dhabi, U.A.E.	
1976	Bayadat/Tawi Al Faqa Road, Dubai, U.A.E.	
1977	Port Roads, Stage 1, Jebel Ali, Dubai, U.A.E.	
1977	Tawi Al Faqr/Al Hair Road, Abu Dhabi, U.A.E.	
1978	Hatta/Agr Road, Dubai, U.A.E.	
1978	Customs and Immigration, Oman	
1978	Port Roads, Stage II, Jebel Ali, Dubai, U.A.E.	
1979	Port Works, State of Qatar	
1979	Hatta/Quimah/Tawi Al Rub Roads, Dubai, U.A.E.	
1980	Dry Excavation, Jebel Ali Harbour, Dubai, U.A.E.	
1980	Hatta Village Roads, Dubai, U.A.E.	
1980	Industrial Area Roads, Jebel Ali, U.A.E.	
1980	Hatta Power Station Extension, U.A.E.	
1980	Housing (25) Tobruk, Libya	
1982	Dubai to Agr Second Carriageway, Dubai, U.A.E.	
1983	Agr to Seeb Second Carriageway, Oman	
1985	Abu Dhabi Town Roads Trip No. 76S, Abu Dhabi, U.A.E.	
1986	Peshawar to Norashera Road, Pakistan	
1986	Minhad Military Airbase, Dubai, U.A.E.	
1987	A Nahda Interchange, Dubai, U.A.E.	
1988	Dubai to Al Ain Road, Dubai, U.A.E.	
1988	Al Garhood Bridge Road, Dubai, U.A.E.	
1990	Bela to Awaran Road Project, NWFP, Pakistan	
1993	Punjab Roadways Projects, Punjab State, India	
1995 (M) (Current)	Tamil Nadu Roads, Tamil Nadu State, India	
1995 (M) (Current)	Madras Coast Road, Madras, India	
1996 (M) (Current)	Rawalpindi to Kharian Highway with NLC, Pakistan	120

(M) - Denotes Management Contract